MICROECONOMIC
ANALYSIS

MICROECONOMIC ANALYSIS

WELFARE AND EFFICIENCY IN PRIVATE AND PUBLIC SECTORS

H. T. KOPLIN
UNIVERSITY OF OREGON

Harper International Edition
HARPER & ROW, PUBLISHERS
NEW YORK, EVANSTON, SAN FRANCISCO, LONDON

MICROECONOMIC ANALYSIS: Welfare and Efficiency in
Private and Public Sectors
Copyright © 1971 by H.T. Koplin

STANDARD BOOK NUMBER: 06-043749-9

LIBRARY OF CONGRESS CATALOG CARD NUMBER: 77-144234

Harper International Edition
INT-35-03935 AINT-35-32595 EINT-35-62576
First printing
Printed in Singapore by Times Printers Sdn. Bhd.

for Bruce, Kathy, and Terry

CONTENTS

4   PRIVATE MARKETS

PREFACE

This text is differentiated from other microeconomic theory texts in two particular ways. First, a major section is devoted to an analysis of the public economy. The almost exclusive concentration on private markets in existing texts is grossly unrealistic, and contributes to the difficulty of persuading students that the theory is useful. Further, recent developments in the field, particularly in the theory of public goods and of voting, are exciting and important, and should be introduced to all students of theory.

Second, this book is oriented to welfare economics. Considerations of welfare, efficiency, and efficiency changes are found throughout this book, in the belief that this reflects the practice of the majority of economists, and that in this way the uses of theory can best be impressed upon the student.

The student of microeconomic theory is typically drilled on techniques, and warned that economics cannot by itself provide answers to public problems, because inadmissible value judgments would be required. But in his courses in applied economic fields, he finds policy questions freely discussed. The treatment of welfare economics in this text attempts to help bridge this gap.

The profession has grown a bit careless in its terminology. It recognizes that the "optimum allocation of resources" may well not constitute a welfare optimum, but the qualification is often absent. "Welfare" gains and losses are calculated, when the economist knows (or should know) he is measuring, not welfare, but economic efficiency. In this text the distinction between welfare and efficiency is carefully drawn and emphasized.

Perfect efficiency is generally defined in terms of a Pareto optimum, a situation such that no one can be made better off without making someone else worse off. The analysis of the necessary and sufficient conditions for achieving a perfectly efficient economy has dominated the literature. This analysis cannot be faulted, so long as it is made perfectly clear that maximum efficiency need not imply maximum welfare, and indeed that an infinite number of perfectly efficient economies can be identified.

For microeconomic theory to be useful, however, it must be applicable to an imperfect and imperfectible world. As Arrow and Scitovsky say, ". . . if the economist is to be something more than a preacher of optimality and market perfection, his policy recommendation in an imperfect, suboptimal world must mostly be based on the measurement of its costs and hoped-for gains."[1]

In this book the phrase "increase in efficiency" is used to describe a change for which benefits exceed costs, each computed in money terms. The excess of benefits over costs is then an objective measure of the efficiency gain resulting from a change.

Consumer, producer, and factor surpluses are employed as the measure of gains and losses. The ambiguities of these concepts are well-known and are recognized explicitly in this text, but the writer agrees again with Arrow and Scitovsky: "The treacherous, many-faced nature of consumers' surplus has often been exposed, but the need for its services seems great enough to overcome scruples about its unreliability."[2]

Because economists deal so often with efficiency, the distinction between efficiency changes and changes in welfare requires constant emphasis. I have tried not to gloss over the incompleteness of economics as a guide to policy, without being nihilistic. It is important to know what economics cannot do, but it is equally important to know what it can do. The teacher no doubt will wish to encourage the students to analyze problems of current interest in class.

I am grateful to many individuals for assistance. In the broad sense, my deepest obligation is to generations of students who have encountered the ideas and, in recent years, preliminary versions of this book. More specifically, I owe a great debt to Robert Fischer, for his encouragement and for his cooperation in testing an earlier draft of this book in his classes. Detailed comments of Dan Blake were most helpful, as were suggestions of Robert Ronstadt, Kent Olson, and Donald Billings. For secretarial services above and beyond the call of duty I thank Elna McNeese, Sue Mitchell, Patty Sweeney, and especially Joyce Sweeney.

H. T. Koplin

[1] Kenneth J. Arrow and Tibor Scitovsky, *Readings in Welfare Economics* (Homewood, III.: Irwin, 1969), p. 3.
[2] *Ibid.*, p. 385.

1

THE
NATURE
AND
METHODS
OF
MICROECONOMIC
ANALYSIS

1

THE ALLOCATION OF RESOURCES

THE NATURE OF MICROECONOMIC THEORY

Economics is concerned with the use of resources to produce goods and services. Because the available resources are insufficient to produce all the goods desired, we must continually choose among alternatives: What goods to produce, how best to produce them, how goods (and work) should be distributed among the people.

Economic theory is the study of the general principles governing the allocation of resources among competing uses. It considers not only how resources are allocated, but how they might otherwise be used. Theory deals with the way in which people as consumers, workers, businessmen, government officials and agencies make choices, what the consequences of their choices are, and how they might choose differently under different conditions.

Microeconomic theory deals with both individual and small groups of persons, firms, industries, products, and prices; it is contrasted with macroeconomic theory, which is concerned with broad aggregates such as the general price level and the total consumption, investment, and income of a society.

Theory is developed in part out of pure curiosity about how the economy works. But because it also describes how the workings of the economy might be changed under different circumstances, it is used and useful for predicting the consequences of changes. The results of theorizing may also influence judgments of the desirability of changes.

Economic theory as such provides no unqualified judgments about whether any specific change would be good or bad. Instead, the theory is likely to say, "If we want to achieve such and such a goal, we can do so by following such and such a policy."

Theory searches for *general* principles. This means that it constitutes a simplified description of economic behavior. From the bewildering array of facts of economic life it attempts to discover certain generalized consistent relationships among variables. Like a model, a theory incorporates certain broad and presumably important characteristics of reality, leaving out many details. This simplification means that theory must be applied cautiously, lest some element omitted from the theory have an unexpected major effect on the conclusions.

Microeconomic theory is by no means a completed, clean body of generalizations. There are many theoretical questions still unresolved, and in many cases theory gives little or no help. Economists are continuously working to improve and extend it. This book at times describes incomplete current research not because it is of current use, but because it shows what is happening, the directions in which theory is moving.

THE METHODS OF THEORY

A theoretical generalization is a statement or proposition about the relationship between two or more variables. It suggests that changes in one variable (for example, the price of a product) are correlated with changes in another (for example, the quantity of the product purchased). An economic model is a set of two or more interrelated generalizations (for example, a demand function and a supply function for the same good).

Induction

Two basic methods of developing theoretical propositions are often used. First, the researcher may employ an inductive approach. He may simply look about him, collect facts, and attempt to perceive general relationships. He may, for example, gather data on two or more economic variables (for example, prices of a good, quantities of that good purchased at those prices, and perhaps the incomes of the purchasers). Then, by arranging the data on a graph or chart, or by performing statistical operations with them, he may perceive some systematic relationships between the quantities and the prices or the incomes. Much empirical work of this inductive type has been done. As more detailed and sophisticated data are available, progress with this method accelerates.[1]

Deduction

In microeconomics recourse is often made to a second method of developing generalizations—deduction. In essence, this "armchair" technique asks what it is reasonable to believe about the relationship between two or more variables. The method begins with basic assumptions, and deduces from them their logical consequences. For example, the economist may assume that every individual seeks to maximize his own welfare; he may then deduce from this by a logical process how the individual will react to a change in price of a good. The deductive method is very commonly used in microeconomic theory and is the basic method developed in this book.

Deduction may be used in preference to induction for several reasons. First, economic situations are so complicated, with so many intertwining influences, that it is difficult to disentangle the separate elements through observation and statistical techniques. The economist is further handicapped, as compared with the physical scientist, in his inability to conduct controlled experiments in which key elements are isolated and manipulated and their interrelationships studied. Second, the deductive method is essential when economists wish to theorize about variables that cannot be observed or measured. The utility and disutility that individuals receive from consumption or effort are the prime examples. Some would argue that economists, as scientists, should not talk about things they cannot observe, but the tradition of economics opposes them. A third justification for the use of deductive techniques is that we often wish to consider hypothetical cases—"What would happen if . . . ?" In such cases the facts obviously cannot be observed and deduction is required.

The dominance of the deductive method should not be overemphasized. Clearly, if through deduction theoretical generalizations that do not accord with the facts are developed, these theories must be abandoned or modified. (Presumably, the assumptions are incorrect.) Conversely, if through induction a useful generalization is developed, it will hardly be abandoned. But the theorist is not likely to be content with his generalization until he is satisfied it is

[1]The statistical testing of economic theories cast in mathematical form is called econometrics.

reasonable, that is, it can be derived by deduction from reasonable assumptions. We want to know *why* as well as *what*. Thus induction and deduction work hand in hand, each supplementing and testing the results of the other.

ECONOMIC GOALS

Economic theory studies alternatives, the conditions under which people will behave one way rather than another, and what consequences that behavior will have on the utilization of economic resources. Knowing this, the economist is able to advise how chosen ends can be achieved efficiently and effectively.

Positive economics is descriptive and deals with what is or could be. *Normative* or *welfare economics* goes beyond positive economics to discuss and analyze economic values and subjective value propositions. Some economists believe that economics should be only a positive science, avoiding any normative aspects dealing with goals. There is general agreement that economists *qua* economists have no special ability to determine values or goals for a society. Nevertheless, the tradition of economics, continued to the present, includes consideration of alternative goals and the best methods of achieving them. A scientist can discuss and analyze goals; he abandons his objectivity only when he espouses particular goals.

The nature of the structure of microeconomic theory has been strongly influenced by a concern with goals. Economists have traditionally identified two major goals of economic life: *efficiency* and *equity*.

Efficiency essentially means obtaining the most output at the least cost; equity means distributing the output and the burden of its production in an equitable or fair manner.

A third goal, concerned with the "noneconomic" aspects of economic life, depends on how economic activity is carried on. It might be termed "environment," or "institutional structure." It is concerned in particular with the freedom or coercion involved in the economic process and with other attributes of the process for which individuals have either a preference or an aversion, and which it is difficult for individuals to influence through normal economic behavior. While something like "environment" appears to play an important part in the satisfactions individuals receive, the concept is difficult to analyze or to discuss objectively. Economics rarely deals explicitly with this third goal, which nevertheless often assumes considerable importance in discussions of public policy. For example, a proposed policy that by general agreement would improve economic efficiency and bring about a more fair distribution of income might be opposed by the public because it involves an undesired degree of governmental coercion.

An economist will often define concepts and formulate theories so that they can with relative ease be related to the goal of efficiency and, less commonly, equity. For example, the economist's concept of profit ("normal profits") is quite different from the accountant's definition—a fact that causes endless confusion among business students (and businessmen) exposed to economics. For each group, the particular definition used seems most appropriate for the purposes to which the concept is put. Similarly, the economist often talks about the "satisfaction" an individual gets from a good, when the individual knows very well that he gets no satisfaction from it in the ordinary sense—for example, spinach to a meat-and-potatoes man. Yet he often may consume the vegetable, which to the economist means that the consumer gets more satisfaction from eating it than he would from not eating it.

The concept of equity is highly subjective. There is no objective way in which one person can evaluate the fairness of a situation or compare his judgments with those of other individuals. No one can really say a given policy is fair; he can only assert that he believes it is (or is not) fair.

Because equity is subjective, it is not amenable to scientific or logical analysis. One can argue philosophically about it, but honest, intelligent, informed men will not necessarily agree. For this reason, economic theory has little to say about fairness. It tends to concentrate instead on the concept of efficiency. A good deal of this book is devoted to that topic: how efficiency can be defined, how efficient various types of behavior and economic institutions are, how inefficiency can be reduced.

This emphasis on the single goal of efficiency causes many people to misunderstand economics and to consider economists as materialists interested only in efficiency. The truth is that as economists, and particularly as economic theorists, they have little to say about equity and not that they feel such a quality is unimportant.[2]

The purpose of economic theory is to *assist* in the evaluation of alternative policies, not to present definitive judgments. As a tool, economics can be of great value. Indeed, one could well argue that without it proper economic decisions can only be made by chance. But it is no more than a tool. To quote a famous passage: "The Theory of Economics does not furnish a body of settled conclusions immediately applicable to a policy. It is a method rather than a

---

[2]In practice, economists often give divergent prescriptions for public policy because they assign different weights to the various goals or have conflicting concepts of fairness.

doctrine, an apparatus of the mind, a technique of thinking, which helps its possessor to draw correct conclusions."[3]

Although economic theory often describes the behavior of individuals—the choices open to them as consumers and workers, and the ways in which they respond to changes in the alternatives available to them—the chief concern of economics is with choices among public policies. It is assumed that the individual makes competent personal choices in his economic behavior in the marketplace, and, therefore, the economist has little advice to give to him. Economic analysis makes its major contribution with questions of public policy in which the nature and implications of the alternatives are far-ranging and of great importance but are obscure.

THE ROLE OF PRICES AND MONEY

One of the most important tasks for the student is to understand the role of prices in an economic system.

Daily, the individual is required to make economic decisions— what products to buy in what quantities, what kind of job to seek, whether to save and in what form. These possible actions lead to pleasures or satisfaction, or perhaps they reduce discomfort. It is assumed by economists that the individual makes his choices on the basis of his own likes and dislikes. Seldom does the economist inquire into the basic determinants of such individual tastes or preferences, usually leaving this task for the psychologist or sociologist.

How does the individual compare two alternatives? In analyzing the process of comparison and choice, the economist introduces money and prices as tools, very powerful but nevertheless not perfect tools. Money can serve as the common denominator, the standard by which the individual compares alternatives. When the individual is weighing a choice between two very similar things (for example, oranges and apples), he may make his decision simply on the basis of his preference for one or the other. But his choices are often much broader and more complex. In such cases, money provides a convenient standard of comparison.

When an individual considers buying a candybar, he is asking in effect whether he would rather spend that 10 cents on the candy than on anything else in the world. A broad question indeed. The question is even broader, for still another alternative may be open to him: forego the candy bar and, concurrently, escape 10 cents worth of effort, the effort he would put forth to earn the 10 cents to pay for the candy.

[3]J.M. Keynes, as quoted in E. A. G. Robinson, *The Structure of Competitive Industry* (New York: Pitman, 1935), pp. viii–ix.

Clearly, even the simplest economic choice involves many possible alternatives. The economist sees money and prices as tools to simplify and clarify the nature of the alternatives. Money is used as a standard of value by the individual. Instead of asking whether he prefers the candy to every other conceivable use of the 10 cents, the individual in effect asks himself whether the candy is worth 10 cents to him. He does the same with other possible purchases and with possible sources of money as well. (Is taking on that extra Saturday job worth the money?) It is this use of money and prices as measuring rods that unifies economic theory.

Lest the reader think there are some things that are priceless—a unique work of art or even a human life—let him ask himself how much money he would be willing to give up to acquire the work of art or save a life. Failure to promote highway safety and a willingness to flood the Egyptian artistic treasures (not to mention the wilderness areas of the United States) deny the existence of a class of "priceless" things. A refusal to employ, because of their cost, known techniques for saving human lives in effect sets a monetary value on human life that is less than the cost of saving it.

The usefulness of money and prices as measuring rods is clear, but it should not be overstated. For many purposes this standard of value breaks down. It is clear that any one individual will find it useful to compare the alternatives open to him in terms of money, that he has a sense of "the value of money" to himself. But it is vital to note that accepting this does not necessarily mean that the value of money is the same to all individuals. Any interpersonal comparison between individuals, then, cannot depend on a money measurement.

WELFARE CRITERIA

If the satisfactions of different individuals in a group cannot be compared objectively, what criterion can be used to determine whether a given change in economic policy will increase or decrease the welfare of the group?

Consider some proposed new economic policy. Assume, even, that perfect knowledge of the effects of the change on all individuals is available. Should the change be carried out? More fundamentally, what criteria may be used to evaluate the desirability of the change?

The easiest case to evaluate is a change that will make one or more persons better off and no one worse off. "Better off" is taken to mean that, given a choice between his economic position before and after the change, an individual would favor the change.

Even a change that makes no one worse off cannot be said to be desirable. Feelings of envy may negate the gains (a fact that parents will readily recognize if they have ever tried to distribute four indivisible pieces of candy among three children). Nevertheless, most economists accept as desirable any change that makes one or more persons better off and no one worse off. This test for an increase in welfare is often called the Paretian welfare criterion, after the Italian economist and sociologist Vilfredo Pareto.

Conversely, Pareto argued that welfare can be said to have decreased when a change makes no one better off and one or more persons worse off, in the sense indicated.

In most cases of public concern, however, a proposed change will benefit some persons and harm others. The Paretian welfare criterion simply ignores such changes.

No objective method exists for comparing the gains and losses of different individuals to arrive at a judgment of whether welfare has been increased or decreased by the change. Faced with this problem and fully recognizing the impossibilty of an objective general solution, the economist suggests that progress can be made by dividing the problem into parts and by then asking whether objective agreement can be reached on some part of the total. The technique to be used has been anticipated: Subdivide the general goal of welfare into partial goals such as efficiency and equity. Then study whether a given situation is more or less efficient than its alternatives. This can be done, for efficiency can be defined as an objective concept.

If a situation B is more efficient than a situation A, one still cannot say that B is preferable to A. But A and B can be compared more easily. Here economics is being used as a tool, as a guide to better choices. Situation A may still be preferred—perhaps on the grounds of equity. But we will now know how much the fairness of A is costing in efficiency terms as compared with B.

EFFICIENCY

The concept of efficiency is central to economics and must be considered with some care. Earlier, efficiency was defined loosely as getting the most output for the least cost. For many purposes this is an adequate and useful definition. The businessman who incurs unnecessary costs in production or produces less with his resources than he could, is not efficient. But when the idea of efficiency is extended to all of economic life, the concepts of *output* and *costs* become difficult to identify, to measure, and to compare. For example, if with a given amount of resources either 100 umbrellas or 50 pair of shoes could be produced, which would be the most efficient use of resources? If another dozen bicycles could be manufactured with an added half dozen man-weeks of labor, would this constitute an increase or decrease in efficiency? If in a different job a man could earn more but only with more effort, would a move promote efficiency?

To provide answers to such questions, the economist defines efficiency in a particular way to suit his purposes. The definition will at first seem awkward to the student, but his growing familiarity with it should bring an appreciation of its usefulness.

A situation is called perfectly efficient if there is no change that can make someone better off without making any other person worse off.[4] An increase in efficiency occurs when, as a result of a change, those who are made better off *could* compensate the losers for their loss and still have net gains left over. Thus, efficiency rises if a change results in *net* monetary gains—the gains exceed the losses when both are measured in money terms. Analogously, efficiency is said to decrease if a change results in net monetary losses, so that the gainers would not be able to compensate the losers.

It is crucial that the student realize from the beginning that by this definition efficiency rises when there are net monetary gains, whether or not the losers are compensated for their losses. Whether compensation *should* be paid or not is a question of equity, not of efficiency. Efficiency asks only whether the gains are great enough that compensation could be paid and still leave the gainers better off than they were before the change.[5]

It is vital to distinguish carefully between the compensation test of an increase in efficiency and the Paretian criterion of an increase in welfare. By Pareto's test, welfare increases as a result of a change only when no one is worse off and at least one person is better off. The compensation test for changes in efficiency is far less restrictive and only requires that the gainers from a change *be able* to compensate the losers.

Any change that satisfies the Pareto welfare test will also pass the compensation test of efficiency. The reverse is not true, for it is quite possible, and in fact no doubt common, for many persons to be made worse off by a change that increases efficiency.

The compensation test is a product of what is often called the

---

[4]This state of perfect efficiency is sometimes referred to as the "optimum allocation of economic resources." This phrase is avoided here because, as we shall see, a situation that is perfectly efficient need not constitute a welfare optimum. In fact, there is not just one but many possible economic states of perfect efficiency. How many "optimum" states can there be?

[5]Note that if compensation is in fact actually paid when a change raises efficiency, no one would end up worse off. The change would then also satisfy the Paretian test for an increase in welfare, as well as represent an increase in efficiency.

"new welfare economics," but it has been implicit in economics ever since Adam Smith. It is in fact the basis of the case for free trade, laissez faire, competition, and many other popular economic causes.[6]

AN ILLUSTRATION OF EFFICIENCY

A very simplified case may illustrate effectively the concept of efficiency. Assume that John has a car he would be willing to sell for $300, and that Andy would be willing to pay $500 for it. If John sells the car to Andy for any price between $300 and $500, it is clear that efficiency has increased. Both John and Andy are better off and no one is worse off. The net monetary gain would be $200, divided between John and Andy depending on the specific price of the car. In fact, the sale satisfies not only the compensation test for efficiency, but also the Paretian criterion for an increase in welfare.

But take the same facts and assume that John is for some reason *forced* to sell the car to Andy for only $200. Has efficiency increased? The rather surprising answer is, yes. Andy is better off by an amount of $300 (the difference between the $500 value of the car to him and the $200 he pays for it); John, on the other hand, is $100 worse off, selling for $200 a car worth $300 to him. The net monetary gain is thus still $200, Andy's $300 gain less John's $100 loss.

Efficiency does not ask whether anyone is worse off. It only asks if the gainer *could* compensate the loser and have gains left over. In this case Andy could compensate John for the latter's $100 loss and still have a gain of $200 left over. Hence, efficiency has increased.

Finally, assume in a third case that Andy buys the car for $600—$100 more than he is willing to pay. (As in the second case, it is clear that some form of coercion must be present.) Here Andy is $100 worse off because of the transaction, but John is $300 better off. John *could* compensate Andy for his loss and still have a net gain of $200. Again, efficiency is increased.

By now, the student will have perceived the crucial facts: Efficiency here depends only on whether Andy ends up with the car. So long as he does, efficiency is increased. The specific price Andy pays for the car appears to be unimportant to efficiency.

This does not mean that in practice the price is irrelevant to

---

[6]On this see E. J. Mishan, "A Reappraisal of the Principles of Resource Allocation," *Economica* 24 (1957), 324–342, reprinted in E. J. Mishan, *Welfare Economics* (New York: Random House, 1964), pp. 155–183.

efficiency. For without coercion, in the second and third cases, the car would not have been transferred to Andy and efficiency would have been defeated. To get this efficiency, when coercion is not employed, a price somewhere between $300 and $500 is required. The important effect of price on efficiency is that some prices induce efficiency while others do not.

Two critically important questions in economic analysis are these: Do the prices that exist in a free market economy encourage efficient production and distribution? If not, how can an efficient set of prices be achieved?

It is possible to achieve efficient allocation of resources without the explicit use of prices, for example by direct allocation of resources.

Lest the reader feel that a foreign element not particularly relevant to the U.S. economy has been introduced with our use of coercion in the examples above, note that coercion in the form of direction of resources by means other than prices is extremely common. Two obvious examples are (1) pervasive government regulation of economic activity (for example, restrictions on entry into professions, minimum or maximum price laws, zoning controls), and (2) direct allocation of resources within an organization without reference to an explicit price system. Within most organizations resources are allocated directly, without use of a price system—particularly in business firms, but in virtually every other organization as well (an army, university, church, or family). A price system is in effect an alternative to direct allocation of goods and resources.

EFFICIENCY AND WELFARE

Efficiency is only one of several goals of economic life. The important question to ask of a proposed change is whether welfare in a broad sense would be increased or decreased by it. Because welfare cannot be measured, an intermediate approach is adopted. The efficiency gains or losses of a proposed change are calculated. The individual then makes a total evaluation of the change, adding to his information of the size of the efficiency change, his subjective judgment of the importance to welfare of efficiency and of the other consequences of a change, such as its effects on the distribution of income.

Many, if not most, proposed changes in public economic policy involve an apparent conflict between efficiency and equity considerations. While economics may not be able to resolve these conflicts, it can help the citizen make a decision by providing him with information on the effects of the proposed change by describing the efficiency gains or losses, and the likely impact of the change on the incomes and prices a citizen may consider relevant to the question of equity.

RECONCILIATION OF EFFICIENCY AND EQUITY OBJECTIVES

Efficiency and equity need not always be in conflict. In this regard, the nature of the Paretian welfare criterion and the compensation test of efficiency leads to two important propositions:

(1)   Whenever there exists a potential change that increases efficiency but is believed to worsen the distribution of income, there exists an alternative change that would increase efficiency without worsening the distribution of income. This second change can in principle be achieved by making the original change and then redistributing gains and losses so that no one ends up worse off.

(2)   Conversely, if a proposed change would reduce efficiency but, by general agreement, improve the distribution of income, an alternative change exists that would not reduce efficiency, but would improve the distribution of income. This alternative change is achieved simply by a redistribution of incomes.

The alternative changes that reconcile efficiency and equity objectives may in practice not be feasible. A particularly interesting aspect of economics, however, is to analyze proposed policy changes that appear to raise conflicts between objectives and to seek to identify policy alternatives that will further both policy objectives.

FREE EXCHANGE AND EFFICIENCY

Finally, a word about the relation of free exchange to efficiency. The genius of Adam Smith, the founder of economics, was to perceive that individuals would be induced by self-interest to engage in transactions of mutual benefit and that efficiency would thereby be promoted. The contribution of such free economic behavior to the promotion of efficiency can hardly be overstated.

This does not mean that a completely free economy leads to a maximum of efficiency or maximum welfare. The complex reasons for this are vitally important to present economic policies. Private markets may not work smoothly, perhaps because of a lack of knowledge by individuals. The presence of monopolistic elements can hinder the achievement of efficiency. Free exchange is not well suited for certain types of economic activities. Public regulation of economic activity or public provision of goods may be desirable to compensate for deficiencies in free exchange or as a means of promoting fairness in the distribution of income. Microeconomic theory is concerned, therefore, not only with the operation of free markets, but with alternatives to them.

REVIEW QUESTIONS

1. Explain the following concepts:
   Economics
   Microeconomics
   Economic theory
   Induction
   Deduction
   Positive economics
   Normative or welfare economics
   Efficiency; perfect efficiency; a change in efficiency
   Equity
   A Pareto optimum
   The Paretian test for an increase or decrease in welfare
2. Explain the functions of money and of prices in microeconomic theory.
3. How is efficiency related to economic welfare?
4. Mr. Smith loses a $10 bill, which Mr. Brown later finds and keeps. What effect does this "change" have on economic efficiency? On economic welfare?
5. Is economics a science? Discuss, making explicit your definitions of science and of economics. Is mathematics a science by your definition?
6. "Efficiency would be increased if everyone gave money for Christmas gifts, instead of useless trivia." Discuss.

FURTHER READING

Marshall, Alfred, *Principles of Economics.* 8th ed., London: Macmillan (1920), bk. I.
Mishan, E. J., "A Reappraisal of the Principles of Resource Allocation." *Economica 24* (1957), 324–342; reprinted in E. J. Mishan, *Welfare Economics.* New York: Random House (1964), pp. 155–183.
Pigou, A. C., *The Economics of Welfare.* 4th ed., London, Macmillan (1932), esp. pt. I.

2 BASIC CONCEPTS AND TECHNIQUES

FUNCTIONAL RELATIONSHIPS

The building blocks of economic theory are propositions about the relationships among economic variables, such as quantities of goods and services, prices, costs and revenues. For ease in combining, manipulating, and perceiving the implications of theoretical propositions, they are often presented mathematically in the form of equations or graphs. Some elementary mathematics of particular use in economic theory will be reviewed in this chapter.

For concreteness, many of the relationships will be illustrated with the use of a production function, relating the quantity of a good produced to other variables, such as the amounts of labor and capital used in production. The general mathematical principles developed are applicable to many other relationships—cost, revenue, and utility functions.

One variable is said to be a function of another if the value of the first is somehow related to that of the second. The statement

$$Q = f(L,\ C,\ T,\ G) \qquad (1)$$

states that the Q, the quantity of a good produced, is a function of the amounts of labor (L) and capital (C) employed, the productive technology (T) available to the firm, and G, a symbol for all the ways in which government affects the firm's production.

Theory is simplification. As Joan Robinson has said, "In order to know anything it is necessary to know everything, but in order to talk about anything it is necessary to neglect a great deal."[1]

The technique used in analyzing the relationships among a limited number of variables is to make the assumption of *ceteris paribus*—that all other variables remain constant. For example, when equation (1) is written

$$Q = f(L; C, T, G) \qquad (2)$$

the terms after the semicolon are assumed not to change. In effect, only the relation between Q and L is being studied.

The relation indicated by equation (2) would hold only for the assumed constant values of C, T, and G.

TWO-VARIABLE ANALYSIS

The relationship between two variables can be represented graphically. The curve OZ in Figure 2.1a illustrates a standard form of the production function $Q = f(L)$, that is, of the relationships between the quantity of a good produced by a firm and the number of workers used in production.

Average Values

From a total function $Q = f(L)$, two other useful relationships can be derived. First, average output per worker for any given number of workers is Q/L. Geometrically, the average product of a given number of workers (L') equals the slope of a straight line (OT) from the origin to a point on the total product curve above L'. OL' workers produce $L'T$ units of product. Average product per worker is thus $L'T/OL'$, which equals the slope of line OT. By drawing (or imagining) a series of lines from the origin to the total curve, one can easily determine the behavior of average product as the number or workers changes, for example, whether the average is rising or falling, and, in particular, the point (T' in Figure 2.1a) at which average product reaches a maximum (or minimum). The extreme values of average product occur when the ray from the origin is tangent to the total curve.

The choice of axes is somewhat arbitrary. Reversing the axes of Figure 2.1a would show the amount of labor required to produce each output. Without reversing the axes, we can note that the *reciprocal* of the slope of a ray drawn from the origin to the total curve equals the average number of workers per unit of output produced.

[1] Joan Robinson, *Collected Economic Papers* (Oxford: Blackwell, 1951), p. 42.

Figure 2.1   *Total, Average, and Marginal Product*

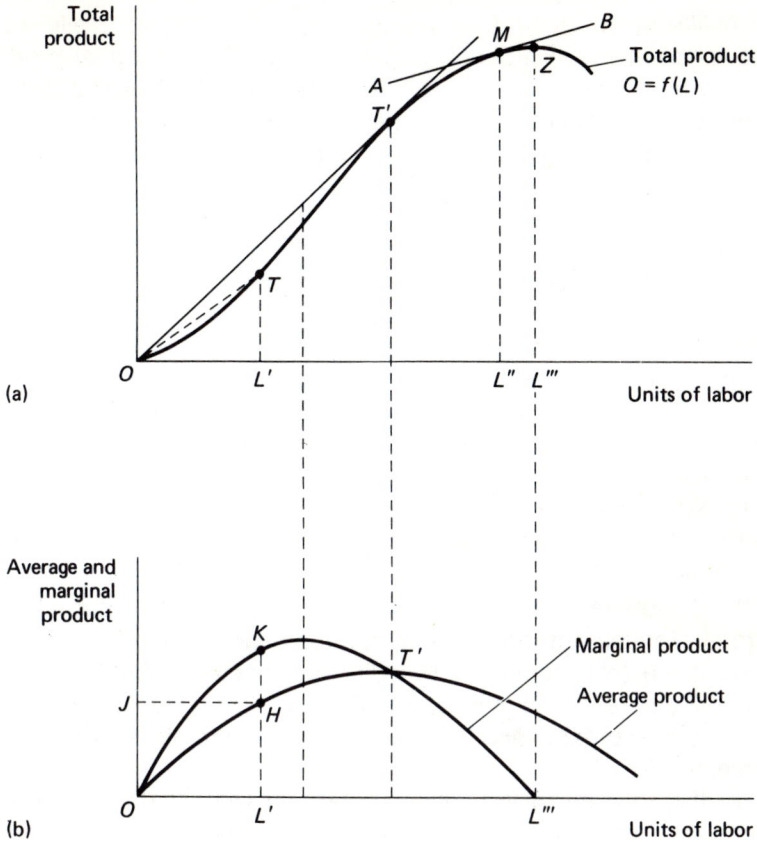

The Concept of the Margin

A second function or curve derivable from a total function is the relationship between *changes* in the two variables. Marginal product of labor, for example, is $\Delta Q/\Delta L$.[2] Geometrically, with a smooth and continuous function, marginal product for any given quantity of labor employed equals the slope of the total product curve at the corresponding point of the total product curve.

In Figure 2.1a, when OL'' workers are employed, the marginal

[2]Marginal product is often defined as the change in product when one additional unit of the factor is employed, with analogous definitions for other marginal concepts—marginal cost, revenue, and utility. When working with continuous functions, as in Figure 2.1a, it is convenient to define marginal product as the limiting value of the change in output divided by the change in labor as the change in labor approaches zero. It is thus the first derivative dQ/dL of the production function.

product of labor is the slope of the total product curve at *M*, that is, the slope of the tangent (*AB*) to the total curve at point *M*. Inspection of the slope of the total product curve thus shows easily the behavior of marginal product, in particular whether marginal product is rising or falling and where it reaches a maximum or minimum.

The following general relationships obtain among total, average, and marginal functions of any type. (Where relevant the relationships may be verified on the graph of total product in Figure 2.1a, and the average and marginal product curves of Figure 2.1b, which are derived from the total curve of Figure 2.1a.)

(1)   When total product reaches a maximum, marginal product is zero (point *Z* of Figure 2.1a, where *OL'''* workers are employed). More generally, the marginal value is zero when the total function reaches either a maximum or a minimum.

(2)   When average product is rising, marginal product exceeds average; when average product is falling, marginal product lies below average.

(3)   When average product reaches an extreme value (maximum or minimum), marginal product equals average product. (See point *T'* in Figures 2.1a and 2.1b.)

(4)   If average product is constant, marginal product must equal average product. The converse is not necessarily true.

(5)   If the total curves of two different functions (for example, total cost and revenues curves) are tangent, the two average curves will also be tangent, and the two curves of marginal value will intersect.

(6)   If a total curve is continuous but not smooth (for example, has a kink), the marginal curve will have a discontinuity, or gap, at the corresponding point.

Average and total curves provide essentially the same information in different forms. Either curve can be derived from the other.

For a given number of workers, total product can be measured directly from the total curve. Alternately, total product can be shown geometrically on the graph of the average product curve as the product of the number of workers times the average product per worker. Thus the total output of *OL'* workers on Figure 2.1b equals the area of rectangle *OL'HJ*.

The marginal curve is derived from the slope of the total curve, but a total curve cannot always be derived from the information given by the marginal curve. The marginal curve shows the slope of the total curve at every point, but it does not indicate the height, that is, the starting point, of the total curve.

Total product for any given number of workers equals the sum of the marginal products up to that point (that is, the area under the marginal product curve), plus a constant, where the constant measures total product when no workers are employed. When, as in Figures 2.1a and 2.1b, the total product curve begins at the origin, the total product for any given number of workers (for example, OL') is the area under the marginal product curve (OKL') up to that point.

ELASTICITIES

Point Elasticity

The elasticity of a function measures the ratio between the *percentage* changes in the two variables. The elasticity of output with respect to labor employed is

$$\frac{\text{percentage change in } Q}{\text{percentage change in } L} = \frac{\frac{\Delta Q}{Q}}{\frac{\Delta L}{L}} = \frac{L\Delta Q}{Q\Delta L}$$

The elasticity of a production function at a point equals $L(dQ)/Q(dL)$, as the assumed change in labor employed approaches zero.[3]

A function is called relatively elastic if the absolute value of the elasticity is greater than one, and inelastic if it is less than one.

Elasticities may be positive or negative depending on whether an increase in one variable leads to an increase or decrease in the other variable. The sign of the elasticity does *not* determine whether the function is elastic or inelastic.

Geometrically, the elasticity of a point on a curve is determined by drawing a tangent to the curve at the indicated point A (compare Figures 2.2a and 2.2b). When the tangent intersects the horizontal axis at point B, and a perpendicular from point A cuts the horizontal axis at point C, the elasticity of the function at point A equals CO/CB.

It is incorrect to associate elasticity with the slope of a curve. Note the three curves of different slopes in Figure 2.3a; each curve has a constant elasticity of one. Conversely, the three parallel curves of Figure 2.3b have different elasticities. Finally, in Figure 2.3c the curve with a constant slope has a different elasticity at every point, whereas the curved line has a constant elasticity but a constantly varying slope.

The elasticity relationship is reversible. The elasticity of B with respect to A is simply the reciprocal of the elasticity of A with re-

---

[3]For $Q = f(L)$, point elasticity is $d(\log Q)/d(\log L)$. A curve of constant elasticity, therefore, is a straight line when the function is graphed on log paper; elasticity is then equal to the slope of the line.

Figure 2.2 *Measuring Point Elasticity*

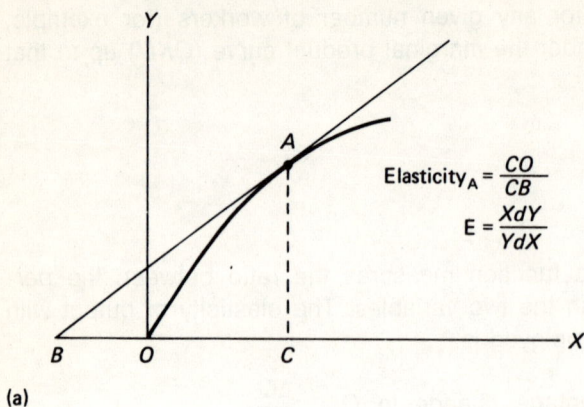

$$\text{Elasticity}_A = \frac{CO}{CB}$$

$$E = \frac{XdY}{YdX}$$

(a)

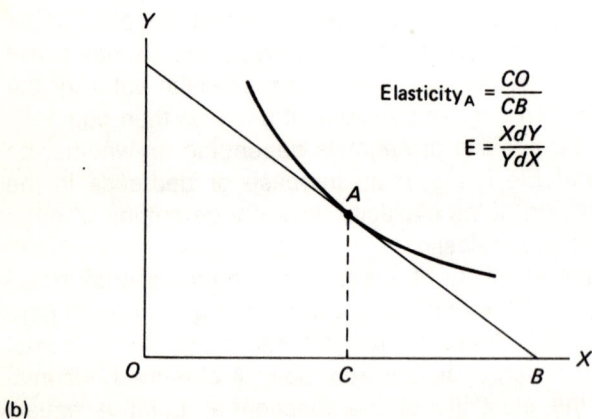

$$\text{Elasticity}_A = \frac{CO}{CB}$$

$$E = \frac{XdY}{YdX}$$

(b)

spect to B. Many of the most commonly used elasticities in economic theory measure the ratio of the percentage change in the variable measured on the horizontal axis to the relative change of the variable measured vertically. Price elasticities of supply and demand are examples. In each case we have

$$E = \frac{\text{percentage change in quantity}}{\text{percentage change in price}}$$

By the usual convention, quantity is measured horizontally and price vertically. These elasticities are therefore measured, in Figure 2.2b, by CB/CO.

Figure 2.3 *Elasticities Compared with Slopes*

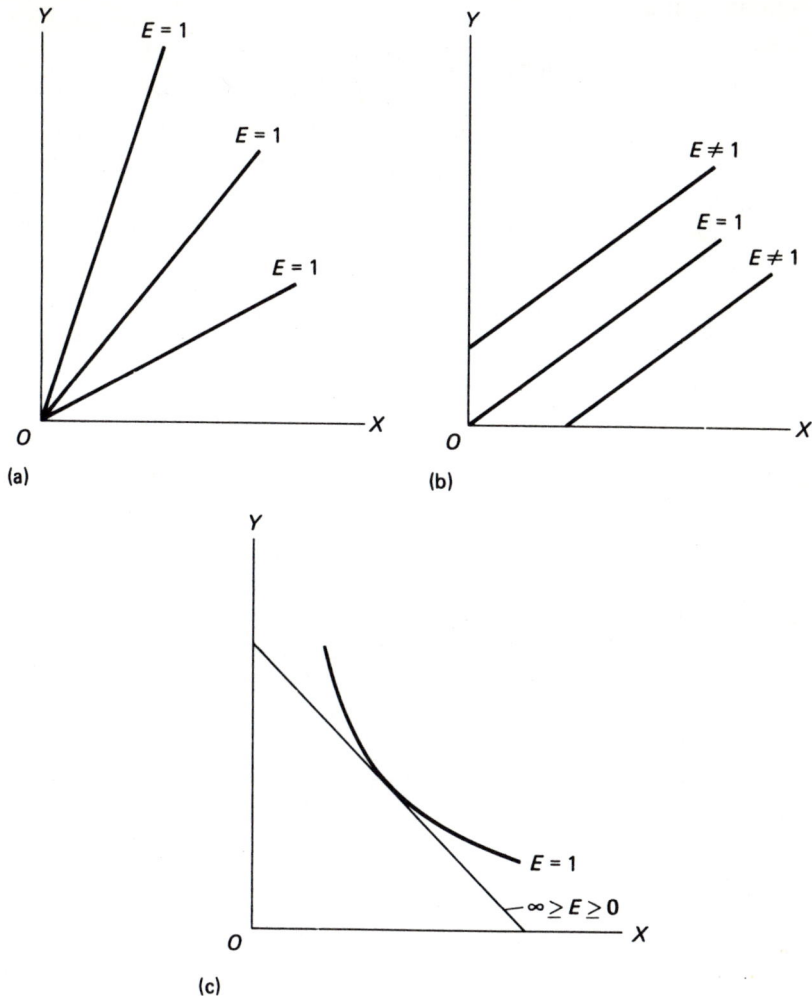

(a)

(b)

(c)

Arc Elasticity

In practice, it is usual to have only partial information on the values of a functional relationship, the values at selected points. Point elasticity, which requires knowledge of the slope of a curve at a point, cannot be determined in such cases. Arc elasticity, a measure of the elasticity of a function over a range between two points, is therefore often used. In effect, it represents an average of elasticities over a range.

Knowledge of arc elasticity enhances the predictive power of economic theory because it is descriptive of a change, a movement from one point to another, whereas point elasticity gives information only about one point.

When Q_1 units of output are produced with L_1 men, and Q_2 requires L_2 men,

$$\text{Arc elasticity} = \left(\frac{Q_2 - Q_1}{Q_2 + Q_1}\right) \div \left(\frac{L_2 - L_1}{L_2 + L_1}\right)$$

Note that in each term the numerator is the change in the value of the variable, and the denominator is the *sum* of the values of the variable at the two points that are observed.

Thus, if it is known that the output of 10 men is 90 and that 12 men will produce 100,

$$\text{Arc elasticity} = \left(\frac{100 - 90}{100 + 90}\right) \div \left(\frac{12 - 10}{12 + 10}\right) = \left(\frac{10}{190}\right) \div \left(\frac{2}{22}\right)$$

$$= \left(\frac{10}{190}\right)\left(\frac{22}{2}\right) = \frac{11}{19}$$

THREE-VARIABLE ANALYSIS

Analysis of three-variable functions can often be conveniently illustrated in two dimensions with isolines—a technique common to cartography. The prefix *iso* means "the same." An isoline on a two-dimensional graph is a locus of all combinations of the two variables plotted, which result in the same value of the third variable. Thus if $z = f(x, y)$, an isoline is a graph of the equation $f(x, y) = a$ constant.

Consider a production function with two inputs, labor and capital, that is, $Q = f(L, C)$. In Figure 2.4 each isoproduct curve (also

Figure 2.4   Three-Variable Representation

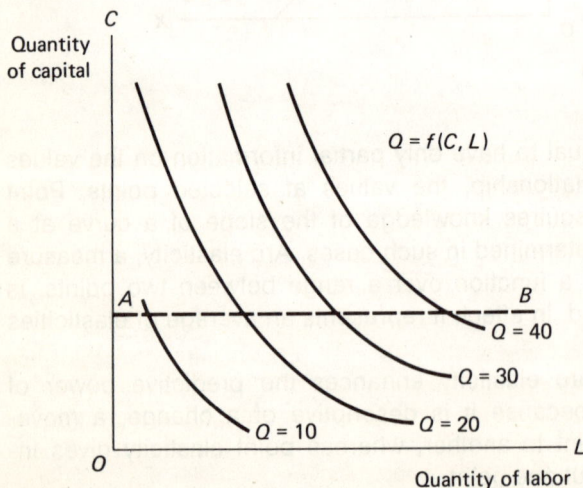

called a production isoquant) represents a specific level of output and shows the various combinations of labor and capital that can be used to produce that output.

Other familiar uses of this technique are indifference curves (which are isoutility curves), isocost curves (for two inputs or two outputs), and isorevenue curves (for two products).

Isoproduct maps can not only be used to analyze the interrelationships of all three variables, but also the relation between any two of them, on the assumption that the value of the third remains constant. Thus labor and capital vary, with output constant, as we move along any isoproduct curve. The two-variable analysis, $Q = f(L)$ (C constant), results by moving along any line parallel to the labor axis, thus keeping the quantity of capital constant. The movement along line AB in Figure 2.4 thus provides the type of information given in Figure 2.1a, that is, the variation in output as the quantity of labor is varied, with the quantity of capital kept constant. Similarly, the function $Q = f(C)$ results from a movement along a line parallel to the capital axis.

The slope of an isoproduct curve equals the negative of the marginal rate of substitution between the two factors of production, the rate at which one factor can be substituted for the other in the production process without affecting the level of output. Analogous rates of substitution between inputs or outputs are found in indifference, cost, and revenue analysis.

REVIEW QUESTIONS

1. Explain the following concepts:
   Functional relationship
   Ceteris paribus
   Production function
   Average product
   Marginal product
   Point elasticity
   Arc elasticity
   Elastic and inelastic functions
   Isoproduct curves or production isoquants
   Marginal rate of substitution
2. Draw a total curve, which includes curved sections, straight stretches, kinks, and several maximum and minimum points. Then construct the average and marginal curves corresponding to the total curve.
3. Similarly, draw an average curve, and construct the corresponding total and marginal curves.
4. Can an average curve be derived from a marginal curve? Why or why not?
5. Construct a map of a production function $Q = f(L, C)$, using iso-

product curves. Then, assuming a constant value of C, derive the appropriate curve showing the relation of Q to L.

FURTHER READING

Allen, Clark Lee, *Elementary Mathematics of Price Theory*. Belmont, Calif.: Wadsworth (1962).

Allen, R. D. G., *Mathematical Analysis for Economists*. London, Macmillan (1938).

Yamane, Taro, *Mathematics for Economists*. Englewood Cliffs, N. J.: Prentice-Hall (1962).

2

PURE EXCHANGE

3 DEMAND OF INDIVIDUALS

The theory of demand describes how individuals and firms decide what goods and services to purchase, and how they respond to changes in the alternatives open to them. The present chapter considers the demand of individuals for goods to be used in personal consumption. Chapter 4 describes individuals as suppliers of goods. In Chapter 5, the interaction of individual demanders and suppliers in markets is considered.

Utility or satisfaction is the capacity of a good to satisfy a human want. The rational individual will choose among the alternatives open to him those that maximize his utility. Economic theory assumes that each individual attempts to maximize his utility. It accepts the preferences of individuals as shown by their market behavior. A further assumption is that the individual has sufficient information about the alternatives open to him to make intelligent choices.[1] The use of such assumptions indicates that the principles of behavior developed in economic theory are best considered as predictions of the tendencies of individuals from which those individuals will diverge at times, but

[1]The analysis of behavior under conditions of uncertainty and the economics of acquiring information are subject to increasing study. See, for example, George Stigler, "The Economics of Information," *Journal of Political Economy* 69 (1961), 213–225.

which, it is hoped, will describe average or typical behavior.

The demand of an individual for a good is a schedule of the quantities, usually per unit of time (for example, per day, month, or year), that he will purchase at various prices. The individual's demand for a good will depend on three basic factors: his tastes or preferences (*T*) for this good as compared with other goods, his income (*Y*), and the prices of alternative goods (*P*$_a$). We therefore have the demand function

$$Q_x = f(P_x, T, Y, P_a) \tag{1}$$

That is, the quantity of good *X* demanded depends on the price of *X*, the prices of other goods, and the individual's tastes and income.

INDIFFERENCE MAPS

The basic construction in modern demand theory is an indifference map. Figure 3.1 is a map showing the preferences of an individual for two goods, let us say apples and bananas. The quantities of the goods are measured along the two axes. Any point on the map represents a particular combination of apples and bananas. The individual is assumed to be able to order or rank all of these combinations, stating with respect to any pair of combinations whether he prefers the first or the second, or is indifferent.

An indifference curve is an isoutility or isosatisfaction curve connecting all combinations of apples and bananas to which the consumer is indifferent. Each such curve represents a constant level of satisfaction. The level of satisfaction represented by one indiffer-

Figure 3.1 *Indifference Map*

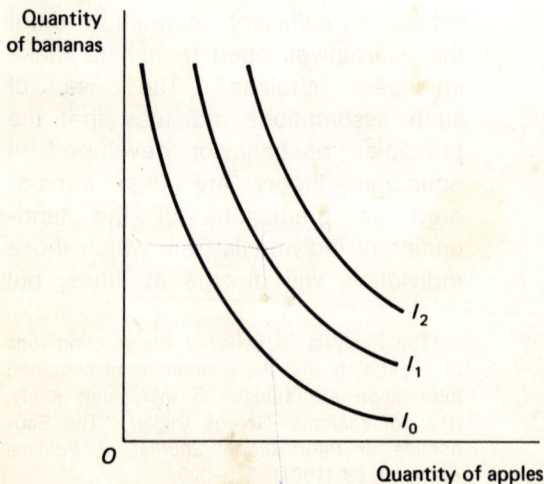

ence curve can be compared ordinally but not cardinally with the level of satisfaction of another curve. The individual ranks one indifference curve as higher or lower than another, but is not assumed to make a quantitative judgment of the difference in the levels of utility on the two curves. Nor is he assumed to be able to rank or order the differences between curves. Thus a movement from curve I_0 to I_1 may represent more or less change in utility than a move from I_1 to I_2.

If the individual gains satisfaction from each of the two goods, the level of his utility will rise as he moves up and to the right on the diagram. In this case the curves will have a negative slope.[2]

For two goods, the curves are usually assumed to be convex to the origin, with a diminishing slope as the individual moves to the right along a curve. Two justifications can be given for this assumption of convexity. First, it is plausible that, as an individual moves along a curve gaining apples and giving up bananas he becomes more and more reluctant to lose still more bananas and, if required to do so, must be given increasing quantities of extra apples to compensate for the loss of each banana. If the individual experiences diminishing marginal utility from added consumption of bananas and apples (that is, if the extra utility he gains from one more unit of each fruit declines as he acquires increasing quantities of that good), and if the utility of each good is independent of the quantity of the other good consumed, the indifference curves will necessarily be convex.

A second justification for assuming convexity of the indifference curves is that, as we shall see, the consumer can be in equilibrium only at a convex point on an indifference curve. The possibility of concave sections of a curve can therefore be ignored.

The rate at which an individual is willing to give up one good (in the previously cited example, bananas) in exchange for another good (apples), while remaining on the same level of utility is called the marginal rate of substitution between apples and bananas (MRS_{ab}). It is the quantity of bananas the individual is willing to give up per unit increase in his quantity of apples.

The MRS_{ab} is equal to the negative of the slope of the indifference curve. In Figure 3.2, as the consumer moves from point 1 to point 2, he gives up BB' of bananas and gains AA' of apples. Thus, MRS_{ab} equals BB'/AA'. This approximates the negative of the slope of the indifference curve between points 1 and 2 and for infinitely small

---

[2]Indifference curves for two goods or services the individual dislikes will also have a negative slope; in that case, utility falls with a movement up and to the right on the map. If one good is liked and the other is not, the indifference curves will have a positive slope. See the indifference curves of Chapter 4 for an individual's preferences between work and income.

changes will equal the negative of the slope. Therefore, the slope of the indifference curve at a point equals $-MRS_{ab}$.

Figure 3.2 *Marginal Rate of Substitution and Slope*

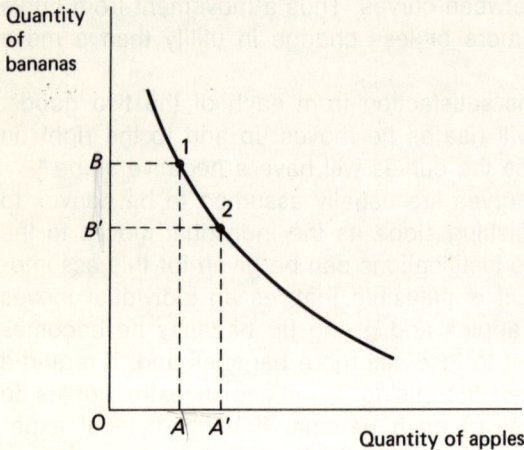

Note that convexity of the indifference curve implies a diminishing marginal rate of substitution as bananas are exchanged for apples.

An indifference curve can be related to the marginal utilities of the two goods. The marginal utility of a good is the change in the total utility of a consumer when he receives or consumes one more unit of the good,[3] quantities of other goods remaining unchanged. The individual is willing to give up ΔQ_b of bananas in exchange for ΔQ_a of apples. The utility he loses from the bananas will equal the marginal utility of bananas times the quantity of bananas given up. Remembering that the change in Q_b is negative, his utility loss is then $-(MU_b)(\Delta Q_b)$. By analogous reasoning the utility gain from apples is $(MU_a)(\Delta Q_a)$. Because the consumer is indifferent about the two positions, his utility gain must equal his loss. Thus

$$(MU_a)(\Delta Q_a) = -(MU_b)(\Delta Q_b) \tag{2}$$

Hence

$$\frac{MU_a}{MU_b} = -\frac{\Delta Q_b}{\Delta Q_a} \tag{3}$$

For small changes $\Delta Q_b/\Delta Q_a$ approximates the slope of the indif-

[3] In the limit, it is the derivative of total utility (U) with respect to the good (G), that is, $\partial U/\partial G$.

ference curve, which equals the negative of the MRS_{ab}. Therefore, in the limit

$$\frac{MU_a}{MU_b} = MRS_{ab} \qquad (4)$$

COMPLEMENTS AND SUBSTITUTES

The degree of curvature of an indifference curve depends on the substitute or complementary relation between the two goods. Two goods are substitutes if an increase in the quantity of one reduces the marginal utility of the second; they are complements if the marginal utility of the second rises when the consumer acquires more of the first good. Butter and margarine, coffee and tea, Fords and Chevrolets are substitutes; razors and razor blades, cars and gasoline, and beer and pretzels, are pairs of complements.

When two goods are perfect substitutes, the consumer remains willing to exchange one for the other at a constant rate of exchange. His marginal rate of substitution between them is constant. The indifference curves for perfect substitutes are therefore straight lines with constant slopes, as in Figure 3.3a. It is rarely useful to distinguish between any two goods that are perfect substitutes; they are therefore treated as a single good.

Figure 3.3 *Indifference Maps for Substitutes and Complements*

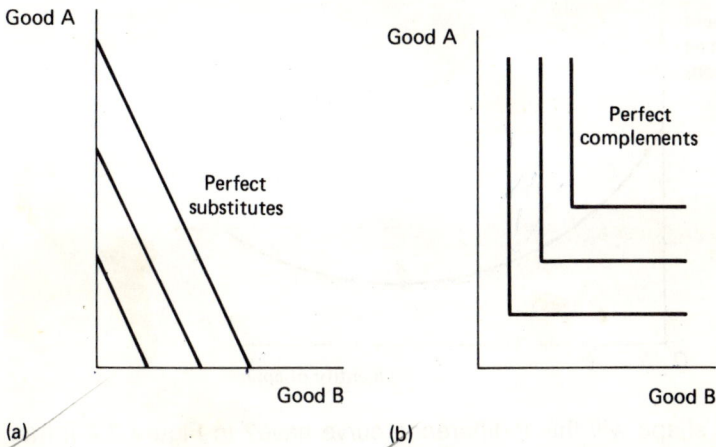

Two goods are perfect complements when they must be used in fixed proportions, and an additional quantity of one is useless unless the quantity of the second is also increased. Left and right shoes· are the obvious examples. Indifference curves for perfect complements are illustrated in Figure 3.3b. Because two perfect complements must be used together, the unit of analysis is usually taken to be a combination of the two goods (for example, a pair of shoes), and neither good is analyzed by itself.

AN INDIFFERENCE MAP FOR ONE GOOD AND MONEY

The analysis can be extended to many goods in many dimensions with the use of equations. The most useful step now, however, is to stay with two dimensions, keeping one good (for example, apples) on the horizontal axis, but measuring all other goods on the vertical axis. A heterogeneous collection of goods can be aggregated into a single measure by using the natural standard of comparison, their money values. To do this requires that the prices of all other goods be assumed given and remain constant. In effect then, money is the variable measured on the vertical axis.

An indifference curve (Figure 3.4) now shows us the combinations of apples and money spent on all other goods at given prices that would give the individual the same level of utility. The slope of the indifference curve at any point is the consumer's marginal rate of substitution between apples and money, that is, the amount of money the individual would be willing to give up for an additional unit of good A.

Figure 3.4   Indifference Curve: One Good and Money

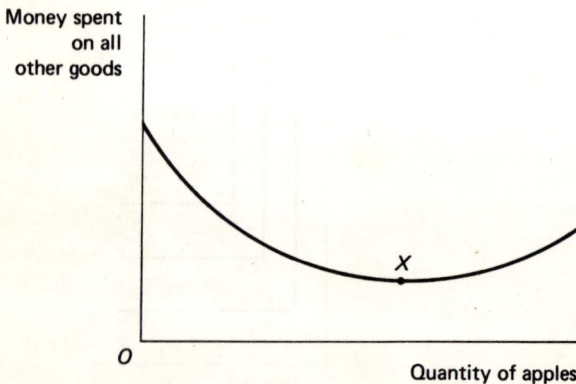

What shape will this indifference curve have? In Figure 3.4 it has been drawn with an initial downward slope, reaching a minimum at X, and then turning up. If the individual is at point X, and is given more A, his utility declines. That means the marginal utility of A is negative beyond X. At point X the slope of the indifference curve equals zero, and hence the MU_a is zero.

It is reasonable to believe that an individual can reach a point of satiety with respect to a particular good, at which its marginal utility is zero. What is not likely is that the marginal utility of money (that is, the marginal utility of goods in general) should ever reach zero. (Thoreau is perhaps the exception who proves the rule.) It is therefore unlikely that indifference curves, when approaching the money axis, will become vertical and turn back to the right. In short, for an indifference map setting money against a good, a set of bowl-shaped indifference curves seems most likely.

Maps are typically drawn showing only the downward sloping portion of the curves because the utility maximizing individual will never move onto the upward sloping sections.

CONSUMER'S SURPLUS

When an individual moves from one point on his indifference map to another, we know whether his utility has increased, decreased, or remained constant. It is not possible, however, to measure the change in utility. But it is possible to measure his gain or loss in money terms.

Consumer's surplus is a measure in money terms of the net gain to a consumer arising from a change in the opportunities open to him. The concept of consumer's (and consumers') surplus is central in the determination of the efficiency gains or losses of an economic change. Efficiency increases as a result of a change in economic activity if the gains of those benefiting from the change exceed the losses of those made worse off when gains and losses are measured in money terms. In the calculation, gains and losses of consumers resulting from the change are measured by the changes in the consumer's surpluses of those individuals.

If, in Figure 3.5, the initial position of the consumer is point Y, with no apples but money of OY, and he is then *given OX* units of apples, he is better off. His gain can be considered conceptually as his increase in utility in moving from point Y on indifference curve I_1 to point M' on indifference curve I_2. This increase in utility cannot be measured. But we can measure from the map the monetary value of the gain. Specifically, the vertical distance between curves I_1 and I_2 is a money measure of how much better off the individual will be when, with the gift of the apples, he is able to move from curve I_1 to curve I_2 (that is, from point Y to point M'). His utility is greater on I_2 than I_1, but the increase in utility cannot be measured.

A difficulty is that the vertical ("money") distance between I_1 and I_2 may vary, depending on where it is measured. For example, the distance YY' may not be the same as the distance MM'. Consider these two in turn.

Figure 3.5   *Measurement of Consumer's Surplus*

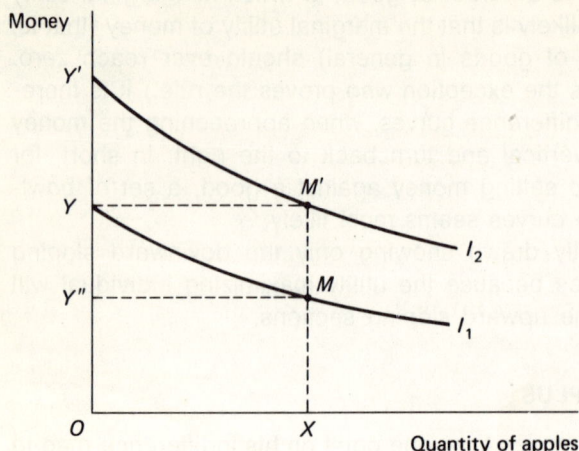

Recall our case: the individual had OY of money, and was *given* OX of apples. He likes apples, so he is better off. The indifference curves tell us that if we took back the apples we would have to give him YY' more of money to keep him as satisfied as he was with the apples   (that is, on indifference level I_2). Distance YY' is therefore one measure of the consumer surplus he receives by being given the apples. It is called the equivalent variation (*EV*), that is, the amount of money that would raise his utility an amount equivalent to the rise due to the gift of apples.

Alternately, having been given the apples, he would be willing to pay up to MM' (= YY") to keep them. Therefore YY" is a second measure of the gain he would receive by being given the apples. Then YY" is called the compensating variation in income (*CV*).[4]

The two measures of gain will be approximately the same if the gain is small as compared with the individual's total holdings of money. A conservative approach would take the smaller of the two values as a measure of the consumer's surplus.

Consumer's surplus is the gain (or loss, if negative) resulting from a change in the opportunities open to a consumer. The value to an individual of free access to public schools or to a park for example, would represent such a surplus which, aggregated over all users, would be compared with the costs of the good to determine whether its provision would promote economic efficiency. In private markets, consumer surplus arises not from free access to goods but from the

[4]If you have trouble remembering terms, try this trick: Alphabetically, *CV* precedes *EV*. CV keeps the individual on his *first* level of utility (that is, in the example, his utility level before he was given the apples); EV keeps him on the second level of satisfaction (which he had reached after receiving the apples).

opportunities to purchase goods at various prices. An important question then is whether a change in the price of a good increases efficiency, which requires measuring consumers' surplus and comparing it with the costs or losses associated with the price change.

THE CONCEPT OF EQUILIBRIUM

In the analysis of consumer behavior, as throughout economic theory, the concept of an equilibrium is fundamental. The term was borrowed from the physical sciences, where it means a balancing of forces. Economics is dealing with individuals, however, and a somewhat different definition is in order. Any equilibrium is a situation that will continue to exist until outside forces arise to disturb it. In terms of human behavior, it therefore means that every individual is satisfied that he has made the best choice among the alternatives available to him. An equilibrium can be said to be a situation in which no one who *can* make a change *wants* to, and no one who *wants* to make a change is *able* to do so.

The nature of any equilibrium is determined by the particular constraints that exist or are assumed to exist. The individuals involved may heartily wish they were in a different situation, that different or fewer constraints restricted their behavior. (They may regret an existing situation, and with hindsight see that they could and should have avoided it.) But, given the existing restrictions, if they can see no way open to them to improve their position, they are in equilibrium. By extension, market equilibrium for a good exists when all individuals in that market as buyers or sellers are in equilibrium.

CONSUMER EQUILIBRIUM

The demand of an individual consumer for a good can be illustrated with his indifference map. Recall that the amount of a good he will demand depends on his tastes, his income, the prices of all other goods, and the price of the good in question. His indifference map is a representation of his tastes. In order to represent all other goods on the vertical axis of his indifference map, it was necessary to assume that the prices of all other goods were known and constant. The individual's income can then be represented by a point on the vertical axis, say point Y of Figure 3.6.

Assume now a given price for apples (P_a). The individual can buy as many pounds as he wishes at this price. The choices now open to him are represented on Figure 3.6 by a line, YX, starting at point Y representing his income (that is, the amount spent on all other goods if he chooses to buy no apples), and ending on the apple axis at point X, which is the quantity of apples he could buy if he spent his entire income on them. Point X is found by dividing his

Figure 3.6 *Equilibrium of the Consumer*

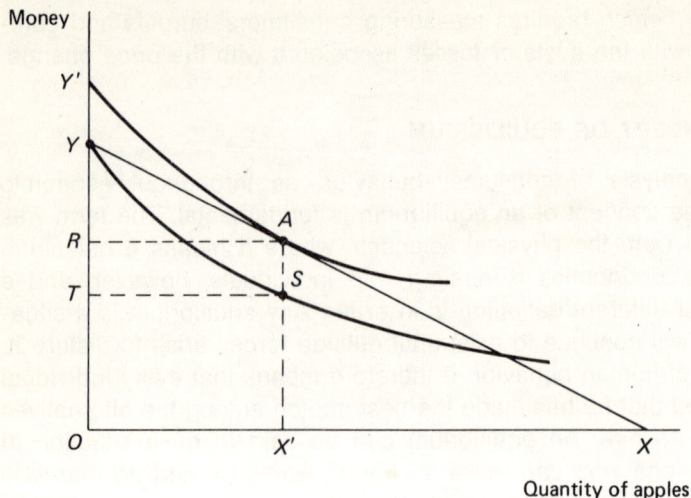

Quantity of apples

income OY by the assumed price of apples. Line YX is called the *budget line*. It may also be called his *opportunity line*. The consumer is free to choose any point (that is, any combination of apples plus other goods) represented by the points on (or below) his budget line.

The slope of the budget line is $-OY/OX$. OX is the amount of apples he could buy with his entire income. Therefore, OX equals OY/Pa. Substituting, the slope of the budget line equals

$$-OY/(OY/Pa) = -(OY/OY)\ (Pa) = -Pa.$$

Thus, the price of apples equals the negative of the slope of the budget line.

The utility maximizing individual will try to reach the highest indifference curve open to him. For a given budget line, this clearly occurs where his budget line is tangent to an indifference curve (point A of Figure 3.6). Point A constitutes an equilibrium position for the consumer. He will buy OX' quantity of apples, paying for them a total amount of YR. (OR represents the income he has remaining after purchasing the apples.) At the point of equilibrium the price of apples (equal to the slope of the budget line) is equal to the individual's marginal rate of substitution between money and apples (equal to the slope of his indifference curve).[5] At any other point along the budget line, the MRS_{am} is either greater than P_a, in which case the individual should buy more apples, or less than P_a, in which case he is buying too many apples.

[5] In both cases the slopes are negative.

By being given the opportunity to purchase apples at this price, the individual receives consumer surplus. His point of equilibrium (A) lies on a higher indifference curve than does point Y, which represents his position if he purchased no apples.

The compensating variation, SA, is the amount he would pay, in addition to the amount he is already spending on apples, to be allowed to continue his present purchases at price P_a. The equivalent variation, YY', is the amount the individual would need to compensate him for the loss of this opportunity to buy apples at this price.

CONSUMER RESPONSE TO PRICE CHANGES

Consider now the consumer's response to changes in the price of a product, other things (that is, money income, tastes, and prices of all other goods) held constant.

Starting with the individual in equilibrium at one price at point E on budget line YA in Figure 3.7, assume that the price of the product is reduced. The new price gives rise to a new budget line YA'. It still starts at point Y (for money income has not changed), but is now flatter, with a slope equal to the new lower price. The consumer has a new equilibrium, at point E'. In the particular case illustrated, the consumer buys more at the lower price (OX' compared with OX), but is spending less on the good (YY') than he would have spent (YY'') at the higher price.

Figure 3.7   *Consumer Response to Price Change*

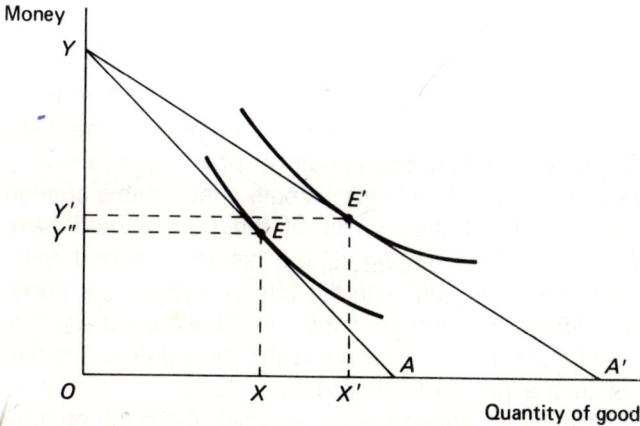

By economists identify two reasons for an individual to change his consumption of a good when its price changes, an *income effect* and a *substitution effect*.

When a price drops, the consumer's real income rises (that is, he can reach a higher indifference curve, representing a higher level of satisfaction) because he can buy more goods with his (constant) money income.

The substitution effect of a price change is the change in the quantity of the good that would be demanded if its price had changed but the individual's real income (that is, his level of utility) had remained constant. The income effect is the change in the quantity demanded, which results from the change in real income due to the price change, even if the price had not changed.

Figure 3.8   *Income and Substitution Effects*

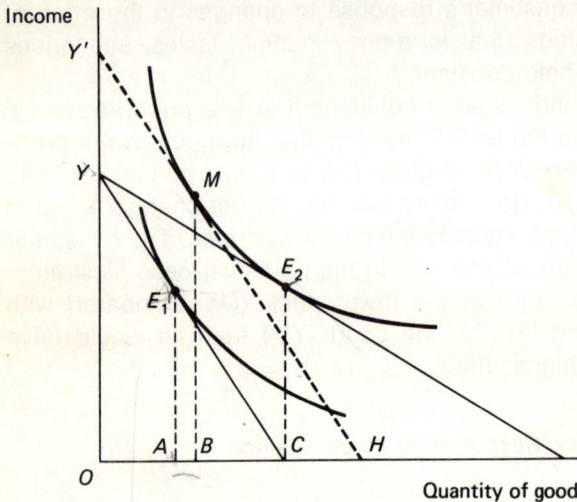

Assume that an individual is in equilibrium in Figure 3.8 at point E_1, purchasing OA units of the good. A drop in the price of the good induces him to move to a new equilibrium at point E_2, consuming OC units of the product. To identify the income effect of this change in price we ask how his consumption of the good would have changed if its price had *not* changed, but his income had been increased enough to enable him, with the former price of the good, to move to the higher indifference curve on which point E_2 lies. In other words, what lump sum change in the individual's income, with no change in the price of the product, would permit him to move to the same higher indifference curve which the price change permits him. To permit him to do this, the consumer's income would have to rise from OY to OY'. At an income of OY', but with the unchanged price of the good, his budget line would be $Y'H$. In this situation he would have moved to point M.

The movement from point E_1 to point M, or, more specifically, the increase in his consumption of the good from OA to OB, is called the income effect of the price change.

Income effects of price changes can be positive or negative. That is, a change in an individual's real income due to a change in the price of a good may cause the quantity of the good purchased to rise or to fall. For *normal* goods, it is positive (that is, the rise in real income resulting from a drop in the price of a good causes the individual to buy more of it). Conversely, the income effect for an *inferior* good is negative. Normal and inferior goods are defined as those for which the income effects are positive and negative, respectively.

The income effects of price changes of typical consumption goods on which the individual spends a small part of his income are not likely in practice to be significant.

The drop in the price of the product increased the consumer's purchases by AC. The distance AB is accounted for by the income effect. The remaining increase, BC, is the substitution effect, the change in quantity demanded resulting from a change in price, real income being held constant.[6]

The substitution effect for a buyer is always negative, price and quantity demanded moving in *opposite* directions. The buyer substitutes the good with the newly lowered price for other goods, the absolute prices of which have not changed; but in terms of relative prices they are now more expensive than before.

For normal goods the income and substitution effects of a price change reinforce each other. Both encourage the consumer to buy more of a good when its price drops, and less when it rises. If the product is an inferior good, however, the two effects run counter to each other. The income effect encourages a drop in consumption of a good when its price falls; but the substitution effect encourages an increase in the good's consumption. The substitution effect is likely in practice to dominate the income effect. Hence the "law of demand": a drop in the price of a good leads to an increase in the quantity demanded.

The so-called "Giffen case" is one where an inferior good has an income effect so strong that it swamps the substitution effect; a drop in price causes a decrease in the quantity of the good demanded, and the demand curve is backward sloping.

[6]The student may well wonder whether the relative sizes of the income and substitution effects in the case illustrated would be the same if we had first shown the substitution effect (that is, a movement along the individual's initial indifference curve), with the income effect accounting for the residual change in the quantity demanded. The answer is "not necessarily." This slight ambiguity in the measurement of the two effects disappears, however, for infinitely small changes.

DERIVATION OF THE DEMAND CURVE

The consumer's demand curve for a product shows the quantities he would demand at all prices, when his money income, his tastes, and the prices of all other goods are given constants.

When on an indifference map the price of a good is varied continuously, the consumer's equilibrium point moves. The line running through the points of equilibrium, as the price changes, is called the *price-consumption line* (see Figure 3.9a).

Figure 3.9 *Price–Consumption and Demand Curves*

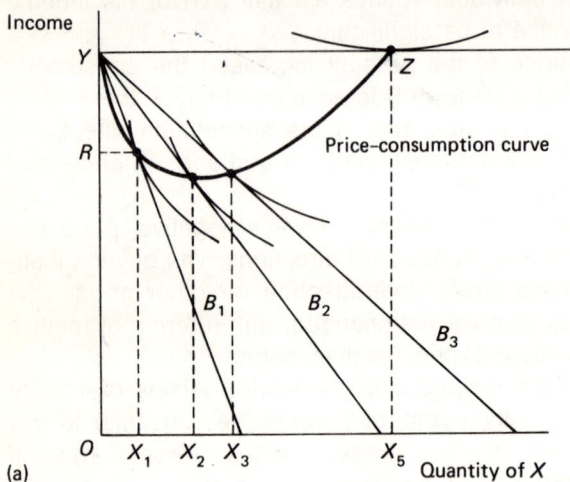

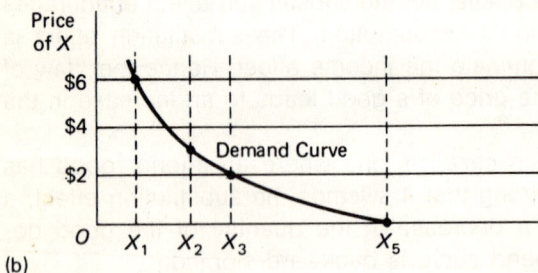

For each point on the price-consumption curve we can determine (1) the price—as indicated by the slope of the budget line and of the indifference curve to which it is tangent at this point; (2) the quantity of X purchased; and (3) the amount of money spent on the good—measured by *YR* (*not OR*), that is, by the vertical distance between the equilibrium point and the individual's initial income level. From this information a demand curve of this individual for the product is constructed.

It is convenient to construct the graph of the demand curve directly below the indifference map because the same variable—the quantity of the good—is measured on the horizontal axes of both graphs. The demand curve of Figure 3.9b is derived from the indifference map of Figure 3.9a. From each equilibrium point on the indifference map simply drop a line to the lower graph. The intersection of this line with a price level equal to the equilibrium price (which equals the slope of the budget line at the equilibrium point) locates one point on the demand curve. By varying price, additional points of consumer equilibrium on the indifference map are determined. These are then translated to the demand curve graph.

Consider now the shape of the price–consumption curve. The highest price the individual will pay for any amount of the good is shown by the slope (*MRS*) of the indifference curve where it cuts the vertical axis at *Y*, the individual's income; for budget lines representing prices higher than this the consumer is in "equilibrium" by staying at point *Y* and consuming none of the good.

The price consumption curve therefore starts at point *Y*. It initially drops to the right, but must rise because when the price of the good is zero, the price–consumption line again reaches the height of *Y*. (See point *Z* on Figure 3.9a, and the corresponding point X_5 on Figure 3.9b—the quantity demanded when the price is zero.)

Generally, therefore, the price–consumption curve will be shaped like a bowl.

The demand curve for an individual shows how much of a good he will buy at various prices. If there are many buyers we can construct a market demand curve for the product summing at each price the quantities of the good all buyers will purchase. The individual demand curves are simply added horizontally.

PRICE ELASTICITY OF DEMAND

Price elasticity of demand is a measure of the responsiveness of the quantity demanded to changes in price. Price elasticity of demand is

$$\frac{\text{percentage change in quantity demanded}}{\text{percentage change in price}} = \frac{\dfrac{dQ}{Q}}{\dfrac{dP}{P}} = \frac{PdQ}{QdP}$$

Because price and quantity will be changing in opposite directions, elasticity of demand will normally be negative. As a convention in economic theory, the minus sign here is commonly ignored.

The price–quantity relationship shown by a demand curve is a schedule of potential expenditures by buyers, and therefore potential revenues for sellers. For the seller who charges all buyers the same price (that is, one who does not practice price discrimination), the demand schedule is a curve of average revenue. A seller is particularly interested in the elasticity of demand for his product and its relation to his revenues.

When the demand for a product is relatively inelastic (that is, when it has an elasticity of less than one), a price reduction leads to a proportionately smaller increase in the quantity sold. The total amount spent on the product and hence the seller's total revenue drop. If demand is relatively elastic, a change in price induces a proportionally greater change in quantity demanded, and the seller's total revenues will increase with a drop in price. Unitary elasticity of demand exists when the percentage changes in price and quantity are equal, so that total revenue remains constant with a change in price.

Elasticity of demand therefore is directly related to marginal revenue, that is, the change in the total revenue of a seller when an additional unit of the product is sold. The relationships between the price elasticity of demand and the behavior of total and marginal revenue of a seller, for a decrease in the price of the product, are as follows:

When the price elasticity of demand is	Total revenue	Marginal revenue
Greater than 1	Increases	Positive
Equal to 1	Constant	Zero
Less than 1	Decreases	Negative

A helpful rule is this: When demand is elastic, price and total revenue move in opposite directions; when demand is inelastic, price and total revenue move in the same direction.

Applying the techniques for measuring elasticity discussed in Chapter 2, the elasticity of a point on a demand curve can be measured by drawing a tangent to the demand curve at that point. The elasticity at point A in Figure 3.10 is then BX/BO.[7]

[7]By the principle of similar triangles, $BX/BO = XA/AP = OC/CP$. Any of these can therefore be used to measure elasticity.

Figure 3.10   *Point Elasticity of Demand*

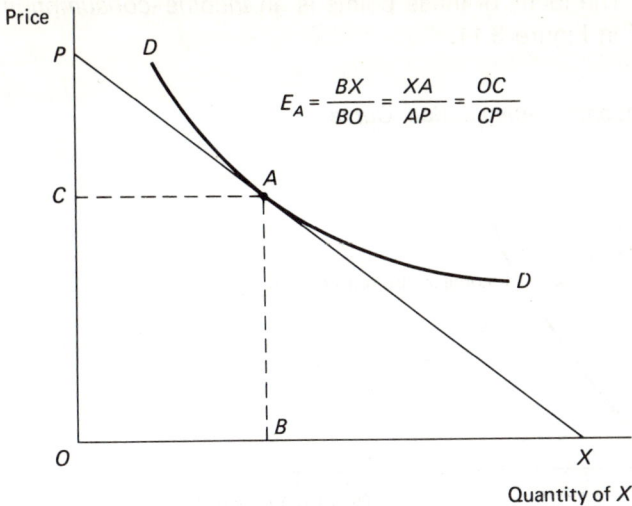

$$E_A = \frac{BX}{BO} = \frac{XA}{AP} = \frac{OC}{CP}$$

DETERMINANTS OF ELASTICITY

The elasticity of demand for a good is closely related to the availability of substitute products. If a good has many readily available close substitutes, elasticity will be high. The elasticity of demand for a single type or brand of goods will be higher than the elasticity of demand for the group of which this good is a part. Thus the demand for meat, in general, is less elastic than the demand for hamburger, which has still less elasticity than the demand for hamburger at a particular market.

The elasticity of demand for a given product is likely to be greater over a longer time period than in the short run. Over a period of time consumers are more able to adjust to price changes.

Further, elasticity of demand will tend to be higher for a good with many uses than for one with a single function. As the price of a multiuse good declines, individuals extend their consumption of it to new uses, thereby increasing the quantity purchased.

RESPONSES TO INCOME CHANGES

The amount of a good demanded by an individual at a given price depends, as noted earlier, on his income. The effects of changing income on the demand for a good can be easily seen on an indifference map. As the individual's income rises, the price of the good being held constant, the budget line shifts up. The vertical intercept of the budget line rises, but the line maintains a constant slope, for the slope depends on the price of the good, which is assumed not to vary. For each income, there will be an equilibrium point for the individual. The locus of these points is an *income–consumption* curve, line *OT* in Figure 3.11.

Figure 3.11 *Income–Consumption Curve*

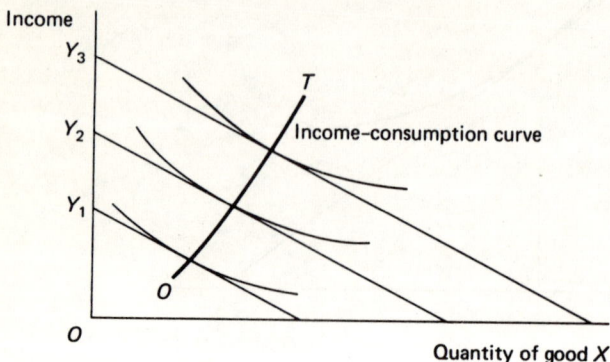

When the income–consumption curve slopes upward to the right, the consumer buys more of the good as his income rises. For such a good, called a *normal good,* the income elasticity of demand is positive. A change of the consumer's income causes the quantity of the good purchased to change in the same direction.

Income elasticity of demand, denoted as E_{qy}, is the responsiveness of quantity (Q) to income (Y).

$$E_{qy} = \frac{\text{percentage change in quantity demanded}}{\text{percentage change in income}} = \frac{\frac{dQ}{Q}}{\frac{dY}{Y}} = \frac{YdQ}{QdY}$$

Inferior goods are those of which less is purchased as income rises, price being held constant. The income–consumption curve for an inferior good has a negative slope, and income elasticity of demand is negative.

A good may be a normal good at some levels of income, and an inferior good at others. Hamburger may be a luxury good for the impecunious student living on beans, but an inferior good when his income makes steak possible. Knowledge of income elasticities is very useful in making long run predictions of the demand for goods. As the per capita real income of a nation rises, the demand for inferior goods declines. The demand for luxury goods (swimming pools, color TV sets) tends to rise proportionally more than income.

CROSS ELASTICITY OF DEMAND

The demand for a good depends on the prices of other goods, in particular those that are close substitutes or complements of the good in question. The strength of the interrelationship between two goods can be measured by the cross elasticity of demand between them.

The cross elasticity of the demand for good A with respect to good B, written E_{ab}, is the percentage change in the *quantity* of A which is demanded in response to a one percentage change in the *price* of good B, when tastes, incomes, and all other prices (including the price of A) are constant. Thus,

$$E_{ab} = \frac{\text{percentage change in } Q_a}{\text{percentage change in } P_b} = \frac{P_b dQ_a}{Q_a dP_b}$$

If goods A and B are substitutes (pie and cake, bicycles and motorcycles), a rise in the price of B will increase the demand for A. The value of the cross elasticity for substitute goods is therefore positive. The greater the absolute value of the cross elasticity between two goods, the closer substitutes they are.

The concept of cross elasticity has been used in antitrust cases. When DuPont was charged with monopolizing the sale of cellophane, for example, the company argued that the cross elasticity of demand between cellophane and other "flexible wrapping materials" was so high that the company could not be considered an effective monopoly.[8]

Cross elasticity of demand between complementary products has a negative value. A *rise* in the price of skis, for example, will *reduce* the demand for such complementary products as ski boots and lift tickets.

A company selling two complementary products (for example, razors and razor blades) may find it advantageous to set an artificially low price on one good to stimulate demand for the other.

THE DEMAND CURVE AND CONSUMERS' SURPLUS

Changes in efficiency are calculated by comparing in money terms the gains and losses resulting from new opportunities available to individuals. As noted previously, changes in consumers' surplus are a measure of the gains or losses to consumers from price changes. Consumers' surplus can be determined from indifference maps. In

---

[8]A majority of the Supreme Court agreed. See *U.S. v. DuPont* 351 U.S. 377 (1956).

practice, however, the maps are not known. What may be known with some degree of accuracy is the demand curve for a product. At any given time it is known how much is being demanded at the current market price. This information provides one point on a demand curve. Past experience with the same and related goods gives some indication of how much would be demanded at other prices. An estimate of the demand curve for a product can thus be developed. The question then is whether, and how, consumers' surplus can be determined from the information provided by a demand curve.

The demand curve is a price–quantity relationship. It shows the quantity demanded at each price, that is, $Q = f(P)$. If quantity is a function of price, price must be a function of quantity, and we can also write a demand equation as $P = f(Q)$. When the demand equation is written in this second form, price takes on a slightly different meaning. Price then is the amount the consumer would be willing to pay for a given quantity. The price associated with a particular quantity is the *marginal value* to the consumer of an additional unit of the product. Marginal value is the amount (in money terms) the consumer would be willing to pay for one more unit. The demand curve is hence a curve of marginal value, showing values to the consumer of each additional unit of the good.

Marginal value is measured in money terms. It should be carefully distinguished from marginal utility (which is not measured in money terms), and also from marginal expenditure and marginal revenue, which measure changes in amount spent. Only if marginal value exceeds marginal expenditure does the individual receive consumer's surplus.

Consider the hypothetical data of Table 3.1. Columns (1) and (2) give the basic price-quantity data of a demand curve. All other columns are derived directly or indirectly from those data.

At a price of $1.00, the consumer buys none. At 80 cents he will buy one unit. The marginal value of the first unit is thus 80 cents to him, and the total value for one unit is also 80 cents. He would buy two if the price drops to 60 cents; the marginal value of the second is therefore 60 cents, and the total value of two units is the 80 cents of the first unit plus the 60 cents of the second, for a total value of $1.40.

But at a price of 60 cents, he spends only $1.20 on the good. The difference between the total value of two units ($1.40) and the amount he spends on them ($1.20) is the consumer surplus, the excess of the value of the good over its cost to him. The demand schedule indicates the marginal value of a third unit of the good to him is 40 cents. At a price of 40 cents he would buy three units, at a total cost of $1.20. But the total value of the three is 80

TABLE 3.1   Consumer's Surplus

(1) Price	(2) Quantity Demanded	(3) Total Expenditures	(4) Marginal Expenditures	(5) Total Value	(6) Marginal Value (= Price)	(7) Consumer's Surplus [= (5) − (3)]
$1.00	0	0		0		0
.80	1	$ .80	$ .80	$ .80	$ .80	0
.60	2	1.20	.40	1.40	.60	$ .20
.40	3	1.20	0	1.80	.40	.60
.20	4	.80	−.40	2.00	.20	1.20
0	5	0	−.80	2.00	0	2.00

cents + 60 cents + 40 cents = $1.80. His consumer surplus is thus 60 cents.

The table then shows the following:

(1) Price equals marginal value.

(2) Marginal value does *not* equal marginal amount spent on the product.

(3) Total value for a given quantity is the sum of the marginal values up to that point. Because the demand curve is a curve of marginal values, total value for a specific quantity is equal to the area under the demand curve up to that point.

(4) Consumer surplus at a given quantity equals total value (that is, the area under the demand curve) minus the amount spent on the product.

Thus the area under a demand curve less the amount spent on the product is a measure of consumers' surplus.

The conclusions derived from the demand curve of Table 3.1 apply equally to a market demand curve, which would approximate a continuous function.

In the earlier analysis of consumers' surplus (p. 36) two measures of surplus were identified. Here only one measure was found. How can one account for the difference?

In the earlier discussion the compensating variation measure of consumer's surplus differed from the equivalent variation when two indifference curves were not a constant vertical distance apart (that is, when an income effect was present and a change in income, with price constant, induces a change in the quantity of the good demanded).

When the income effect is zero, the two measures are equal, and the consumer's surplus measured from the demand curve will be equal to the consumer's surplus shown on the indifference maps. Measures of consumer's surplus are not likely to differ significantly for products taking a small portion of the individual's budget or for small changes in the prices of goods. But consider the case of an automobile. Assume that an individual would buy one car at a price of $3000 or less. What price would he pay for a second car? That is, what would be its marginal value to him? He might well say that the amount he would pay for a second car would depend on how much the first cost him. If he had to pay $3000 for it, he would pay only $500, say, for a second. On the other hand, if he could get the first car for only $1000, he might be willing to pay up to $800 for a second.

Thus the marginal value of the second car here depends on the price paid for the first. Should the consumer be given a second car free of charge, the consumer surplus he would receive from it would depend on how much he had been charged for the first car.

The measurement of consumer's surplus by subtracting the amount spent on the good from the area under a demand curve, then, may be imprecise when a strong income effect of this type is present. For practical purposes, however, such possibilities are ignored because they are significant only for very major changes in price of products on which a significant portion of the individual's income is spent.

REVIEW QUESTIONS

1. Explain and give examples of the following:
    Utility
    Demand
    Indifference curve
    Marginal rate of substitution
    Marginal utility
    Complements
    Substitutes
    Consumer's surplus
    Compensating variation
    Equivalent variation
    Equilibrium
    Budget line; opportunity line of consumer
    Income effect
    Substitution effect
    Normal good
    Inferior good
    Price elasticity of demand
    Income elasticity of demand
    Giffen case
    Price–consumption line
    Income–consumption line
    Marginal revenue
    Average revenue
    Cross elasticity of demand
    Marginal value

2. (a) Draw an indifference map for an individual, showing his preferences between one good and all other goods.
    (b) Assuming an income level for the individual and a price for the single good, construct the budget line. Show the consumer's equilibrium point, the quantity of the good purchased, the amount spent on the product, and the two measures of the consumer's surplus he receives.
    (c) Assume a change in the price of the product and show the new equilibrium. What has happened to the consumer's surplus? Show the income and substitution effects of the change in price. Is the product a normal or an inferior good? How do you know?

3. If income elasticity of demand is unity, what shape will the income–consumption curve have?

4. If price elasticity of demand is unity, what shape will the price–consumption curve have?
5. A demand curve can be derived from an indifference map. How much of an indifference map can be derived from a demand curve?
6. Construct an indifference map for a Giffen good. What shape will the price–consumption curve have? What is the shape of the income–consumption curve?
7. Moving from left to right, are two indifference curves likely to be closer or farther apart vertically? horizontally? On what factors do the answers to these questions depend?

FURTHER READING

Henderson, James M., and Richard E. Quandt, *Microeconomic Theory: A Mathematical Approach.* New York: McGraw-Hill (1958), chap. 2.

Hicks, J. R., *A Revision of Demand Theory. London:* Oxford University Press (1956).

Hicks, J. R., *Value and Capital.* 2nd ed., London: Oxford University Press (1946), pt. I.

Marshall, Alfred, *Principles of Economics.* 8th ed., London: Macmillan (1920), bk. III.

Stigler, George J., "The Development of Utility Theory." *Journal of Political Economy 58* (1950), 307–327, 373–396; reprinted in Alfred N. Page, ed., *Utility Theory: A Book of Readings.* New York: Wiley (1968).

4

SUPPLY
OF
INDIVIDUALS

THE INDIVIDUAL AS A SELLER

The analysis of the supply functions of individuals offering goods or services is similar to demand analysis, utilizing essentially the same techniques. After a generalized analysis of individual supply, two particular cases will be considered: supply of labor services and supply of savings by individual lenders to borrowers.

As in demand analysis, the quantity of a good or service an individual will supply depends on his preferences, his income, and all prices. An individual supplier has a choice of supplying some good or service he controls or retaining it for his own uses. An indifference map will show his preferences for retaining the good or service for his own use, as compared with giving it up and enjoying the money paid him for supplying the good or service.

An indifference map (see Figure 4.1) plotting income on the vertical axis and quantity of the good or service which he retains for his own use,[1] summarizes his preferences. Prices of all other goods are assumed given and constant. The initial position of the individual is a point representing the

[1]Alternately, the quantity supplied could be measured from left to right on the horizontal axis, in which case the indifference curves would have positive slopes. The method used in the text will facilitate the analysis of the theory of pure exchange of Chapter 5.

Figure 4.1   *Equilibrium of the Individual Seller*

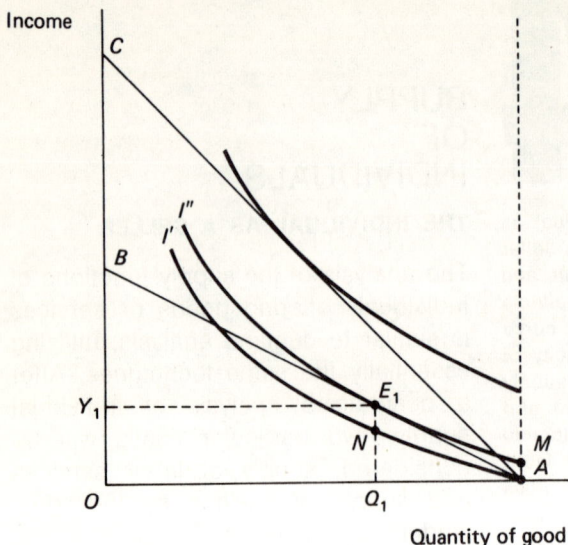

Quantity of good

amounts of income and the good he would have if he supplied none of the good to others.

If, as in Figure 4.1, the individual has no income other than he would receive from selling his product and has *OA* units of the product available for sale his initial position is point *A*.

The quantity of the good the individual will supply depends on the price he can receive for it. His opportunity line will begin at point A and rise to the left. The negative of the slope of his opportunity line equals the price of the product. If the opportunities available to him are represented by line *BA*, he could move to point *B*, selling his entire stock of the good *OA* in exchange for income of *OB*. Then *OB/OA* is the slope of line *BA*[2] and *OB/OA* is also the total income received from the sale divided by the quantity sold; that is, the price of the good.

A higher price would be represented by a steeper opportunity line beginning at point *A* (for example, line *CA*).

Equilibrium for the individual occurs at a point of tangency between an indifference curve and his opportunity line. With the price (P_1) represented by opportunity line *BA*, equilibrium is at point E_1. The supplier sells AQ_1 units of the product (note the quantity supplied is measured from right to left, beginning at point *A*), and receives OY_1 in income from the sale.

The seller's surplus, analogous to consumer's surplus, is meas-

[2]The negative sign of the slope of *BA* is ignored because the seller moves from right to left along the line.

ured by the vertical distance between indifference curve I' running through point A and indifference curve I'' which he reaches at his equilibrium point E_1. As in demand analysis, this surplus can be measured in two ways: (1) the compensating variation, distance E_1N, which is the amount of income he could give up after the sale and be as well off as he was before the sale; and (2) the equivalent variation, distance MA, the amount of money he would require if not permitted to make the sale, which would make him as well off as he became by having the opportunity to sell his product.

INCOME AND SUBSTITUTION EFFECTS

The effects on the seller's equilibrium position of a change in price are illustrated in Figure 4.2, showing the seller's equilibrium positions E_1 and E_2 at prices represented by the slopes of the two opportunity lines, BA and CA. The higher price permits the individual to move to a higher indifference curve. In the case illustrated, he sells more at the higher price than at the lower price (AQ_2 compared with AQ_1), and his income from sale increases from OY_1 to OY_2.

Figure 4.2   *Income and Substitution Effects for a Seller*

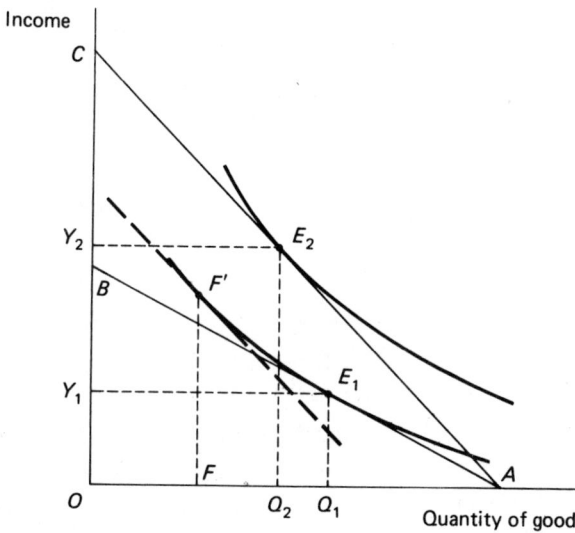

The change in quantity sold from Q_1 to Q_2 results from a substitution effect and an income effect. The substitution effect is the move from Q_1 to F. It is the change in the quantity the individual would have supplied with the assumed change in price if his real income had not risen as a result of the price change (that is, if he stayed on the indifference curve through his original equilibrium point E_1). The substitution effect for a seller is always positive—a change in price causes a change in the quantity supplied in the same direction.

Note that in the case illustrated the substitution effect by itself was larger than the total effect of the price change. The income effect alone, OF to OQ_2, would induce the seller to supply *less* at the higher price. This result is expected. For a normal good, an individual will wish to retain for his own use a larger quantity of the good when his income rises. This requires that he offer less of it for sale.

In the case of demand analysis, the income and substitution effects of a price change for a normal good worked in the same direction. For a fall in price, for example, both effects encouraged an increased demand for the good. In supply analysis of a normal good, however, the two effects have opposite influences: the substitution effect of a price rise increases the amount supplied, while the income effect decreases it.

In demand theory it was noted that the income effect of a price change is not likely to be significant, and that the substitution effect would dominate. For this reason an inverse relation between price and quantity demanded is likely, and the demand curve will be downward sloping. It cannot be assumed, however, that the income effect in supply analysis will be insignificant. If the good or service being supplied provides a large share of the individual's income, as with a worker's supply of his own labor, the income effect can be substantial.

In the supply of a normal good or service, a strong income effect can overpower the substitution effect. The result then is an inverse relation between price and quantity supplied: a higher price reduces the amount offered for sale; the supply curve is backward bending.

THE SUPPLY CURVE

A supply curve is derived from an individual's indifference map by the same technique used in the derivation of a demand curve. Variation in the price results in a succession of opportunity lines for the seller and a set of equilibrium points showing the quantity that would be supplied at each successive price, as in Figure 4.3. The locus of these points of equilibrium is called a price-supply curve or, alternately, the seller's offer curve. It is comparable to the price–consumption curve of the buyer, which may also be called the buyer's offer curve.

Figure 4.3 *Seller's Offer Curve*

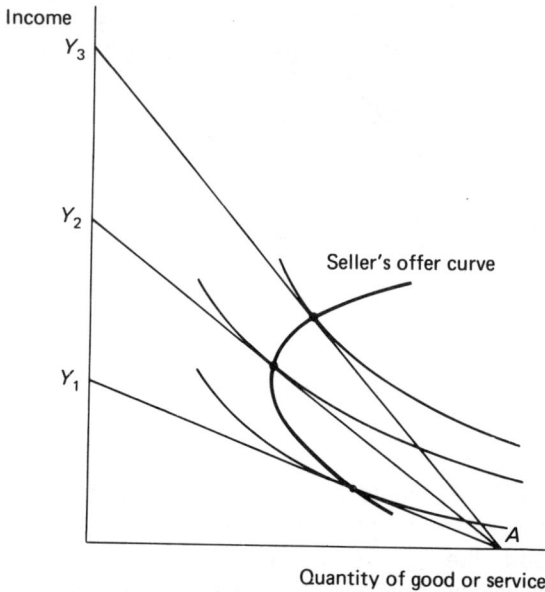

Quantity of good or service

The price–quantity data taken from each of the seller's equi-librium positions provide the points on a supply curve. Because the amount supplied is shown from right to left on the indifference map illustrated, while it appears from left to right on the usual supply diagram, it is not convenient to construct the supply curve diagram directly below the indifference map as was done in the de-mand analysis; otherwise the technique and results are analogous.

A buyer receives consumer surplus when he pays less for a good than he would be willing to pay. A seller receives a surplus[3] when he receives more than the amount for which he would have been willing to supply the good or service. A supply curve shows the marginal supply price for each quantity (that is, the price at which he would be willing to supply the marginal unit). The area under a supply curve up to a point therefore shows the minimum total payment he would require for supplying that quantity without mak-ing himself worse off by the sale.

If, as in Figure 4.4, the price is P_1, the supplier will offer amount OQ_1, and total receipts from the sale are $OP_1E_1Q_1$. The area under the supply curve up to this quantity, area OSE_1Q_1, is the minimum total amount for which the individual would have been willing to supply this quantity. Therefore, the difference between the two quantities, area P_1E_1S, is a measure of the supplier's surplus.

[3]Supplier's surplus is usually called rent or quasi-rent. See Chapter 16 for a discussion of these concepts.

Figure 4.4 *Seller's Surplus*

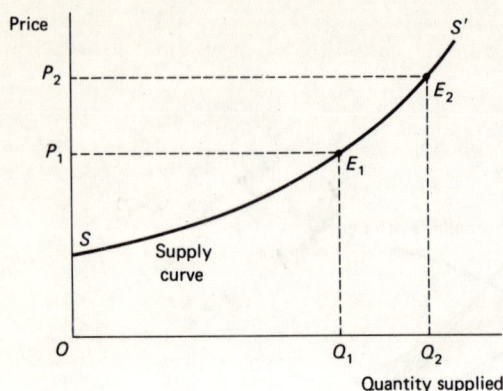

An increase in price to P_2 would raise the amount supplied to OQ_2 and increase the seller's surplus by area $P_1P_2E_2E_1$.

For the normal good, the area of surplus measured from the supply curve diagram will be between the compensating variation and the equivalent variation. If the vertical distance between any two of the seller's indifference curves is constant (that is, if one curve is a vertical displacement of the other), all three measures of surplus will be equal.

PRICE ELASTICITY OF SUPPLY

Price elasticity of supply is a measure of the responsiveness of amount supplied to a percentage change in price.

$$\text{Elasticity} = \frac{\text{percentage change in quantity supplied}}{\text{percentage change in price}} = \frac{PdQ}{QdP}$$

For the normal upward sloping supply curve, price elasticity is positive. Arc and point elasticities of supply are computed with the same formulas as is elasticity of demand.[4]

Except for perfectly vertical or horizontal supply curves, for which the elasticities are zero and infinity respectively, the price elasticity of supply cannot be inferred from the slope of the supply curve alone. For example, every straight line supply curve extending from the origin has a constant elasticity of one at every point, although each curve has a different slope. It is true, however, that if two supply curves pass through the same point other than the

[4]For the geometric technique see Chapter 2.

origin, the steeper of the two will have the lower elasticity at that point.

Price elasticity of supply is likely to be greater over a longer period than in the short period because suppliers have more opportunities to adjust the quantity supplied to new price opportunities. Elasticity of supply is greater the more narrowly the good or service being supplied is defined. For example, the elasticity of supply of labor as a whole for a nation is low; the elasticity of supply of a particular type of labor to a particular firm will be higher because of the alternative opportunities open to the supplier of the labor.

INCOME AND QUANTITY SUPPLIED

A supplier's response to changes in his income from other sources, when the price of the good or service supplied is held constant, is shown by the succession of equilibrium points on his indifference map which result from vertical shifts of the opportunity line. Because price is constant, all opportunity lines will have the same slope, but their origin will change. In Figure 4.5, as the individual supplier's income *from other sources* rises from A to B to C, his equilibrium shifts from E_1 to E_2 to E_3. The curve connecting points of supplier equilibrium as his income changes is an income–supply line.

Figure 4.5 illustrates the income–supply line for a normal good. As the individual's income rises, he supplies less of the good, retaining more of it for his own use. Income elasticity of supply for

Figure 4.5 *Supplier Response to Income Changes*

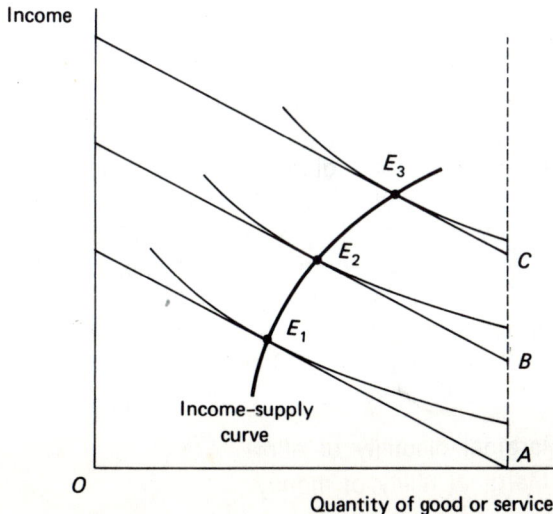

a normal good is therefore negative. For an inferior good, income elasticity of supply is positive, and the income–supply line would have a backward slope.

SUPPLY OF LABOR SERVICES

The analysis of the supply of labor services by an individual follows closely the general theory of individual supply. An individual has twenty-four hours a day that he can offer for sale or retain for his own use. He is assumed to have certain abilities, and a set of preferences among leisure, work, and income. These preferences are summarized on an indifference map. Income from all sources is measured on the vertical axis. The horizontal axis measures twenty-four hours. Hours of work could be measured in either direction, with the remainder measuring hours of leisure. In Figure 4.6 leisure is measured from point P to the right.

Figure 4.6 *Individual Labor Supply*

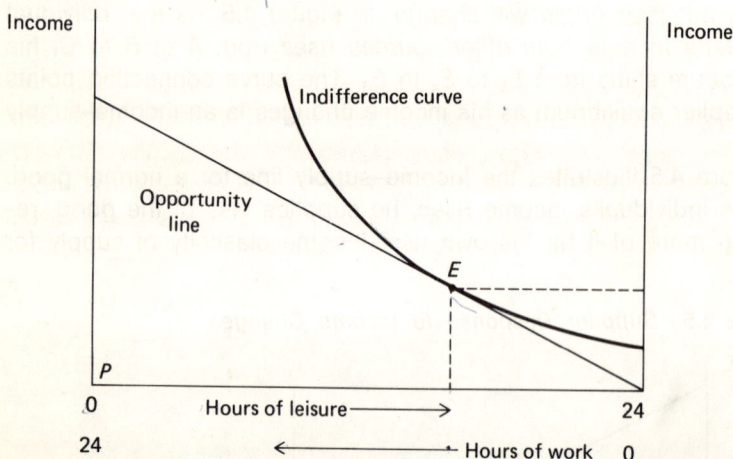

The negative of the slope of the indifference curve equals the individual's marginal rate of substitution between money and leisure. It is the amount of money the individual is willing to give up (in foregone earnings) in exchange for another hour of leisure. Alternately, the negative of the slope is a measure of the individual's supply price of an additional hour of labor. It is therefore in effect a monetary measure of the marginal disutility of effort. More specifically, the slope of the indifference curve at a point is

$$\frac{\text{Marginal disutility of effort}}{\text{Marginal utility of money}}$$

The marginal rate of substitution between income and leisure is likely to increase substantially as the individual moves to the left along any indifference curve. The first few hours of work each day may be almost pleasant, but as a normal work day is exceeded the *MRS* is likely to rise sharply until at the hours of work that would involve physical exhaustion the curve may become vertical.

The analysis of income and substitution effects and of price and income elasticities of the supply of labor services is analogous to that of previous sections. Leisure is likely to be a normal good, more of which is desired as income rises. The income effect of a rise in the wage rate is likely to reduce the quantity of labor supplied and may in some cases, or over some range of wage rates, swamp the substitution effect so that less labor is offered at higher wage rates, and the supply curve is backward bending.

For similar reasons, the income elasticity of supply of labor may be negative, individuals working fewer hours per day as income from other sources rises. The decline in the average hours worked per week since the nineteenth century suggests an income effect is at work.

An indifference curve analysis shows neatly the effects of differential overtime pay on the hours of work an individual will be willing to supply. The opportunity line in this situation will be kinked. Assume, for example, the standard rate of pay is $5 an hour, with double pay ($10 per hour) for all hours over eight a day. The opportunity line *ABC* of Figure 4.7 illustrating this case has a kink at eight hours. From *A* to *B* the slope is $5; beyond point *B* the slope is $10.

Figure 4.7   *Overtime Pay*

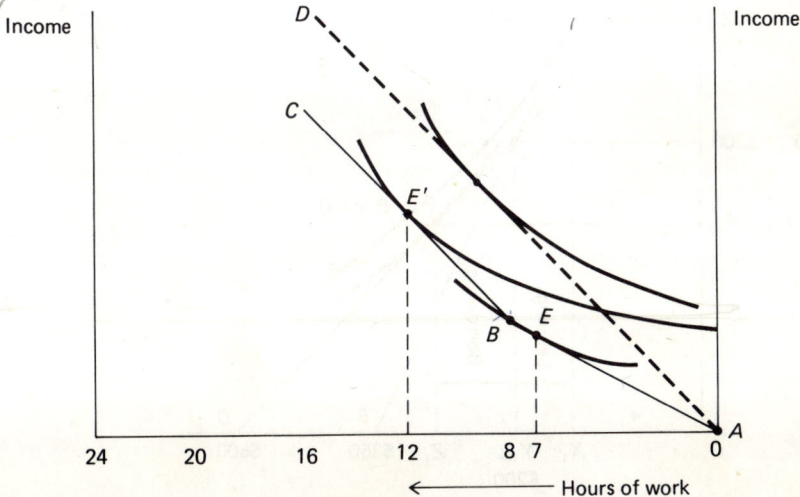

At a straight pay rate of $5 an hour, the equilibrium of the worker would be at point E; he works 7 hours. With overtime, however, he moves to point E', working 12 hours. It is interesting to note that had the straight pay rate been $10 for any number of hours, as along opportunity line AD, he would have worked fewer than the 12 hours he works under the overtime pay scheme. It is in fact quite possible that, at a straight rate of $10 an hour, he would offer fewer hours of labor than at a straight hourly rate of $5.

THE THEORY OF LENDING AND BORROWING

Lending and borrowing are special kinds of exchange, where money in one period of time is exchanged for money in another period. The lender is a supplier and the borrower a demander of funds.

The borrowing and lending behavior of an individual are pictured in Figure 4.8. To simplify the example, only one year loans are considered here. The indifference map show the preferences of an

Figure 4.8   *Borrowing and Lending*

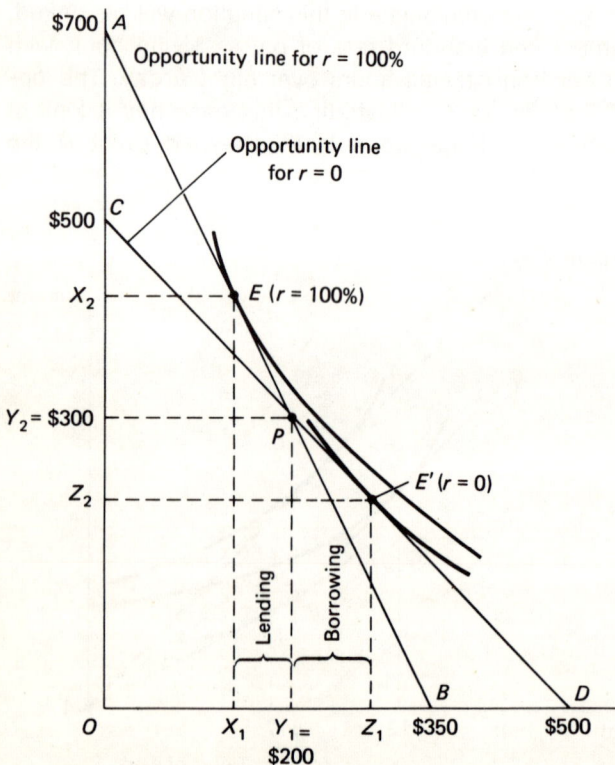

individual for *consumption* in period one (measured on the horizontal axis) compared with *consumption* in period two (on the vertical axis).

The individual is assumed to know what his income will be in each of the two periods. The alternative consumption patterns open to the individual are then described by an opportunity line. He may simply choose to consume whatever income he has in the period he receives it. One point on his opportunity line, therefore, is found by making consumption in each period equal to that period's income. Assuming incomes of OY_1 ($200) and OY_2 ($300) in the two periods, point P of Figure 4.8 is one consumption pattern available to him.

He may, however, choose to save some of the income of the first year to enable him to increase his consumption of the second year. He may then lend the excess of the first year's income over his consumption of that period. In return, his loan will be repaid with interest the following year when, by assumption, he will spend it, along with his second period income, on consumption.

Alternately, he may borrow in the first period, spending more on consumption than his current income. In the second period, then, part of his income must be used to repay that loan, plus interest on it.

If the rate of interest is, say, 10 percent for every dollar of the first year's income which he saves and lends, he will receive $1.10 in the second period. For every dollar he reduces first period consumption, second period consumption can rise by $1.10. Therefore, to the left of his initial point P on the diagram, his opportunity line rises with a negative slope of 1.10, (that is, $1.10/$1.00).

Conversely, if in period one he spends beyond his first period income, he must borrow. For every $1 he adds to that year's consumption through borrowing, he must in the second period pay back $1.10, and hence reduce his consumption in period two by that amount. To the right of point P, therefore, his opportunity line drops, also with a negative slope of $1.10/$1.00 or 1.1. The slope of the individual's opportunity line is −(1 + the rate of interest).

In Figure 4.8 opportunity line AB shows the consumption alternatives open to the individual when the rate of interest is 100 percent.[5] If the individual consumed nothing his first period, loaning his entire first period income of $200, he could in the second period consume $700—his second period income of $300, plus the repayment of his $200 loan, plus interest (at 100 percent) on the loan of a further $200. Point A represents this consumption plan. At the other extreme, he could borrow $150 and add it to his first

[5]This unrealistic rate is used only to make the diagram clear.

period income of $200 to finance consumption of $350. His entire second period income of $300 would then be required to repay the loan with interest, and his second period consumption would be zero. Point B shows this consumption plan.

Opportunity line AB shows the range of alternatives open to the individual. He maximizes his utility by moving to that point on the opportunity line which is tangent to an indifferent curve. Point E, on line AB, is his equilibrium when the rate of interest is 100 percent. In this instance he is saving (and lending) amount Y_1X_1, that is, the difference between his first period income (OY_1) and first period consumption (OX_1). In return for his saving he will receive Y_2X_2 the next period, which, added to his second period income of OY_2 gives him second period consumption of OX_2.

In contrast, consider the equilibrium of the consumer when the rate of interest is zero. The individual's new opportunity line CD still goes through point P (where he would be neither lending nor borrowing), but its slope is now less, equal to minus one. His new equilibrium is at E'. He is now a borrower, in the amount of Y_1Z_1. His second period consumption is then OZ_2.

The single diagram thus applies to borrowing and lending, to "buying" and "selling" a loan.

The income and substitution effects on lending and borrowing resulting from a change in the rate of interest are found with the familiar techniques.

The substitution effect of a rise in the rate of interest will always cause an increase in lending or a decrease in borrowing (that is, the individual would move to the left along an indifference curve). The impact of the income effect is uncertain. As noted earlier, with normal goods, the income effect of a price rise causes demanders to demand less, and suppliers to supply more, of the good. The individual who is lending or borrowing is sometimes a "buyer" (borrower) and sometimes a "seller" (lender). The income effect of a rise in the rate of interest will help the lender (that is, raise him to a higher indifference curve) but harm a borrower. Therefore, if the rules for normal goods apply to borrowing and lending, the income effect of a rise of interest will encourage the lender to lend less, and the borrower to borrow less.

Both income and substitution effects of a rise in the rate of interest cause a borrower to borrow less. It is fairly sure therefore that the *demand* curve for consumption loans has the standard downward slope.

For the seller (lender) the two effects run in opposite directions. It is therefore not clear (for the normal good) whether the supply curve of loans will rise to the right or the left.

The theory of borrowing and lending by the utility maximizing individual can be extended to other cases, for example, to multi-period analysis; to the effects of rising incomes on saving and borrowing; to the realistic case in which the individual pays a higher rate of interest when borrowing than he receives from lending (where the opportunity line has a kink). Perhaps enough has been said, however, to suggest the applicability of standard maximization principles of microeconomic analysis to this area.

REVIEW QUESTIONS

1. Explain the following concepts:
    Marginal rate of substitution for a seller
    Seller's offer curve
    Income–supply curve
    Income and substitution effects for a seller of labor services
    Seller's surplus
    Price elasticity of supply
    Income elasticity of supply
    Seller's opportunity line
    Income and substitution effects for a lender and a borrower
2. Construct an indifference map for a seller of labor services and derive the seller's offer curve from it.
    Construct the graph of the corresponding supply curve.
    Show the seller's surplus, at some assumed price, on the two diagrams.
3. Assume an individual with given preferences for consumption in each of two periods, and known income levels in the two periods. Assume further that he can borrow at 12 percent but is paid only 5 percent for lending. Draw his indifference map and opportunity line, and show his equilibrium position.

FURTHER READING

Leontief, Wassily, "Theoretical Note on Time-preference, Productivity of Capital, Stagnation, and Economic Growth." *American Economic Review 48* (1958), 105–111; reprinted in Wassily Leontief, *Essays in Economics.* New York: Oxford University Press (1966).

Perlman, Richard, *Labor Theory.* New York: Wiley (1969), chaps. 1–2.

5

THE THEORY OF EXCHANGE

THE EDGEWORTH BOX DIAGRAM

A market is any set of conditions in which economic agents meet to engage in economic transactions. A market may be identified by the type of product being traded, the number of transactors on either side of the market, a geographical area, or other characteristics. The simplest market involves two individuals engaged in pure exchange of a good for money. No production is assumed to take place.

The analysis in Chapters 3 and 4 of the behavior of individual buyers and sellers leads to a discussion of pure exchange between individuals. Under what conditions will two individuals engage in exchange? What will the terms of exchange be? Will their behavior result in economic efficiency?

The basic analytical device used in the theory of pure exchange is an *Edgeworth box diagram*,[1] an ingenious combination of the indifference maps of two individuals.

Begin with the indifference maps of two individuals. Call them B (for buyer) and S (for seller), showing their preferences for two goods, (*M* and *X*). It is convenient (although not essential) to assume one of the goods is money, which is measured on the vertical axis on each indifference map. On the hori-

[1] Named after the originator, Francis Y. Edgeworth, an English economist (1845–1926).

zontal axis quantities of some good X are measured. The two individuals are assumed to possess specific initial quantities of money
and good X. The particular quantities for each individual are represented, as before, by a point on his indifference map.

The indifference map of individual S is then rotated by 180 degrees, and placed on top of B's indifference map in such a way
that the point representing S's initial holdings of money and good
X coincides with the point on B's indifference map representing B's
initial holdings of money and the good.

Figure 5.1 *Edgeworth Box Diagram*

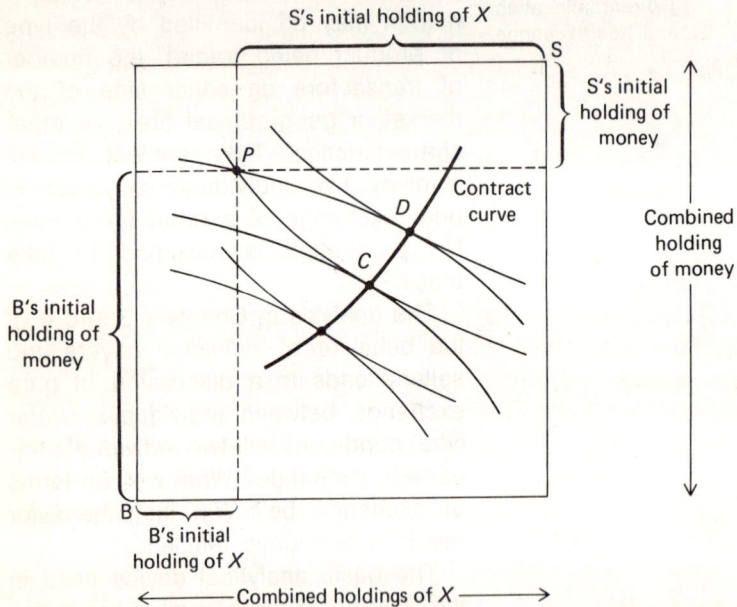

The result is a box, Figure 5.1, the width of which equals the
total quantity of X held jointly by B and S, and the height of which
equals the combined amount of money held initially by B and S.

B's holdings of money and X are measured up and to the right
from the lower left hand corner of the box, while S's holdings are
measured down and to the left from the upper right hand corner.
In Figure 5.1, point P represents the initial holdings of the two
persons. If B started out with no X but had some money, while S
started out with no money but a stock of X, the point representing
their initial holdings would lie on the upper left hand corner of the
diagram.

Any point in the box then defines a distribution of money and
good X between the two individuals. A movement from any one

point to another within the box defines a change in the distribution between B and S of the fixed total quantities of money and X. By comparing any two points, we can see whether B, or S, would be made better or worse off by a movement between those points, that is, whether the change would move B or S to a higher or lower indifference curve.

THE CONTRACT CURVE

In Chapter 1 an efficient situation was defined as one in which there is no change that can make one person better off (that is, move him to a higher indifference curve) without making another person worse off. Such an efficient situation is often called a *Pareto optimum.* On the box diagram, distributions of money and good X between B and S, which are efficient (that is, Pareto optima) are easily identified. They occur at every point at which an indifference curve of B is tangent to an indifference curve of S. From any such point of tangency there is no move, no redistribution of money and the good that can make one individual better off without at the same time making the other person worse off. An inspection of the box diagram shows that at all other points in the box (that is, with any other distribution of money and good X between B and S) some change exists that could make either B or S better off without hurting the other individual.

If any indifference curve of B is nowhere tangent within the box to an indifference curve of S, the highest indifference curve of S which can be reached by moving along B's indifference curve is found on the border of the box. Such a point is also a Pareto optimum, or point of efficiency.

The locus of these efficient points is called a *contract curve.* No point off the contract curve is efficient.

The tangency of the indifference curves along the contract curve means that, at any point on that curve, the marginal rates of substitution between money and good X are the same for the two individuals. A condition for efficiency in exchange, therefore, is that the *MRS* between any two goods be the same for all individuals.[2]

In terms of welfare analysis, it is perhaps worth emphasizing the following:

(1) There are many points of efficiency, not just one; all points on the contract curve are efficient.

(2) A welfare comparison of the various distributions represented by points on the contract curve must be made on grounds other than efficiency, for example, of equity.

---

[2]Exceptions occur when the efficient points lie on a border of the box.

(3) A point *off* the contract curve *may* represent higher welfare than some point on it if one believes the efficiency of the latter is more than offset by its unfairness (or some other undesirable characteristic), compared with the point off the curve.

(4) The point of maximum welfare, however, will lie somewhere on the contract curve, and cannot lie off it. The reason is that, for any point *off* the curve, there is some other point *on* the curve which makes someone better off and no one worse off.

It is therefore a necessary but not sufficient condition for maximum welfare for all individuals consuming a good to have the same marginal rate of substitution between the good and money. A significant question to ask of any economic system, then, is whether it encourages individuals to reach positions of efficiency on the contract curve.

EQUILIBRIUM IN EXCHANGE

What happens when a buyer meets a seller? The results depend a good deal on personal and institutional factors, of course: whether there are other buyers and sellers; how strong, smart, aggressive, and knowledgeable the buyer and seller are; and, of course, the preferences of the two individuals. We will examine five possibilities with the use of the box diagram, being particularly interested in whether the resulting equilibrium represents an efficient outcome (that is, whether it lies on the contract curve).

Figure 5.2 *The Feasible Region for Voluntary Exchange*

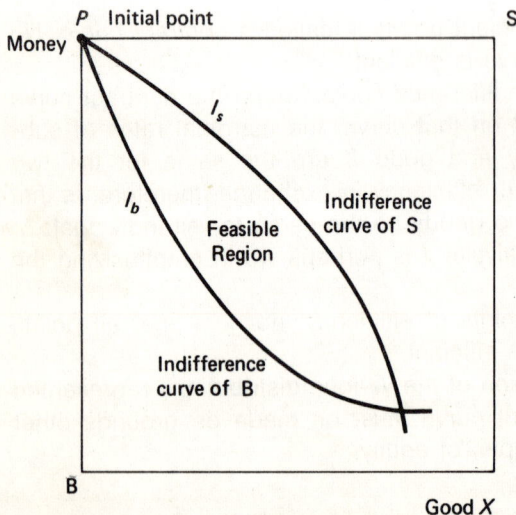

For simplicity, assume the potential buyer initially has money but none of the good X involved, and the seller has a supply of good X but no money. On the box diagram, the initial position (P) thus lies in the upper left hand corner, as in Figure 5.2.

It is immediately apparent that, unless some form of coercion is present, no equilibrium in exchange can exist outside the area between the indifference curve of the buyer (B) and the indifference curve of the seller (S), which run through the initial position. In Figure 5.2, voluntary exchange can take place only in the feasible region between these two curves.

CASE 1   Competitive behavior by buyer and seller   An individual buyer or seller will be said to behave competitively if he believes he cannot affect the market price. He may be called a "price-taker" rather than a "price-maker." If neither the buyer nor the seller feels he can influence the price of X, but simply behaves competitively by responding to prices offered to him, the equilibrium of exchange is found by using the standard price–consumption curve or offer curve of the buyer and the offer curve of the seller, which are derived as described in Chapters 3 and 4 and are illustrated in Figure 5.3a.

Competitive equilibrium in exchange requires that both buyer and seller be in individual equilibrium (that is, at a point on their offer curves). It further requires that the amount one person wishes to buy be equal to the quantity the other offers to sell. An equilibrium price, then, will equate the quantity supplied with the quantity demanded.

On Figure 5.3a three price lines are illustrated: PO_1 representing a low price, PO_2 an intermediate price, and PO_3 a high price. Price is equal to the negative of the slope of the price line, which constitutes a budget line for the buyer and an opportunity line for the seller. At any price, the buyer wishes to purchase the amount indicated by the intersection of the price line with his price-consumption or offer curve; the seller wishes to sell the amount shown by the intersection of the price line with his offer curve.[3] The *intersection* of a price line with an offer curve is a point of *tangency* of the price line with the individual's indifference curve.

With a price equal to the slope of price line PO_1, the buyer wishes to purchase BZ' of the good, while the seller wants to give up PY'. Clearly price P_1 is not an equilibrium price.

Figure 5.3b shows the same situation in terms of supply and demand curves derived from the buyer and seller indifference maps

---

[3]Because the seller's indifference map has been inverted the quantities he is willing to suppy are measured from left to right, from point P.

Figure 5.3   *Competitive Exchange Equilibrium*

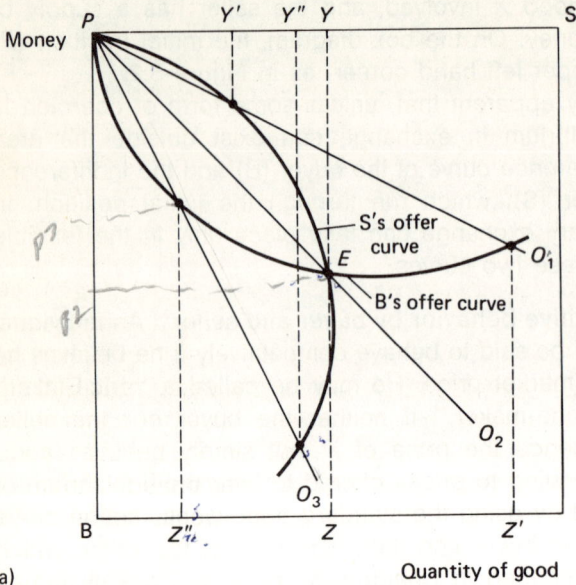

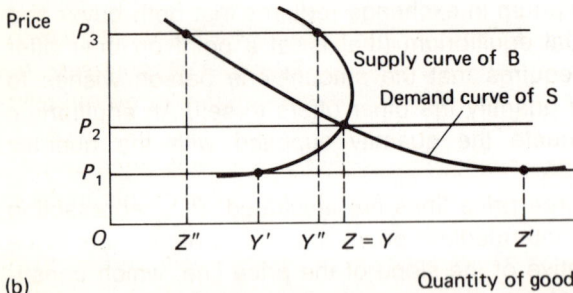

(b)   Quantity of good

of Figure 5.3a. At price PO_1, demand and supply are not in equilibrium.

At the higher price P_3, equal to the negative of the slope of line
PO_3, the buyer wishes to purchase only BZ'', while the seller is
willing to sell PY''. At this high price there is excess supply.

At the intermediate price P_2, equal to the slope of price line PO_2,
the amount supplied (PY) equals the amount demanded (BZ). At
this price both buyer and seller wish to move to point E of Figure
5.3a, the intersection of their offer curves. Price P_2 thus constitutes
an equilibrium price for competitive exchange.

The distribution of money and good X between the buyer and
seller represented by the equilibrium point E is an efficient situation
(that is, a Pareto optimum), and lies on the contract curve. At point
E the price line (PO_2) is tangent to an indifference curve of the

buyer because point E lies on the buyer's offer curve, and every point on an offer curve represents a tangency of a budget or opportunity line with an indifference curve. For analogous reasons, at point E the price line is also tangent to an indifference curve of the seller. Therefore, at point E the buyer's and seller's indifference curves are both tangent to the same price line and hence must be tangent to each other. Point E must lie on the contract curve.

A competitive equilibrium in pure exchange is thus shown to be efficient. This conclusion would hold for any number of buyers and sellers. It also is true regardless of the location of the point representing the initial distribution of money and the good between the buyer and the seller. If the initial point were different, the buyer and the seller would have different offer curves. The intersection of these new curves would not be likely to occur at point E. But the intersection of the new offer curves representing the competitive equilibrium appropriate to the new initial distribution of assets would still lie on the contract curve. It must be emphasized that the particular point on the contract curve which would be reached through competitive exchange will vary depending on the initial distribution of assets among the transactors.

CASE 2   Monopolistic seller, competitive buyer   For the second case, assume that the seller is a monopolist who has the power to set the price and exercises that power. The buyer responds competitively to the price set by the seller, buying his preferred quantity at that price. The seller is here a price-maker, and the buyer a price-taker. The utility-maximizing seller will set that price which, combined with the buyer's response, puts the seller on his highest possible indifference curve.

The points to which the buyer will move when confronted with various prices are shown by the buyer's offer curve (that is, price–consumption curve). By choosing the appropriate price, the seller can induce the buyer to move to any point on that curve. The buyer's offer curve therefore represents an opportunity line for the seller. The seller will choose the price that will induce the buyer to move to that point on his (the buyer's) offer curve at which the seller reaches his highest attainable indifference curve.

The buyer's offer curve will intersect many indifference curves of the seller. But at one point on the buyer's offer curve, an indifference curve of the seller will be tangent to the buyer's offer curve. In Figure 5.4 this is point E. This point is the highest level of satisfaction this monopoly seller can reach. His policy would then be to set the price represented by the slope of the line PA. This price induces the buyer to move to point E, buying quantity BZ of good X, for which he pays the seller amount PY.

Figure 5.4   *Simple Monopoly*

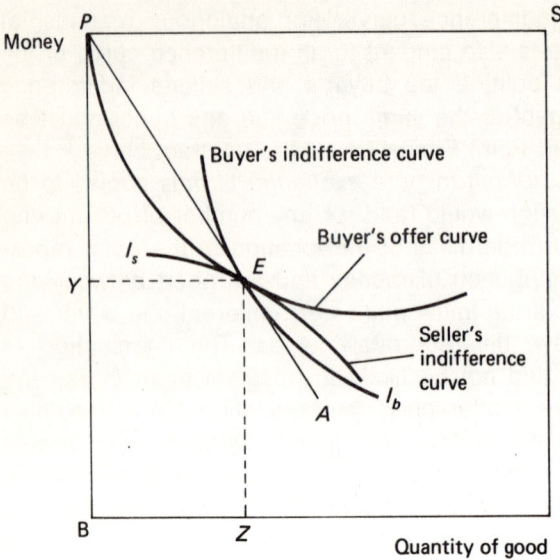

The monopoly equilibrium position point *E* will not lie on the contract curve, and is not an efficient result. At point *E*, the buyer's indifference curve (I_b) is tangent to the opportunity line *PA*. But at point *E* the seller's indifference curve (I_s) is tangent not to the opportunity line but to the buyer's offer curve. The buyer's and seller's indifference curves cannot be tangent at point *E*, but must intersect at *E*. Point *E* cannot lie on the contract curve and the result therefore cannot be efficient. Either the buyer or the seller or both could be made better off than at point *E* if they moved somewhere within the inner area bounded by the buyer and seller indifference curves I_b and I_s, which go through point *E*.

In short, simple monopoly in exchange does not lead to an efficient result.

CASE 3   Competitive seller, monopsonistic buyer   In this case, illustrated in Figure 5.5, the buyer is assumed to be the price-maker and the seller a price-taker. The offer curve of the seller constitutes an opportunity line for the buyer. Results are analogous to those of Case 2. By setting the appropriate price, the buyer can induce the seller to move to any point on his (the seller's) offer curve. The buyer sets the price which causes the seller to supply amount *BX*, and move to point *E*, where an indifference curve of the buyer is tangent to the seller's offer curve. As in Case 2, the two relevant indifference curves intersect at point *E*, and the result is not efficient. Any further movement within the area bounded by the buyer and

Figure 5.5   *Simple Monopsony*

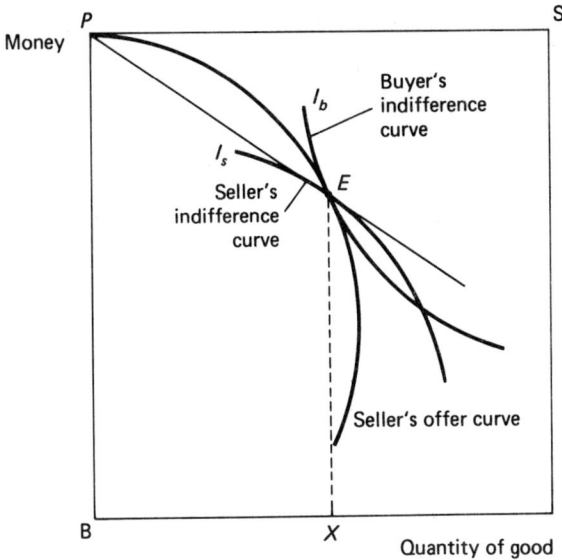

seller indifference curves through point *E* would make neither worse off, and one or both of the parties better off.

CASE 4   **Perfectly discriminating seller**   A very strong seller may be able to exact more favorable terms from the buyer than did the simple monopolist of Case 2. He may practice price discrimination, setting not just one price for the buyer, but charging the purchaser different prices for different units of the good. In the limit, the seller may charge the maximum the buyer is willing to pay for every unit of the good. This technique is called *perfect price discrimination*.

This limit to which the seller can force a buyer is represented by the indifference curve of the buyer, which goes through the initial point. The buyer will refuse any transaction which would put him on an indifference curve lower than this. That curve of the buyer (I_b in Figure 5.6) thus represents the limits of the alternative positions open to the discriminating seller and constitutes the opportunity line for the perfectly discriminating supplier.

To which point along this buyer indifference curve will the seller wish to move the buyer? The seller's best position along this curve is that point at which he (the seller) has an indifference curve tangent to the limiting indifference curve of the buyer. This is point E_s in Figure 5.6, which is the equilibrium point for the perfectly discriminating seller.

The seller can reach point E_s with either of two techniques, both of which have the same results. First, he may in effect move the

Figure 5.6 *Perfect Discrimination*

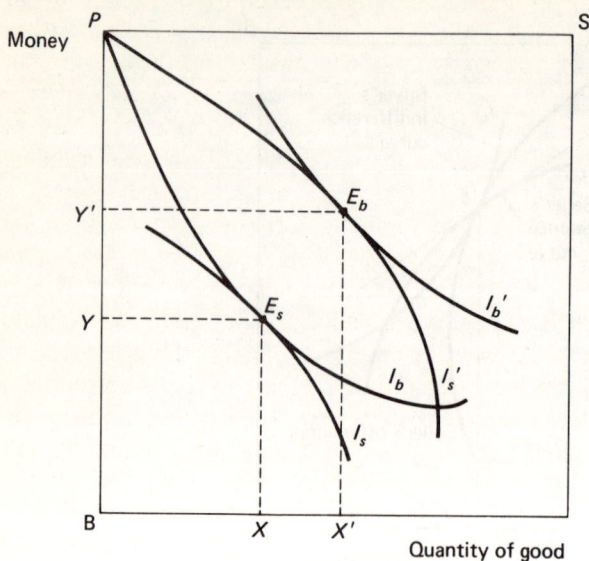

buyer down the latter's indifference curve (I_b) from the initial point P to point E_s, at each step charging the buyer for the next unit of good X the highest price he will pay for it, thus keeping the buyer on this indifference curve. The price charged for any particular unit of good X is equal to the *slope* of the buyer's indifference curve at that point (that is, the buyer's marginal rate of substitution between money and the good at each point).

This tactic of the seller is of course complicated and in practice could only be achieved approximately. A second and much simpler technique exists by which the seller can reach point E_s—the *all-or-none* offer. Instead of one price or a set of different prices for successive units of good X, the seller makes one offer, to sell OX quantity of the good to the buyer for a lump-sum price of PY, on a take-it-or-leave-it basis.[4]

With both techniques, the seller is appropriating for himself all the surplus, all of the gains of trade.

Rather surprisingly, the equilibrium at point E_s is efficient. At that point indifference curves of the buyer and seller are tangent, and E_s lies on the contract curve. Hence a strong monopolist is more likely to lead to efficient results than a weak monopolist!

CASE 5 **Perfectly discriminating buyer** Case 5 is analogous to Case 4, and is also illustrated in Figure 5.6. Here, the strong buyer sets the terms of exchange and is able to appropriate all the gains

[4]In practice, the seller would probably offer a little bit more to induce the buyer to deal.

of trade. The buyer may use perfect price discrimination to move the seller along indifference curve I'_s, the seller's indifference curve through the initial point. That curve represents the perfectly discriminating buyer's opportunity line. Alternately, the buyer may set an all-or-none offer.

The buyer wishes to reach an equilibrium position at point E_b, at which a buyer indifference curve (I'_b) is tangent to the base indifference curve (I'_s) of the seller. This result can be reached through a series of discrimination prices or through an all-or-none offer by the buyer to the seller to buy OX' units of the good for a lump-sum of $\dot{P}Y'$. As in Case 4, the equilibrium position is efficient, lying on the contract curve; a strong buyer leads to more efficient results than the buyer of Case 3 who had weak monopsonistic power.

In summary then, in free exchange an equilibrium will be reached somewhere within the feasible region; with competitive behavior by both buyer and seller, there is a determinate equilibrium on the contract curve, its location depending on preferences and on the initial position of buyer and seller; in other situations, buyer and seller will attempt to push each other to the edges of the feasible region; with perfect discrimination by either buyer or seller the equilibrium lies on the contract curve; when a single price is set by a simple monopolist or monopsonist, however, the equilibrium position does not lie on the contract curve and is not efficient.

DIRECT ALLOCATION AND FREE EXCHANGE

Free competitive exchange tends to lead to an efficient allocation of goods. This suggests that, when an authority such as the government, a business firm, or a head of a family wishes to induce an efficient allocation of resources within the organization, it should restrict itself to some overall allocation of purchasing power, and not prohibit voluntary exchanges among recipients. In wartime rationing, for example, an authority may wish to influence the allocation of goods in the interests of fairness by distributing rationing points. But efficiency is more likely to be achieved if the recipients are then permitted to engage in exchange of points (or of the goods secured with the rationing points). It would be a wise authority indeed that could so perfectly determine preferences that an efficient distribution would be achieved by direct allocation. Black markets have their uses.

Within a firm, or even a university or a church, the theory of exchange suggests that budget allocations to departments are more likely to lead to efficient use of resources when the allocations are very broad rather than detailed, and departments are permitted to engage in exchange.

Consider the distribution of candy among children in a particular family. For efficiency, make an overall allocation (say, the equal amounts of every kind to each child), and then let the children make any further deals they desire—watching, perhaps, that the older or more aggressive do not exploit the weaker with unfair discrimination.

REVIEW QUESTIONS

1. Explain the following concepts:
   Edgeworth box diagram
   Contract curve
   Price-taker
   Price-maker
   Competitive behavior
   Price discrimination
   Perfect price discrimiation, by seller or buyer

2. Construct an Edgeworth box diagram similar to that of Figure 5.1, and show the competitive equilibrium. Compare with this the offer curves and competitive equilibrium which would result if the two individuals had started with a different initial distribution of the same total quantities of money and the good. Will this change in the initial distribution affect the location of the contract curve?

3. Under what conditions will a buyer and seller not engage in exchange? Where does the contract curve lie in such a case?

4. A strong monopoly leads to efficiency in exchange, a weak monopoly does not. Should strong monopolies therefore be encouraged?

5. Assume a seller knows the preferences of a buyer and can set a two-part price, one price for the first X units of the good (a quantity chosen by the seller), and a second price for all units of the good in excess of X. Show on a box diagram the seller's optimum pricing strategy.

6. If a buyer and a seller have identical preferences (i.e., the same indifference maps), what will be the shape and location of the contract curve? Will a change in the distribution of the initial holdings affect the nature of the resulting competitive equilibrium? Demonstrate.

7. To individual A but not to individual B, money and good X are perfect substitutes:
   (a) Show A's offer curve.
   (b) Show the competitive equilibrium in exchange.
   (c) Show the results of cases 2 through 5 of the text.

FURTHER READING

Edgeworth, F. Y., *Mathematical Psychics*. London: Routledge & Kegan Paul (1881).

Newman, Peter, *The Theory of Exchange*. Englewood Cliffs, N. J.: Prentice-Hall (1965), chaps. 3–5.

Scitovsky, Tibor, *Welfare and Competition*. Homewood, Ill.: Irwin (1951).

3

THE
FIRM

6 PROFIT MAXIMIZATION AND OPPORTUNITY COSTS

□ profit maximization
□ the sales maximization assumption
□ identification of costs and revenues
□ private and social costs and benefits

PROFIT MAXIMIZATION

The business firm is an organizational device, an economic and legal institution. It incurs costs in acquiring inputs, which are factors of production such as labor, land, and capital, or intermediate goods purchased from other firms. The inputs are converted into output through a production process. The firm receives revenues by selling its outputs to individuals, other firms, or government and nonprofit agencies.

Profits are the excess of revenues over costs. The standard assumption of microeconomic theory is that a firm attempts to maximize its profits. This is a shorthand way of saying that the controllers of the firm direct it in such a way as to maximize the firm's profits.

The firm as such is not human. It has no utility function and no preference maps. The firm is a tool designed to further the interests of individuals. It is difficult but essential to distinguish between the interests and objectives of individuals, who are assumed to be utility maximizers, and the objectives of the firm. The behavior of the firm is directed by those in control of it, presumably to further their own interests.

The realism of the profit maximization assumption is often questioned. Profit maximization is, at best, an objective which, because of incomplete knowledge and managerial inefficiencies, is imperfectly achieved. The important question, however, is whether

firms do in fact attempt to maximize profits, or whether other objectives are sought.

Some alternative objectives will be considered after a discussion
of the appropriateness of the profit maximization assumption under
three types of control of the firm: (1) control by owners who receive
the profits of the operations of the firm, (2) control by an owner
who also manages the business (the proprietorship), and (3) control by hired managers.

CASE 1   Owner control   This is the standard case of economic
theory. By assumption, the interest of the owners in the firm is
solely to make money; they have no other involvement in the firm.[1]
The owners maximize their utility vis-a-vis the firm if the firm maximizes profits. Utility maximization by the owners thus leads to
profit mazimization for the firm. Note that it is not necessary that
profit maximization be independently assumed to be the firm's objective. The standard assumption that the owners as individuals
maximize their utility leads to profit maximization by the firm. In this
case, it is correct but misleading to say that the owners are maximizing profits. They are maximizing utility but, since the firm affects
them only through the profits earned by the firm, the owners achieve
their goal of utility maximization by having the firm maximize profits.

CASE 2   Control by the owner-manager   Can one say the objective of the firm is to maximize profits, when an individual both owns
and manages the firm? Interestingly, and somewhat surprisingly, the
answer is yes.[2] In this case also, utility maximization by the owner
is the equivalent of profit maximization of the firm.

The key to this symmetry lies in the recognition that the supply
price of the owner (that is, the amount for which he would be willing
to provide his services) is included in the costs of the firm, which
must be deducted from revenues to arrive at profits. The utility
maximizing owner-manager does not want simply to maximize the
net money receipts from his business; he may have to work harder
to increase those receipts, and the increase in receipts may not
be worth the effort. In such a case, if he does work the longer hours,
the costs to the firm include the costs of persuading him to work
the extra time. If these costs of the owner's effort exceed the increase in receipts that his efforts would bring forth, he will not be
maximizing his utility, nor can we say that the firm is maximizing
profits. For the firm, the extra costs exceed the extra receipts, and

[1]If the owners have any interest in the firm other than in its profits (that is, if
they receive any utility or dis-utility from their association with the firm other
than from their money income from it) their behavior is better described by
case B.

[2]See H. T. Koplin, "The Profit Maximization Assumption," *Oxford Economic
Papers*, n.s. *15* (1963), 130–139.

profits are reduced; for the individual, the extra receipts are not worth the extra work, and he would not be maximizing utility.

Thus, when the supply price of the services of the owner is included (as it should be) in the costs of the firm, profit maximization of the firm leads to the same pattern of behavior as does utility maximization by the owner-manager.

Because utility maximization and profit maximization induce the same behavior in the owner-managed firm, the case can be described either in utility or in money terms. In utility terms, the individual owner-manager weighs the disutility of the added effort against the utility of the additional income he would receive from the effort. In money terms, he compares the extra money receipts he would receive by working longer with the amount of money he would demand to be persuaded to supply the additional effort.

Analogous reasoning applies to other types of behavior by individual proprietors of businesses (for example, giving special treatment to friends, refusal to work on Sunday, keeping on an inefficient employee because of friendship). In each case, utility maximization by the individual and profit maximization for the firm call for the same behavior.

In short, "making money," that is maximizing money returns, is not necessarily "maximizing profits"; nor need it be consistent with utility maximization by the individual.

The principle is general and should be emphasized. Economists are sometimes accused of assuming that all individuals either do, or should, maximize money returns, that somehow there is waste if, for example, a man does not take the highest paying job he can find, or if the farmer refuses to switch to an urban job which would give him higher money income. This is poor economics. Both utility maximization and economic efficiency are violated if a rational, informed individual is required to act contrary to his own preferences.

The assumption that firms attempt to maximize profits can thus be applied with complete consistency to the owner-manager firm.

CASE 3   Control by managers   The idea that a business firm is controlled by its owners is supported in law but often not in fact, particularly in the modern large corporation with thousands of stockholders. The firm can be viewed as an organization controlled by its officers and managers. The question here is whether and to what extent the profit maximization assumption is relevant to such firms.

Consider managers seeking to maximize their own utility. Because the owners do have the technical power to remove them from office and to hire new managers, the managers must placate the owners and provide sufficient earnings or dividends to discourage stockholder revolt. Managers can be viewed as hiring or renting capital from the owners and paying them the minimum price (in the form of earnings) which will enable the firm to attract the desired amount of capital from this source.

Earnings in excess of this level go by law to the owners. Will managers seek to maximize earnings? They do not receive them themselves, so the question can be asked whether they would not simply work to achieve the "satisfactory" level of profits, rather than maximum profits.[3] One suspects this is often the case. And, if so, the profit maximization principle is weakened.

How seriously the principle is weakened in practice is a question of fact rather than theory. Since the profit maximization assumption is basic to most of economic theory, it is perhaps worthwhile to consider here some of the factors that could encourage a manager-controlled firm to maximize profits or, conversely, to follow a path on which profits are not maximized:

(1) To the extent that competition is effective, managers may have no choice, for maximization of profits may be essential to survival of the firm.

(2) Managers may be induced to seek maximum profits if their salaries or status are determined by the profits of their companies. To the extent that managers can, directly or indirectly, appropriate any profits (returns above the necessary payments to owners), they may well seek to maximize profits.

(3) On the other hand, managers often are unable to appropriate monetary returns. They may therefore have an incentive to substitute other goals for profits and to guide the company in the direction of these goals and away from profits. For example, executive amenities —plush offices and expense accounts—may be expanded beyond the level necessary to command the services of the executives.

Perhaps more important is the alleged propensity of executives to pursue the goal of growth for the company, whether or not it is profitable. The status of an executive is closely tied to the size and growth path of his company. The investor is presumably interested in earnings and might happily turn profits earned in one company into investments in other companies with greater profit potential, rather than reinvest in the firm in which they were earned. But usually the interest of an executive is tied to the company he manages. Hence, profit maximization in a general sense may be sacrificed for growth of one company.

THE SALES MAXIMIZATION ASSUMPTION

Research is now being conducted to explore the extent to which objectives other than profit maximization influence the conduct of

[3]See H. A. Simon, "New Developments in the Theory of the Firm," *American Economic Review, Papers and Proceedings 52* (1962), 1–15.

firms.[4] Several alternative hypotheses have been advanced. None has yet gained general acceptance. Perhaps the most popular suggestion is that in many types of situations businessmen attempt to maximize their sales rather than profits. Because a minimum level of profits is necessary for the survival of a firm, the sales maximization hypothesis is often advanced subject to a minimum profit constraint.[5] That is, the businessman is assumed to attempt to maximize his sales so long as he is concurrently able to achieve some minimum "satisfactory" level of profits.

To some observers, the sales maximization hypothesis is attractive because it seems to describe the actual behavior of many businessmen. Note that the hypothesis fits well with case C of the preceding section. Managers maintain the minimum profit level necessary to satisfy their owners, beyond which they may seek sales rather than extra profits. The reason for this is that their own incomes and status are often more closely related to the size of the business than to its profit rate.

The sales maximization assumption may also be defended as a useful managerial tool, even in a profit maximization context. The profits of a division of a company for example are often difficult to determine, especially on a day-to-day basis. Instructing a division manager to maximize sales rather than profits gives him a more easily defined goal to pursue. Higher management may establish further constraints on his behavior, which cause sales maximization to lead to profit maximization. In this sense, sales maximization is an example of the many operating rules useful in management. They are imperfect in principle, but given the imperfect knowledge of business life may lead to better results than a rule that in principle is superior.

No general alternative to the profit maximization assumption has gained wide acceptance in economics, however, and the main body of microeconomic theory is based squarely on that assumption.

IDENTIFICATION OF COSTS AND REVENUES

Not all accounting costs and revenues are relevant to profit maximization by the firm or to the determination of the economic efficiency of the firm's operations. Costs that cannot be escaped and revenues that will inevitably be received are (and should be) ignored in determining the behavior that will maximize profits or minimize losses.

[4]See Kalman J. Cohen and Richard M. Cyert, *Theory of the Firm* (Englewood Cliffs, N.J.: Prentice-Hall, 1965), chaps. 16–17, and the references cited there on pp. 382–383.

[5]See William J. Baumol, *Business Behavior, Value and Growth* (New York: Macmillan 1959).

The firm makes profits by pursuing any policy for which the additional revenues exceed the added costs due to that policy. The costs and revenues that determine whether a policy will increase profits (or reduce losses) are those that would not have existed if the policy had not been followed.

Many of the costs of a firm are quite obvious, while others are subtle and difficult to determine. One can almost define a good businessman as one who through skill, experience, or intuition successfully identifies the costs and revenues associated with any given policy.

The cost of using a resource is often defined in terms of alternative or opportunity costs; that is, the cost of one use of an input is the best alternative use to which the input could be put. To the child with a penny clutched in his hand, the cost of a licorice stick is not a penny, for he intends to give that up in any case; the cost of the licorice is, rather, the bubble gum that the child could buy if he foregoes the licorice. The cost of spending an evening at the movie is not just the price of admission, but also the monetary value of the alternative use of the time. The cost of using a piece of land that would otherwise lie vacant is zero.

Opportunity costs often do not correspond to accounting or historical costs. This fact might suggest that the introduction of the opportunity cost concept by economists is foreign to business operations. This is not true. The costs relevant to profit maximization *are* opportunity costs, as successful businessmen realize.

Costs can be explicit or implicit. The cost to a firm of most factors of production and of intermediate goods used in its own productive process is explicitly paid in money—a cost that can be avoided by the firm simply by not hiring or buying the input.

If, however, the firm already possesses some input (say, a warehouse), the cost of using that warehouse for storing one product would be the value the firm would obtain by using it to store some other product, or the value the firm could get by renting the warehouse out to another firm, whichever is greater. If there is no alternative use for an input its cost is zero, regardless of how much the firm may have paid for it.

The cost of an owner's time or capital to his firm is not the amount the owner actually withdraws from the business, but the return on these services he could get from the next best alternative. More correctly and precisely, the cost is measured by his supply price, below which he would wtihdraw his labor or capital.[6]

[6]It is often stated that the cost of an owner's time is the amount he could earn if employed as a manager elsewhere. This ignores the fact that he may be willing to work for less if he can be his own boss. Only if the two alternatives give him the same utility do the foregone managerial earnings measure the cost of his services to his own firm.

If there is no present alternative use for a factor of production, but its use in one period reduces its value in the future, that discounted reduction of future value must be recognized as a current cost of using the factor. This is called *user* cost.

To summarize, the opportunity cost of acquiring an input to use in production is its current market supply price. The opportunity cost of employing an input already acquired by the firm is not its historical or accounting cost, but the highest of the following: (1) the amount for which it could be sold or rented in the market, (2) its value to the firm in the production of some other product, and (3) the decrease in the future value of an input held by the firm, which is due to current use of the input, which would be avoided if the input is held out of current use.

The identification of the revenues relevant to profit maximization has the same complexities as identifying costs, although perhaps in a lesser degree. If selling a product to one individual at a special price makes other buyers reluctant to pay the standard price, the reduction in revenues from the other buyers must be subtracted from the price paid by the favored customer in calculating the revenue from his sale. (A businessman may attempt to avoid this secondary revenue reduction by keeping the sale secret, or by arguing that the favored buyer has some particular characteristics justifying a lower price to him than that paid by other customers.) Conversely, if a special price today leads to increased revenues in the future (for example, selling equipment below its cost to encourage future sales of supplies used with the equipment, as razors and blades), the present discounted value of the increased future revenues should be accounted as part of the revenues of the current sale (or alternately and with equivalent effect as reductions in current costs) when the profitability of the policy is evaluated.

PRIVATE AND SOCIAL COSTS AND BENEFITS

Firms determine their behavior in accordance with the costs which they pay and the revenues they receive. The analyses of Parts III, IV, and V are conducted in terms of these private costs and revenues. In any evaluation of the performance of private firms, however, it is important to note that the costs and benefits to society, which may be called *real* or *social costs* and *benefits,* resulting from a firm's operations[7] may be larger or smaller than the private costs and revenues of the firm. The causes of these possible divergences, and the public policies which may be instituted in response to these conflicts, are discussed in detail in Part VI.

The excess of social over private costs is called an *external cost;*

---

[7]Or from the behavior of an individual consumer.

the excess of social benefits over benefits accruing to the customers of a firm is an *external benefit*. The existence of these externalities has the effect of impairing the efficiency of the operation of private markets. Economic efficiency calls for the production of a good if its benefits (in money terms) exceed its costs. A good that has external costs will be overproduced by private firms; conversely, from the viewpoint of the efficient allocation of resources, not enough of a good with external benefits will be produced in private markets.

Air and water pollution are prime examples of external costs. There is no doubt that the existence of externalities is currently a problem of major public concern. Economic analysis can make a significant contribution to the solution of these problems.

REVIEW QUESTIONS

1. Explain the following concepts:
   Profit maximization
   The sales maximization assumption
   Alternative or opportunity costs
   Explicit and implicit costs
   Private and social costs and benefits
   External cost; external benefit
2. Discuss the relevance of the profit maximization assumption to the corner grocery store, and to General Motors.
3. Devise examples of divergences between private and social costs, and discuss the consequences of these divergences.

FURTHER READING

Baumol, William J., *Business Behavior, Value and Growth.* New York: Macmillan (1959).

Coase, R. H., "The Nature of the Firm." *Economica*, n.s. *4* (1937), 386–405.

Coase, R. H., "The Problem of Social Cost." *Journal of Law and Economics 3* (1960), 1–44.

Cyert, Richard M., and James G. March, *A Behavioral Theory of the Firm.* Englewood Cliffs, N. J.: Prentice-Hall (1963).

Koplin, H. T., "The Profit Maximization Assumption." *Oxford Economic Papers*, n.s. *15 (*1963), 130–139.

Simon, H. A., "New Developments in the Theory of the Firm." *American Economic Review 52* (1962), 1–15.

7 LONG-RUN PRODUCTION AND COST FUNCTIONS

THE PRODUCTION FUNCTION

A production function is the relationship between quantities of inputs and outputs. It tells us what quantities of various inputs can be used to produce a given output, and what outputs can be produced with a given set of inputs. The concept can be applied to the economy as a whole or to an individual firm.

The production function for an individual firm producing one product (where Q is the output of the product, L, C, and N stand for three factors of production, labor, capital, and land respectively, and T represents the technology available to the firm) may be written

$$Q = f(L, C, N; T) \qquad (1)$$

The nature of the production function depends on the technology existing at any time. The word "technology" refers to the whole range of productive techniques known at any given time, regardless of whether any particular technique is in actual use or not. Conventionally, when discussing a production function, technology is assumed fixed or given, just as in demand theory tastes were assumed constant. The semicolon before T in equation (1) means that technology is assumed constant. The effects of changes in technology on the production function may be analyzed, but at any given time the state of technology is assumed not to change.

In practice, firms produce with varying degrees of internal efficiency. In economics it is usually assumed that the firm produces with perfect internal efficiency, that is, that managers produce any particular level of output at the lowest cost available to them, given the constraints within which they are operating. This assumption perhaps is justified by the principle of the division of labor—leaving the study of internal inefficiency to the field of business administration—as well as the lack of any generally accepted alternative.

The ability of a firm to convert inputs into outputs depends in large part on the firm's existing organization and ownership of factors. Economics distinguishes between the *short run* and the *long run*. In the long run, the firm has no prior commitments and is free to adopt whatever productive organization and processes it chooses. In the short run, the firm has one or more constraints on its behavior, which it does not have in the long run. The constraints may be major or minor, and there is hence a whole universe of different short runs, each defined by a particular set of constraints. In calendar time, the short run may be very brief or extended, depending on how long it takes for constraints to be removed, for example, how long it takes to construct expanded facilities, or to depreciate existing capacity.

Long-run production functions and the cost functions derived from them are considered in the present chapter; the following chapter takes up short-run production and cost functions.

The theory of production and costs can be developed for any number of inputs and outputs. Largely because it is difficult to represent more than three variables graphically at any one time, the theory is usually illustrated for only three variables with the understanding that it can be generalized if needed. The two input-one output case is developed here, although this tends to cause economists and students to think too much in terms of a single product firm.

THE PRODUCTION MAP

In the long run the firm can choose any productive techniques it desires, subject to existing technology. Assume that the firm produces one product Q and can use various quantities of two factors, C and L (for example, capital and labor). The production function $Q = f(L, C)$ can be illustrated on a production map, measuring quantities of L and C on the horizontal and vertical axes respectively, as in Figure 7.1.

For any given combination of quantities of L and C represented by a point on the production map, there will be a maximum quantity of the good Q that can be produced given existing technological knowledge and assuming internal efficiency. That same quantity of Q could be produced with other quantities of L and C. A line can be drawn (for example, line XX_{50} in Figure 7.1) connecting all combinations of L and C with which this quantity of Q could be produced. This line is an *isoproduct curve,* or a *production isoquant.* Unlike an indifference curve representing a level of utility that cannot be measured, the production isoquant represents a definite measurable level of output and can be labeled as such.

Figure 7.1   *Production Isoquant*

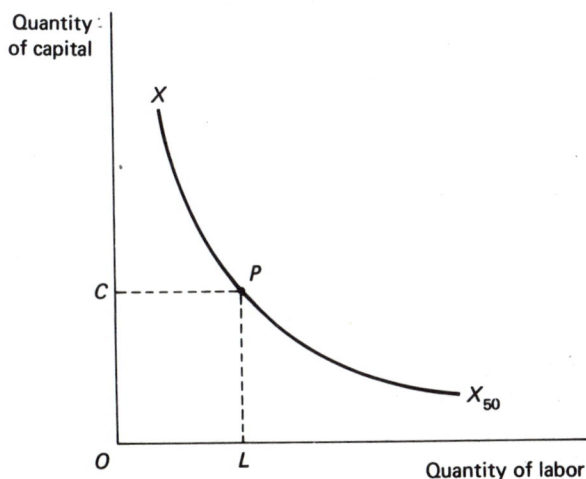

In general, the production isoquants will have a negative slope. This simply means that if the quantity of one factor of production is reduced the amount of the other factor must be increased if the existing level of output is to be maintained.

As with indifference curves, the isoquants are likely to be convex to the origin. Moving along one isoquant, as quantities of one factor continue to be removed, ever increasing amounts of the other factor must be added to maintain production of the fixed output.

The negative of the slope of the production isoquant is called the marginal rate of technical substitution of factor C for factor L (MTS_{LC}), and equals the amount of C (measured on the vertical axis) that can be withdrawn when one unit of L (measured on the horizontal axis) is added, the level of production being held constant.

The slope of the isoquant at any point equals the negative of the ratio of the marginal products of the two factors. The marginal product of a factor is the increase in total product per unit increase in a factor when the quantities of all other factors are held constant (that is, it is $\Delta Q/\Delta F$, with Q as product, and F as any factor).

In the limit, for infinitely small changes the marginal products of capital and labor are $\partial Q/\partial C$ and $\partial Q/\partial L$ respectively, the partial derivatives of output with respect to each factor.

The proof that the *MTS*, or negative of the slope of the isoquant, is equal to the ratio of the marginal products of the factors[1] is analogous to the proof that the slope of an indifference curve equals the ratio of the marginal utilities of the two goods. On Figure 7.2,

Figure 7.2   *Marginal Rate of Technical Substitution*

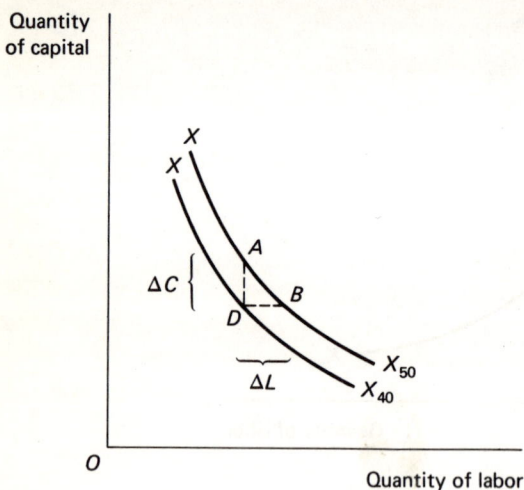

the slope of the isoquant XX_{50} between points A and B approximates $-AD/DB$ which equals $\Delta C/\Delta L$. When starting from point A the quantity of capital is reduced by ΔC, production would move to isoquant XX_{40}, at point D; output declines by 10 (that is, ΔQ equals -10). The marginal product of capital here is $\Delta Q/\Delta C$. Similarly, a move from point B to point D, reducing the quantity of labor by ΔL, brings a reduction in output by the same ΔQ ($= 10$). The marginal product of labor is thus $\Delta Q/\Delta L$.

The movement from point A to point B can then be considered in two steps, moving first from A to D, and then from D to B. In each move, output changes by the same amount, first dropping by ΔQ, and then rising by the same amount. Thus

[1]In terms of the calculus, when $Q = f(C, L)$, the total differential is $dQ = (\partial Q/\partial C)dC + (\partial Q/\partial L)dL$. Along an isoquant $dQ = 0$. Thus, $-(\partial Q/\partial C)dC = (\partial Q/\partial L)dL$ and $-dC/dL = (\partial Q/\partial L)/(\partial Q/\partial C) = MP_L/MP_C$.

$$MP_x = \frac{\Delta Q}{\Delta C} \quad \text{or} \quad \Delta C = \frac{\Delta Q}{MP_C}$$

and

$$MP_L = \frac{\Delta Q}{\Delta L} \quad \text{or} \quad \Delta L = \frac{\Delta Q}{MP_L}$$

$$MTS_{LC} = \frac{\Delta C}{\Delta L} = \frac{\dfrac{\Delta Q}{MP_C}}{\dfrac{\Delta Q}{MP_L}} = \frac{\Delta Q}{MP_C} \cdot \frac{MP_L}{\Delta Q} = \frac{MP_L}{MP_C} \qquad (2)$$

An isoquant may have a positive upward slope when relatively large quantities of one factor are combined with relatively small quantities of another. This occurs when the marginal productivity of the abundant factor becomes negative; the addition of still greater quantities of this redundant factor (keeping the quantity of the other factor constant) causes total output to decline. In Figure 7.3, the marginal product of labor has become zero at points G, beyond which the marginal product of labor is negative; the marginal product of capital reaches zero at points H.

Figure 7.3   Ridge Lines

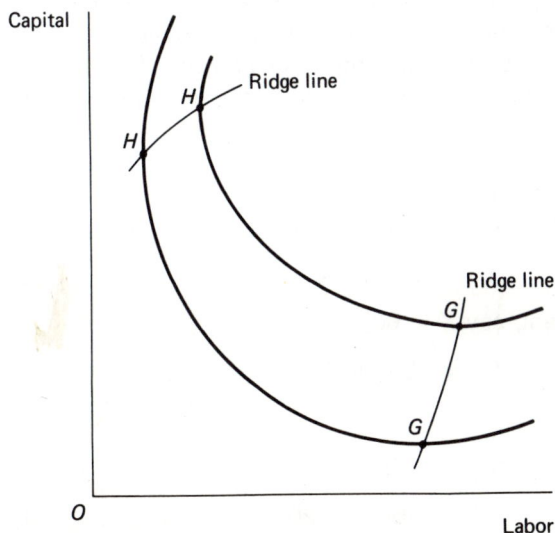

Lines connecting points of zero marginal productivities of capital and labor respectively are called *ridge lines*. The so-called "economic region" for the firm lies between these lines.

ELASTICITY OF SUBSTITUTION

The curvature of an isoquant indicates the degree to which two factors can be substituted, in the production of the product. The *elasticity of substitution* (E_s) between two factors is a measure of the relative change in the ratio in which the two factors are employed, compared with the relative change in the slope of the isoquant, that is, the marginal rate of substitution between the two factors. The flatter the isoquant, the more easily factors can be substituted for each other, and the greater will be the elasticity of substitution. The elasticity of substitution is the percentage change in the ratio of the factors employed divided by the percentage change in the marginal rate of substitution between the factors when product is held constant along an isoquant. Thus

$$E_s = \frac{\dfrac{d(C/L)}{C/L}}{\dfrac{d(MTS)}{MTS}} = \left(\frac{MTS}{C/L}\right)\left(\frac{d(C/L)}{d(MTS)}\right)$$

Perfect Substitutes

Two limiting cases for the degree of substitutability can be noted. First, two factors are perfect substitutes if the ratio of their marginal products remains constant as the ratio of their quantities changes. As we move along an isoquant, adding labor and reducing capital, the slope of the isoquant does not change; the marginal rate of substitution between the factors is constant. When two factors are perfect substitutes, the isoquant is a straight line and the elasticity of substitution is in the limit infinite.

An illustrative production function with perfect substitutes is

$$Q = .5C + 3L \tag{3}$$

Along any one isoquant, say $X = 60$,

$$60 = .5C + 3L$$

or

$$.5C = -3L + 60$$

$$C = -6L + 120 \tag{4}$$

Equation (4) is that of the isoquant. It has a constant slope of -6. Six units of capital can be substituted for one unit of labor at any point on the isoquant while maintaining output at its constant level of 60 units. As in demand theory, two factors that are perfect substitutes are typically treated as a single factor in production theory. Unless the prices of two perfect substitutes are equal, the more expensive of the two simply will not enter into production (or consumption) plans.

Fixed Production Coefficients

The second limiting case with respect to the elasticity of substitution arises when no substitution between or among factors is possible. This case is called fixed coefficients of production. To produce a given amount of a product, certain quantities of each factor are required, and no increase in one factor can compensate for the loss of the other factor. In the two-factor, fixed coefficients case, the isoquants are L-shaped. The elasticity of substitution is zero. The two ridge lines coincide, and only points along this combined ridge line are "economic" (see Figure 7.4).

Figure 7.4   Ridge Line with Perfect Complements

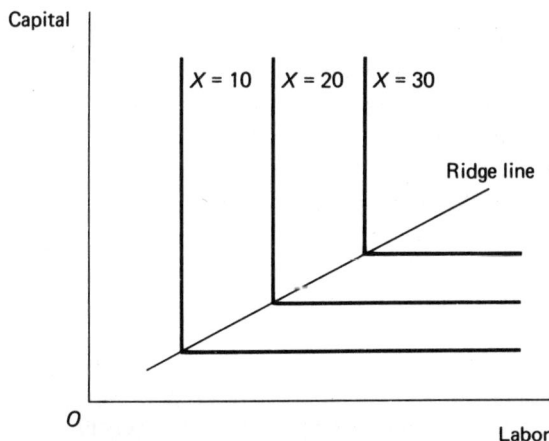

As an example, assume that two units of capital and five units of labor are required for each unit of output, and no substitution between capital and labor is possible. The production function is written

$$Q = \min\left(\frac{C}{2}, \frac{L}{5}\right) \tag{5}$$

Output will be equal to the minimum of $C/2$ or $L/5$, whichever is smaller.

Along the horizontal sections of the isoquants the marginal productivity of labor is zero; additions to the quantity of labor have no effect on the volume of output. Along the vertical sections, the marginal product of capital is zero. At the corners of the isoquants the marginal products of capital and labor cannot be separately determined. Because the factors must be used together, only the added productivity of additional "package" of capital plus labor can be determined.

Engineers and businessmen often think that the possibilities for substitution of one factor for another in the productive process are slight; economists are more convinced that substitution can and does take place. It is likely that the time period under consideration is important; the shorter the time period the fewer opportunities there are for substitution, that is, the lower the elasticity of substitution.

In some modern theories of production (for example, linear programming) and of growth, fixed production coefficients are assumed. One may question the realism of this assumption, but it certainly simplifies the analysis.[2]

RETURNS TO SCALE

The returns to scale of a firm describe the behavior of output as the quantities of the inputs are increased in a given proportion. If, when all inputs of a firm are increased by a given percentage, output rises by the same percentage, the firm has constant returns to scale. Increasing returns mean that output increases proportionally more than inputs; decreasing returns cause output to increase less proportionally than inputs have increased.

A firm may have increasing returns over one scale of operations (that is, in one portion of its production map) and decreasing returns in another.

On a production map, along any ray from the origin the proportion of factors remains constant. Constant returns to scale are then shown on a map if a movement along such a ray (see line OA of Figure 7.5, for example) cuts isoproduct curves measuring regularly increasing output at equal intervals along the ray from the origin. Each movement of a given distance along the ray is accompanied by the same increase in output. Along line OA, the same increase in factors each time raises output successively by ten units:

$$OA_1 = A_1A_2 = A_2A_3$$

For increasing returns, isoproduct curves with equal product increases become closer together for a movement along a straight

---

[2]In short-run analysis, fixed coefficients are plausible over a range of a firm's production. In a given plant, for example, additional output may require only the addition of relatively constant amounts of labor and raw materials.

line from the origin; the added product requires a less than pro-portional increase in inputs. See line OB of Figure 7.5, on which $OB_1 > B_1B_2 > B_2B_3$. Decreasing returns, on the other hand, are indicated along line OD, where isoproduct curves become farther apart as inputs are increased: $OD_1 < D_1D_2 < D_2D_3$.

Figure 7.5 *Constant, Increasing, and Decreasing Returns*

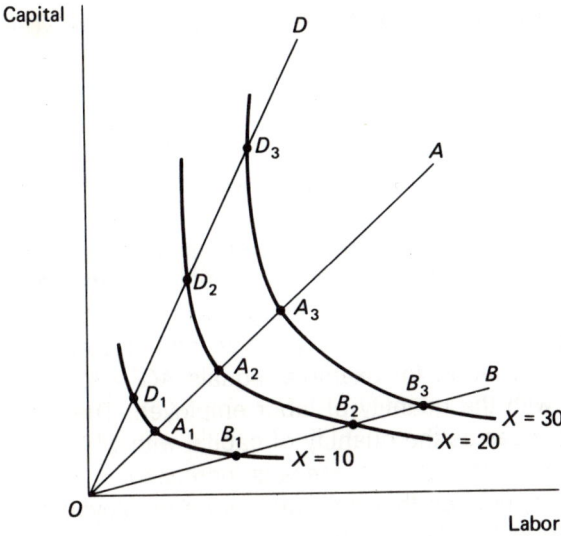

Figure 7.6 *Variable Returns to Scale*

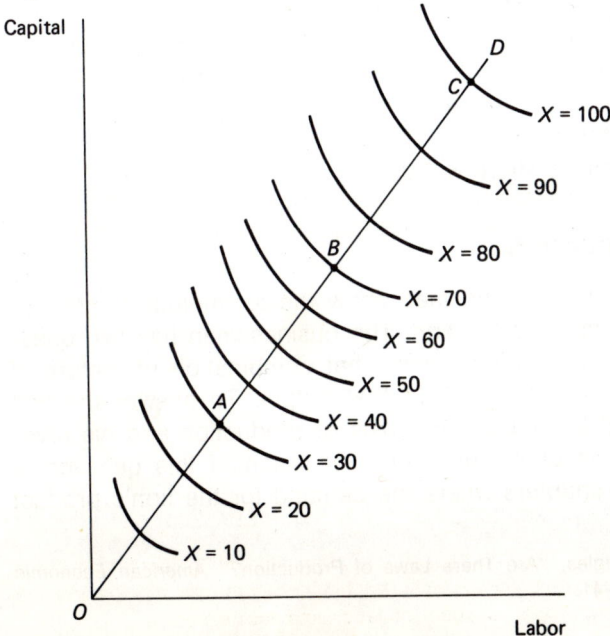

Perhaps a more common case is illustrated in Figure 7.6, which along ray *OD* shows first increasing returns (from *O* to *A),* then a region of constant returns (*A* to *B*), and finally decreasing returns (*B* to *C*).

THE COBB-DOUGLAS PRODUCTION FUNCTION

The Cobb-Douglas production function has many uses in economic analysis, in both microeconomic and macroeconomic theory. The form of the function is

$$Q = AL^\alpha C^{1-\alpha}$$

where *A* represents a constant, and α has a positive value less than one.[3] Empirically, the value of α for the United States has been found to be approximately .7.

The Cobb-Douglas function has constant returns to scale with any factor proportions. Elasticity of substitution between labor and capital has a constant value of one. The marginal productivities of both capital and labor are continuously positive and decreasing. The marginal product of labor, for example, equals $AC^{1-\alpha}/L^{1-\alpha}$. It thus varies inversely with the quantity of labor employed. The marginal product of labor rises as the quantity of capital with which the labor is combined in the production process is increased.

Note that production requires that both factors be employed. No production is possible with only one factor.

Finally, the Cobb-Douglas production function has the interesting characteristic, quite useful in macroeconomic growth models, that if each factor of production is paid a price equal to the marginal productivity of the factor, the share of total income received by one type of factor will remain constant for any changes in the quantities of factors employed. The share of income going to labor will equal α; capital's share will be $1 - \alpha$.

COSTS OF PRODUCTION

The production function and map show the technological production possibilities open to the firm. The businessman has two questions: how much to produce, and what combination of factors of production to employ to produce that output. To answer the first question he must know both his costs of production and his revenues from the sale of the product. Discussion of this question is deferred to later chapters where the demand for the firm's product

[3]See Paul H. Douglas, "Are There Laws of Production?" *American Economic Review 38* (1948), 1–41.

is combined with its costs. However, the second question—what combination of factors to employ for any given output—requires only a knowledge of the costs of producing various outputs with various combinations of factors of production, and can be answered as soon as information on the costs or prices of factors of production is added to the information on technological production possibilities provided by the production map.

The costs of production of a firm thus depend on (1) the production function and (2) input prices. Data on the costs of inputs can be added to the production map. From the combinations the firm's cost function can then be derived.

In the two-factor case, assume the firm may use labor (L) and capital (C), the prices of which are P_l and P_c respectively.

It is convenient to indicate costs with appropriate *iso curves*, in this case isocost curves. Each curve is the locus of the combinations of the inputs which, *for given prices of these inputs*, have the same total cost.

Those combinations of capital and labor which would cost a total of $100, for example, are found by the following process. If the price of labor is $1 a unit, $100 will buy 100 units of labor and no capital. One point on the $100 isocost curve is therefore point P, in Figure 7.7. Alternately, if the price of C is $2 per unit, the entire $100 spent on capital will purchase 50 units of capital, giving point P', a second point on the $100 isocost curve.

Figure 7.7 Isocost Curves

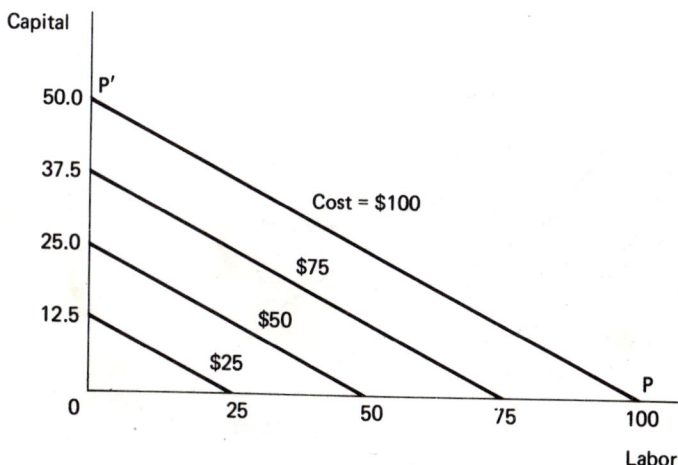

So long as the prices of C and L are constant, all other combinations of C + L that would cost $100 lie on a straight line connecting the two points P and P'.

The negative of the slope of an isocost curve when factor prices are constant is equal to the ratio of the prices of the two factors. The negative of the slope of the $100 isocost curve of Figure 7.7, for example, is OP'/OP.

$$OP' = \frac{\$100}{P_C} \quad \text{and} \quad OP = \frac{\$100}{P_L}$$

Thus

$$\frac{OP'}{OP} = \frac{\$100/P_C}{\$100/P_L} = \frac{P_L}{P_C}$$

Lines for other total cost figures can then be constructed easily. The $75, $50, and $25 isocost curves are also shown in Figure 7.7.

THE FIRM'S EXPANSION PATH

A combination on one diagram (see Figure 7.8) of the isocost lines with the isoproduct curves of the production function shows both output and costs as functions of the quantities of the two factors employed.

Figure 7.8   *Expansion Path*

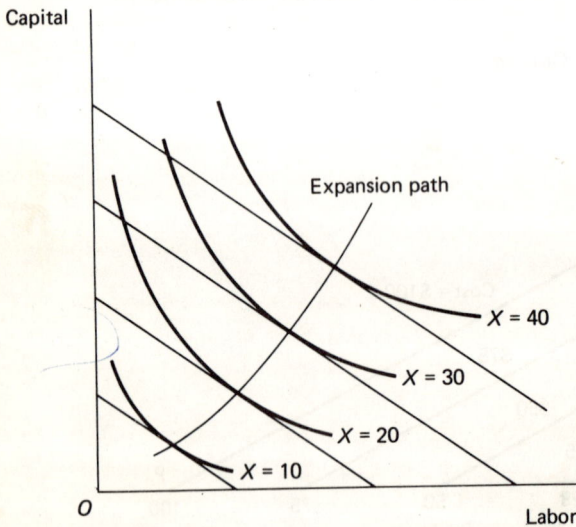

The producer will wish to minimize the cost of producing any output. The minimum cost of any output occurs where the isoproduct curve for that output is tangent to an isocost curve.

The locus of the points of tangency between isoquants and isooutlay curves is the firm's *expansion path*. Points on this line show the factor quantities that provide the minimum cost of producing each output given the production function and the prices of the inputs. The expansion path thus answers one of the two production questions of the businessman: what factor proportions to use to produce any given output.

At each point on the expansion path where isoproduct and isocost curves are tangent the slope of the isoproduct curve equals the slope of the isocost curve. At these points the ratio of the marginal products of the two factors is equal to the ratio of their prices. As noted earlier, the negative of the slope of the isoproduct curves equals the ratio of the marginal products of the two factors, and the negative of the slope of the isocost curve equals the ratio of the factor prices. Therefore, where the two curves are tangent with equal slopes,

$$\frac{\text{Marginal product of labor}}{\text{Marginal product of capital}} = \frac{\text{Price of labor}}{\text{Price of capital}}$$

A rule for minimizing the cost of any given output when factor prices are given, therefore, is to use factors in a proportion that equates the ratio of their prices with the ratio of their marginal products.

Changes in factor prices will shift the location of the isocost curves and the expansion path. On Figure 7.8, for example, a rise in the price of labor will cause each isocost curve to become steeper, pivoting on its intersection on the vertical (capital) axis. The expansion path will tend to shift to the left, which means that the minimum cost combination of factors for any given output will, after the rise in the price of labor, use less labor and more capital than before.

If the firm's production function shows constant returns to scale, the expansion path will be a straight line through the origin. For given factor prices, the same factor proportions will minimize the cost of producing any output. A change in relative factor prices will shift the location of the expansion path, but the new path will also be a straight line out of the origin.

If the production function has fixed production coefficients, the firm's expansion path will be a straight line through the corners of the isoproduct curves regardless of changes in relative factor prices. The rule that on the expansion path the ratio of the factor prices is equal to the ratio of the marginal productivities of the factors does not hold in this case because the separate marginal products of the two factors are not defined at the corner points of the isoproduct curves.

If the two factors are perfect substitutes, isoproduct curves are straight lines. In this case, the firm's expansion path (except for one exceptional case) will lie completely along one or the other axis. The minimum cost of producing any output results from using only one of the two factors. A shift in relative factor prices may cause the expansion path in this case to shift from one axis to the other.

The exceptional case with perfect substitutes arises when the ratio of the prices of the two factors is exactly equal to the marginal technical rate of substitution between the two factors. The slopes of the isoproduct and isocost curves will be equal. In this situation the costs of producing a given output are the same whatever factor proportions are used and, in effect, the entire map constitutes an expansion path for the firm.

The expansion path for the firm with a Cobb-Douglas production function will always be a straight line through the origin because that function has constant returns to scale. The lower the price of one factor relative to the price of the other, the closer the expansion path will lie to the axis on which units of the cheaper factor are measured.

LONG-RUN COST CURVES OF THE FIRM

From a production map with overlaid isocost curves, the long-run total costs of the firm of producing various outputs can be determined. It is convenient, however, to transfer this cost information to a graph on which costs are plotted against the output of the firm. The analysis can be simplified because for given prices of factors only points along the expansion path need be considered.

Two general propositions about the cost curves may first be noted.

(1) Cost curves are derived from the production function and knowledge about factor prices; changes in either of these will affect the cost curves.

(2) Although the quantities of factors used in production do not appear explicitly on cost curve diagrams, they are there implicitly; the decision of a firm to produce a given output at minimum cost automatically implies the use of particular quantities of the factors of production (that is, the quantities shown on the expansion path for that output).

From the expansion path of a firm a graph is constructed plotting the output of the firm against its total costs.

An important question in both theory and practice is whether total costs increase proportionally with output, or whether total costs rise faster or more slowly than does total output. Another way of stating the same question is to ask whether average costs per unit of output are constant, increasing, or decreasing. The phrases "constant," "increasing," and "decreasing costs" refer to the behavor of average cost as output increases.

When the prices of factors of production are given constants, constant average costs implies constant returns to scale for the firm; increasing returns implies decreasing average costs; and decreasing returns means rising average costs.[4]

. Constant, increasing, and decreasing costs, respectively, are illustrated in parts (a), (b), and (c) of Figure 7.9, where in each section the upper diagram shows the total cost as output increases, and the lower shows the average cost and marginal cost derived from the corresponding total cost curve.

Part (d) of Figure 7.9 illustrates a commonly used composite case. At small scales, the firm has decreasing costs where marginal cost is less than average cost. After a point, however, average cost rises, with marginal cost in excess of average cost. At the minimum point of average cost, marginal cost is equal to average cost.

The long-run average cost curve is often called a planning curve. It is a basic tool for a firm deciding what scale of plant to build, for it shows the minimum average cost for producing each possible output.[5]

THE SIGNIFICANCE OF THE LONG-RUN COST FUNCTION

What long-run cost function a firm will have is an empirical question depending largely on its technology. There is general agreement that most firms have decreasing costs over at least an initial range of outputs.

Long-run average costs of production decrease for technological reasons. The existence of indivisibilities of types of equipment or techniques that cannot be subdivided is often cited: a railroad cannot have half a track between two points. Pure indivisibilities in production are rare. Much more common is the technique or item of machinery that has significantly lower average costs per unit of output for larger than for smaller scales of output.

[4]When factor prices are not assumed constant, the correlation between returns and costs may not hold (for example, average cost may rise for a constant returns firm if the prices of factors increase as the firm expands its output). For the present, however, it will be assumed that factor prices do not change as the firm varies its level of production.

[5]Note that the long-run planning curve has been derived solely from the production map and input prices; no reference to short-run curves is necessary to construct this long-run curve.

Figure 7.9 *Long-run Total, Average, and Marginal Cost Curves*

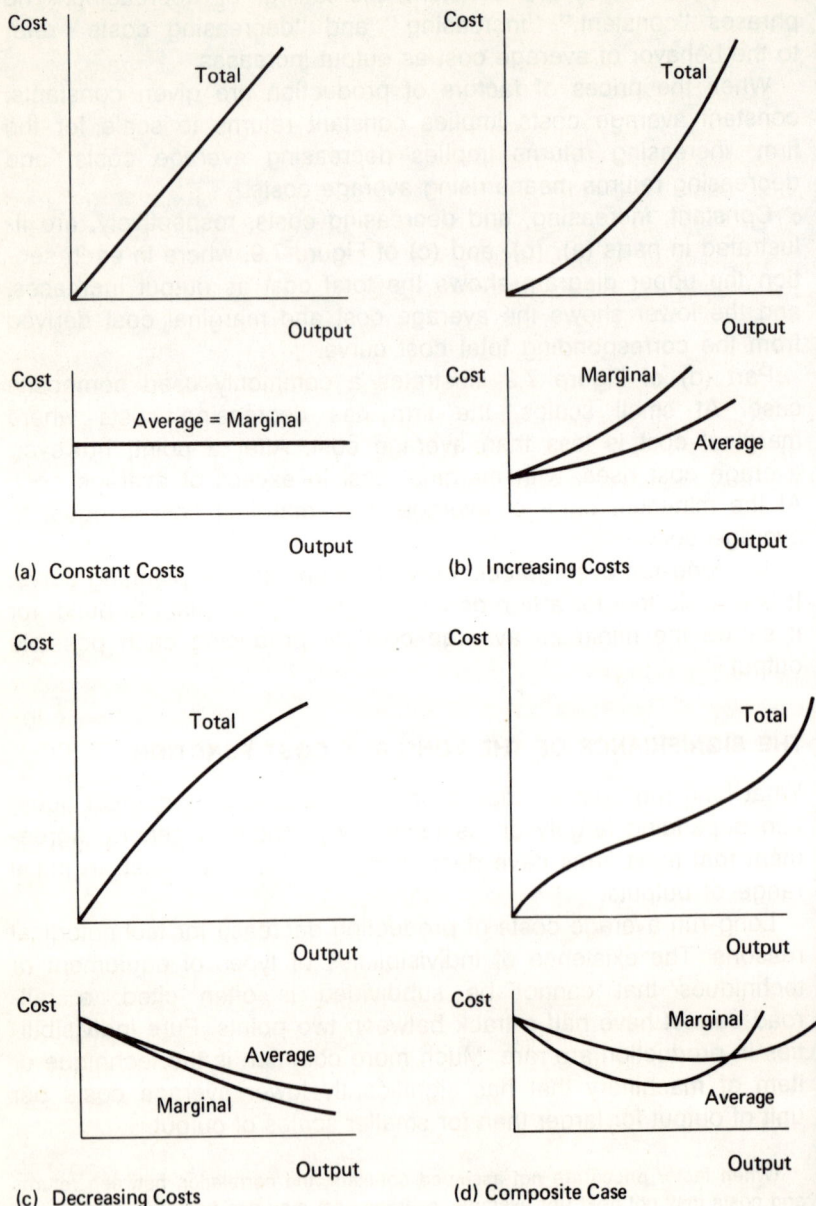

(a) Constant Costs

(b) Increasing Costs

(c) Decreasing Costs

(d) Composite Case

The larger firm thus can use any technique available to the smaller firm; the small firm cannot feasibly use some techniques open to the larger firm. The firm therefore encounters decreasing costs as it expands its scale of operations.

The existence of an initial phase of long-run decreasing costs for most firms is widely recognized. More important questions are whether and at what point the firm's average costs tend to level out, and whether firms will incur increasing costs at large scales of output.

A firm that has continuously decreasing costs over the entire range of output that it is likely to want to produce (the firm would expect to exhaust the market for its product while still in the decreasing cost range) is called a *natural monopoly*. The lowest possible cost of production of that product requires a single firm. Public utilities are examples of natural monopolies. Such firms raise difficult /problems of public policy. Competition between firms in the production of the good is not feasible. In addition, serious questions arise with respect to the optimum pricing policy for the natural monopoly. The decreasing costs of the natural monopoly mean, by definition, that the firm's marginal cost is less than its average cost of production. A price that would cover average cost will exclude from the market some customers who would be willing to pay a price equal to the marginal cost of production, an exclusion that conflicts with economic efficiency.[6]

Do firms ever have increasing costs? At this point there is a division in the literature of economics. One could almost say a choice exists between (1) a theory unsupported by facts, and (2) some facts without a supporting theory.

The theory is that any firm will eventually run into increasing costs because of the rise in administrative costs. The problems of integrating the operations of a firm often appear to increase more than proportionately with size. In the large firm or organization, operating procedures must be formalized and standardized. Employees must "go by the book." This can make the organization inflexible and inefficient. Everyone has his own candidate for the role of lethargic giant. The writer's favorite is the U.S. Army.

Many studies have been made of the costs of firms.[7] Although the results are inconclusive, one pattern appears quite often: long-run decreasing costs up to a point, at which average costs level off and remain relatively constant over a wide range of outputs.

This existence of such constant returns to scale over a range of sizes is also supported by an argument (made most notably by George Stigler) known as the *survivor principle*.[8] If an industry is

[6]These problems are discussed further in Chapters 10, 11, and 17.

[7]See, for example, J. Johnston, *Statistical Cost Analysis* (New York: McGraw-Hill, 1960); P. J. D. Wiles, *Price, Cost and Output*, 2nd ed. rev., (Oxford: Blackwell, 1961), appendix to chap. 12; Joe S. Bain, *Barriers to New Competition* (Cambridge: Harvard University Press, 1956); A. A. Walters, "Production and Cost Functions: An Econometric Survey," *Econometrica* 31 (1963), 1–66.

[8]George J. Stigler, "The Economies of Scale," *Journal of Law and Economics* 1 (1958), 54–71, reprinted in George J. Stigler, *The Organization of Industry* (Homewood, Ill., Irwin, 1968), chap. 7.

observed over extended periods of time, and firms of varying sizes do in fact survive, this evidence suggests that the costs of firms of different sizes are approximately equal. Over a period of time, higher cost firms would fail to survive. The argument is persuasive but not conclusive because there may be other reasons for the success or failure of a firm.[9]

The question of the nature of the cost functions of firms has great practical importance. The possibilities for a competitive economy depend on the presence of constant or increasing costs.

The theoretical interest in the nature of firms' cost functions lies in this question: What determines the size of firms? The question can be answered fairly easily if firms have the U-shaped cost curve of Figure 7.9d. In particular, in the long run under perfect competition, firms with U-shaped average cost curves will adopt the scale at which their average cost is at a minimum. But if firms have constant costs, there is really nothing within the existing body of economic theory to explain why an individual competitive firm will be one size rather than another.

In this case one might well ask, if firms have constant costs what difference does it make what size a firm is? The answer is partly economic: Large firms are likely to have market power that has undesirable economic results. This question also raises grave political and social issues, for large firms have an influence on the political and social fabric of society quite different from that of smaller firms.

The implications of the long-run cost curve for the functioning of an economy cannot be discussed fully without a concurrent description of the kind of markets facing firms. Before entering this area, however, the short-run production function and the nature of short-run cost curves will be analyzed.

REVIEW QUESTIONS

1. Explain the following concepts:
    Internal efficiency
    Technology
    Short run
    Long run
    Production map
    Marginal rate of technical substitution
    Ridge line
    Elasticity of substitution

[9]In addition, different firms in a given industry do not produce the same collection of goods or sell in the same market areas, so they are not strictly comparable in terms of cost functions.

Perfect substitutes in production
Fixed production coefficients
Perfect complements in production
Returns to scale: constant, increasing, and decreasing
Cobb-Douglas production function
Isocost curve
Expansion path
Constant, increasing, and decreasing costs
Planning curve
Natural Monopoly
"Survivor principle"

2. "Long-run decreasing costs are incompatible with a decentralized, competitive economy." Explain.

3. What are the implications for public policy and for economic efficiency if, in fact, firms' long-run average cost curves are essentially horizontal?

4. On appropriately constructed production maps, show the effects on the firm's expansion path resulting from a change in the price of one factor of production, assuming in turn the production function

   (a) is a Cobb-Douglas.

   (b) has fixed production coefficients.

   (c) has perfect substitutability between factors.

FURTHER READING

Arrow, Kenneth J., Hollis B. Chenery, Bagicha Minhas, and Robert M. Solow, "Capital-Labor Substitution and Economic Efficiency." *Review of Economics and Statistics 43* (1961), 225–250.

Carlson, Sune, *A Study on the Pure Theory of Production.* London: Staples Press (1939).

Douglas, Paul H., "Are There Laws of Production?" *American Economic Review 38* (1948), 1–41.

Frisch, Ragnar, *Theory of Production.* Chicago: Rand McNally (1965).

Henderson, James M., and Richard E. Quandt, *Microeconomic Theory: A Mathematical Approach.* New York: McGraw-Hill (1958), chap. 3.

Johnston, J., *Statistical Cost Analysis.* New York: McGraw-Hill (1960).

Leibenstein, Harvey, "Allocative Efficiency vs. 'X-efficiency.' " *American Economic Review 56* (1966), 392–415.

Walters, A. A., "Production and Cost Functions: An Econometric Survey." *Econometrica 31* (1963), 1–66.

8 SHORT-RUN PRODUCTION AND COST FUNCTIONS

THE NATURE OF THE SHORT RUN

The long-run cost curves of the firm show how its costs change as it varies output, when the firm is able to vary all inputs. Once a firm has committed itself to a particular scale and has negotiated contracts with suppliers of various inputs, it no longer has the freedom to vary production, which is assumed in long-run theory. These further restrictions on its behavior are termed short-run constraints and its behavior under these constraints is called short-run behavior.

The short run is defined as that period of time within which at least one of the inputs of the firm cannot be varied, and at least one input is variable.[1] The definition indicates that the short run covers a wide range of conditions. For this reason, short-run behavior of a firm is less predictable than long-run behavior. How the firm will react in the short run to some change in the conditions affecting it (for example, a change in technology,

[1]The definition is arbitrary and is a simplification to replace the more complex idea that in short periods of time inputs can be varied only at a higher cost than in the long run. A firm can withdraw from almost any commitment, but often only by incurring a penalty fee of some type. It may buy out of a long-term contract for the supply of some raw material; it may convert an existing plant to an alternative use. At best, by definition, it will not be able to recoup all of the costs committed to a fixed factor.

or in supply or demand curves of inputs or outputs) will depend on the particular short-run constraints under which it operates.

The costs of the firm may also be classed as variable and fixed. A fixed cost is one that does not vary with a change in the output of the firm. A variable cost does change as the output level of the firm varies. Variable costs are therefore avoidable costs; the firm can escape them by reducing its level of production. In the long run, all costs and inputs are variable. In the short run, some costs and some inputs are variable, while others are fixed. Because the fixed costs are independent of the level of production of the firm, however, they do not influence the firm's behavior in the short run.

The usual characteristics of a fixed input are that the quantity of the input available to the firm has a limit and by definition cannot be increased beyond that point, and that the total cost of this fixed input is a given constant. It may be possible, however, to use less than the fixed available quantity of the input in production, although this will not reduce the cost. The firm with a dozen lathes, for example, is not required to use them all, but their fixed cost remains unchanged no matter how many are used. The point is that it may sometimes be advantageous to the firm to keep some of its fixed inputs unused.

Ordinarily, the costs of a variable input vary only with the quantity of the input employed, and its costs are zero if none of the factor is used. If the supply of the factor to a firm is perfectly elastic, the cost of the input is simply its price times the number of units used, where the firm may use any quantity of this variable input. If the supply of the factor to the firm is not perfectly elastic, however, the price of the factor will rise as the firm uses more of it, and the total variable cost of this factor will rise faster than the quantity employed.

Cases may also arise in which some or all of the costs of a variable input are fixed to the firm. For example, the firm may have a contract that provides for a lump sum payment for the use of a given type of factor whether the factor is used or not, with an additional variable payment depending on the quantity used. Electricity and telephone rates are common examples, as are legal fees to the firm paying a retainer to a law firm.

Unless otherwise noted, it will be assumed here that fixed and variable inputs give rise only to fixed and variable costs respectively.

THE MARKET PERIOD

The *market period* is a limiting case of the short run. In the short run some inputs are fixed and others are variable: some costs are fixed and others will vary with output. In the limit, all inputs and all costs can be considered fixed. This is the "market period."

Three alternative concepts of the market period are formulated in the literature:

(1) Since all inputs are fixed, so is output. Only one quantity can be supplied, and it is put on the market for whatever price it can bring. While these assumptions are consistent with competitive behavior, they are not consistent with behavior under imperfect competition or monopoly.

· (2) The second form of the concept of the market period is similar to the first, except that firms have the option of withholding some of their current output for sale in a future peroid. These assumptions are no doubt realistic, but as formulated the case can (and should) be handled in terms of short run rather than the market period. For, as already noted, future revenue that would be lost if current output is sold instead of being held for future sale is properly counted as a part of the marginal cost of current sales. Thus, in this second formulation of the market period concept, not all costs are fixed. This interpretation is, however, the one most commonly found in the literature.

(3) In the definition of the market period adopted in this book, all costs are assumed fixed in the market period and the firm cannot produce more than a given output (which can be called the "constrained" output). But the firm does have the option of producing less than that amount.[2] Total costs are fixed, regardless of the amount produced, up to the constrained output. For greater outputs the total cost cannot be defined, since it is physically impossible to produce more than the constrained output. Marginal cost is zero up to the constrained output, after which it is undefined.

The market period cost curves of the firm are illustrated in Figure 8.1. Output OX is by assumption the maximum quantity the firm can produce. Because all the firm's costs are fixed, its average total cost curve is identical with its average fixed cost curve. Up to output OX, this average cost curve has the shape of a rectangular hyperbola: Output times average cost equals a constant total cost. At output OX a dotted vertical line is shown for the average curve; no more than OX can be produced at any cost.

The market period marginal cost curve lies along the horizontal axis for all outputs up to OX; marginal cost is zero. At output OX, marginal cost in effect becomes infinite, as indicated by the vertical line.

---

[2]Alternately, the full amount can be considered to have been produced, with some portion of it disposed of costlessly.

Figure 8.1 *Market Period Cost Curves*

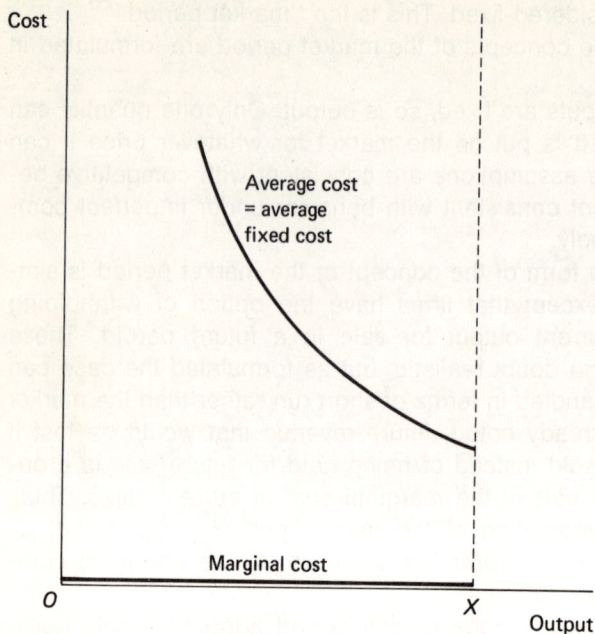

THE SHORT-RUN PRODUCTION FUNCTION

It is possible to derive a firm's short-run production function, for the two input case, from the long-run production map of Chapter 7. On that map the points at which the quantity of one of the factors remains the same give a relationship between output and the variable quantities of the other input. This is done by moving along a hori-

Figure 8.2 *Derivation of Short-run Production Function*

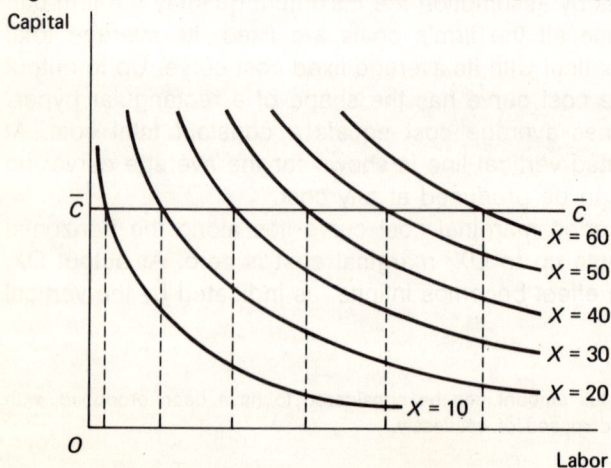

zontal line in Figure 8.2 if the fixed input is capital, and along a vertical line if labor is assumed constant with capital variable. The resulting information about the relationship between the quantity of the variable input (say, labor) and the output of the product (from the successive isoproduct curves as they are crossed) can best be illustrated on a graph showing only these two variables. Figure 8.3a shows a typical total product curve derived in this way; below it on Figure 8.3b are drawn the average and marginal product curves derived from the total product curve of Figure 8.3a.

Figure 8.3 *Total, Average, and Marginal Production Curves*

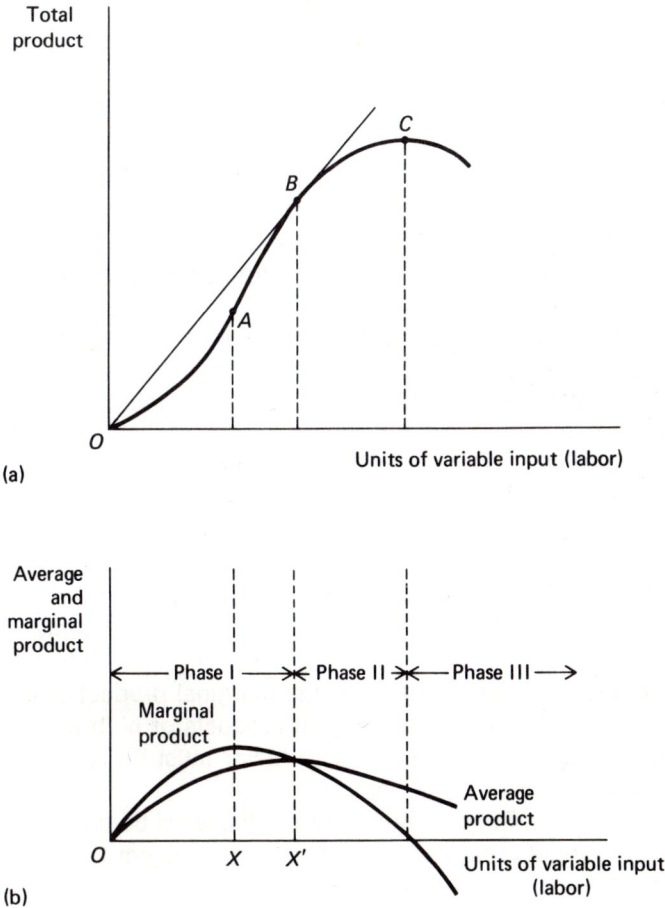

THE PRINCIPLE OF DIMINISHING RETURNS

The curves of Figure 8.3b show the familiar principle of diminishing returns: If one factor or group of factors of production is held constant and another is varied the marginal product of the variable factor will eventually diminish. On Figure 8.3b, diminishing returns set in when OX units of the variable factor are employed. The justification for the principle is simply that both reason and evidence suggest that output cannot increase indefinitely when there is a restriction on one of the inputs used in its production.

Three "phases" in the behavior of short-run average and marginal product curves are distinguished in Figure 8.3b. Phase I extends to the point of maximum average product; within it, the average product of the variable factor is rising; marginal product first rises and then falls to a point of equality with average product.[3] In Phase II, average product declines continuously, while marginal product falls and reaches zero at the end of the phase. In Phase III, the marginal product of the variable factor is negative, and average product continues its decline. Phase III would end where total and average product reach zero.

Note that marginal product reaches a maximum at the steepest point (point A) on the total product curve. Average product is highest at that point on the total curve (point B) at which a ray from the origin is tangent to the total curve. At this same point, marginal product equals average product. When total product reaches a maximum (point C), marginal product is zero.

The significance of the three phases appears most strongly in considering in later chapters the behavior of the perfectly competitive firm. One technical point can be noted here. If a long-run two-factor production function has constant returns to scale (as, for example, the Cobb-Douglas production function discussed in Chapter 7), it can be shown that at any point on the production map the phases of the two factors are symmetrical: where one factor (the other constant) is in Phase I, the second factor (holding the first constant) will be in Phase III. If either factor is in Phase II, however, the other will also be in Phase II. In terms of marginal products in this case of constant returns to scale, when the marginal product of one factor exceeds its average product, the marginal product of the other will be negative. Where the marginal products of both factors are positive, the marginal product of each factor must be less than the average product of the same factor.

As we shall see later, the competitive firm will always be operating in Phase II for all inputs (that is, all factors will be subject to diminishing returns).

---

[3]Recall that for smooth and continuous functions, when any average curve reaches a maximum it will be intersected by the corresponding marginal curve.

CONVERSION OF PRODUCT CURVES INTO COST CURVES

As noted in Chapter 7, the cost functions of a firm can be derived from a production function plus knowledge of input prices. We now demonstrate this transformation for the short run. The total product curve of Figure 8.3a is used. In addition to the information given by that total product curve, only the total cost of the fixed factor (= TFC) and the price per unit of the variable factor (P_v) must be known.

The horizontal axis of Figure 8.3a measures units of variable factor employed. That same axis can be converted to a measure of the cost of the variable factor employed simply by multiplying the units of factor by its price (P_v, which is assumed constant). The result is Figure 8.4, plotting total product against total *variable* cost.

Figure 8.4 *Output as a Function of Total Variable Cost*

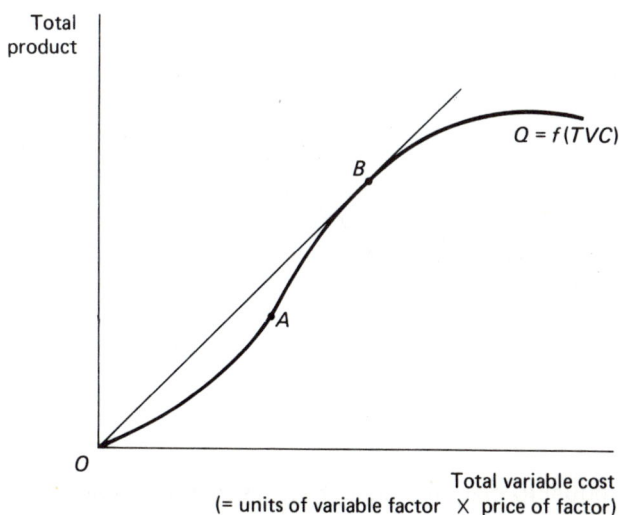

Total variable cost
(= units of variable factor X price of factor)

If now the axes of Figure 8.4 are reversed, Figure 8.5a results, a graph of total variable cost at various levels of output.

From this graph of total variable costs can be derived (with the familiar techniques of Chapter 2) the average variable cost and marginal cost curves of Figure 8.5b.

Note the symmetry of the cost and product curves: marginal cost reaches a minimum at the point A on the total curve at which marginal product reaches a maximum; average variable cost reaches a

Figure 8.5   *Variable Cost Curves*

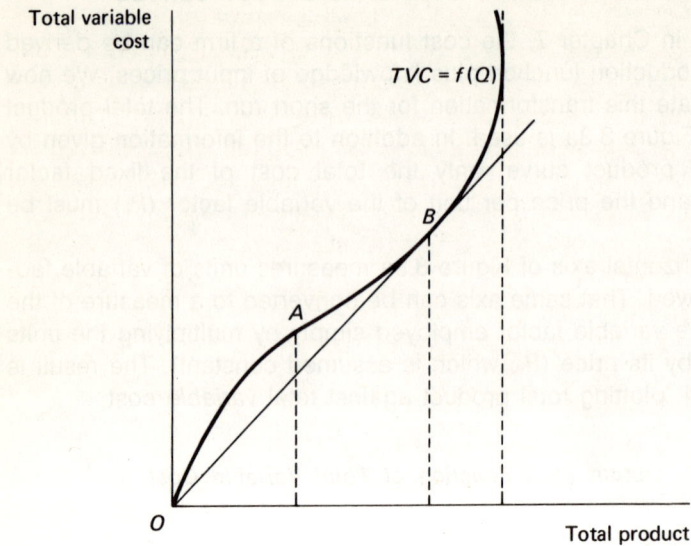

(a)

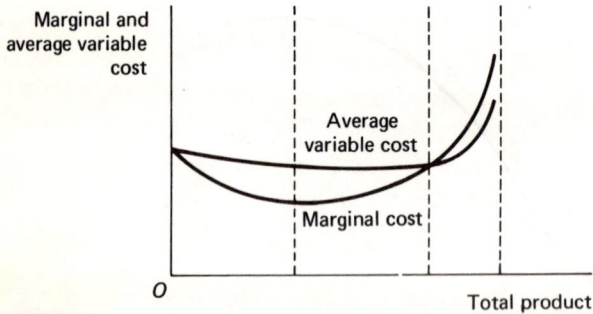

(b)

minimum and is equal to marginal cost at the same point *B* at which average product reaches a maximum and is equal to marginal product. Cost curves for points at which marginal product is negative are not constructed. The firm would never operate in this region; those same outputs can be produced at lower cost with the use of fewer units of the variable factor.

The next step in the development of the firm's short-run cost curves is to add the fixed costs of the constant factor. Total fixed costs are a constant and could be added above the total variable costs of Figure 8.5a. It is more convenient however to place total fixed costs below the total variable costs. The result is Figure 8.6a, on which total fixed and total fixed plus variable costs are measured vertically from point O, while total variable costs are computed vertically from point Z.

Figure 8.6b now gives the whole family of short-run average and marginal cost curves derived from the total curves of Figure 8.6a. Note that while there are three average curves, there is only one marginal curve. Marginal fixed costs are of course zero; marginal variable costs are therefore the same as marginal total costs. When the total cost curve is shifted up by the additional of fixed costs, its *slope* at any output does not change; since marginal cost is measured by slope, the addition of fixed costs does not affect the marginal cost curve.

Figure 8.6   *Short-run Cost Curves*

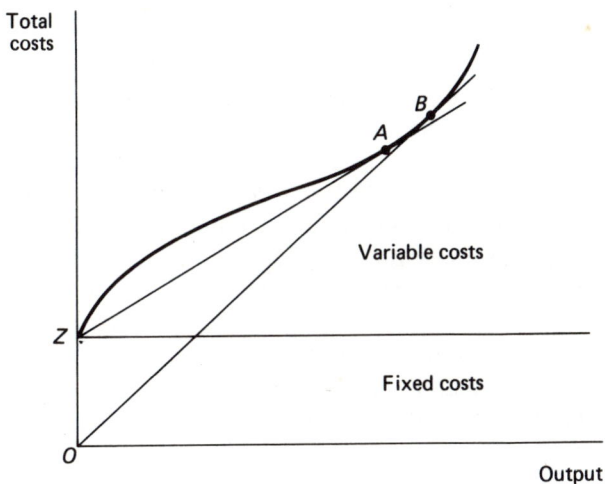

(a)

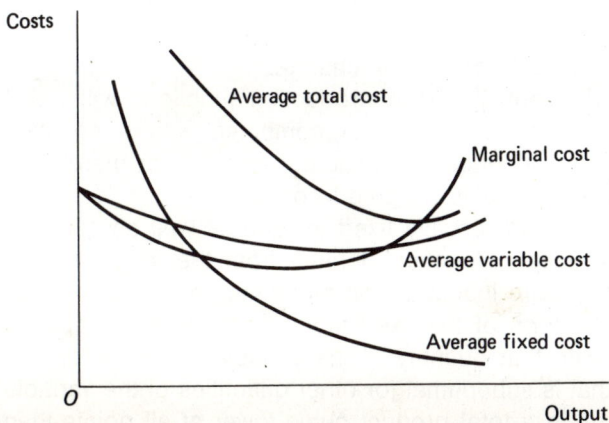

(b)

On the other hand, the addition of fixed costs does change the shape of the average cost curve. Compare the average total cost (*ATC*) with the average variable cost (*AVC*). Note, first, that the *ATC* reaches a minimum at a greater output than does the *AVC*. Second, note that the marginal cost curve goes through the minimum points of both average variable and average total cost.

Given any two of the average curves, the third average curve can be derived.

One final geometrical point: since marginal costs are variable costs and vice versa, the marginal cost and average variable cost curves must start together. The marginal cost of the first unit of output produced must equal the average variable cost of producing one unit.

THE FIXED FACTOR ASSUMPTION

Short-run cost functions are derived from short-run production functions. To determine the possible shapes of the cost curves the forms of the production function must be considered. To this point the short-run production function has been derived from the long-run production map by a movement along a path that keeps one of the inputs constant. An important question, however, is whether the constant input is assumed to be fixed in quantity only, or if it is also fixed in a specific form. For example, consider capital as the fixed factor. Capital may have many forms, and it is unlikely that the particular form of a fixed quantity of capital that would be chosen when the firm is employing it with 10 workers would be the same as the form of capital the firm would choose if it were restricted to the same overall quantity of capital, but planned to employ 100 workers. In other words, as the firm conceives of a movement across the long run production map, keeping the *quantity* of capital constant, it is likely that the specific *form* of the constant quantity of capital the firm would choose will change.

Clearly, very different short-run production functions will result from varying quantities of one input combined with a constant quantity of the other depending on whether the form or merely the quantity of the fixed factor is assumed constant.

In practice, factors are usually fixed in form as well as quantity. The short-run production function derived from the long-run production map is therefore inaccurate at all points except the one (or ones) at which the form of the fixed factor happens to be optimal for combination with that quantity of the variable factor. A form of the fixed factor that is suboptimal for other quantities of the variable factor would result in a total product curve *lower* at all points than the total product curve derived from the long-run production map except at the one point at which the *form* of the capital is optimal.

Figure 8.7   *Alternative Total Product Curves*

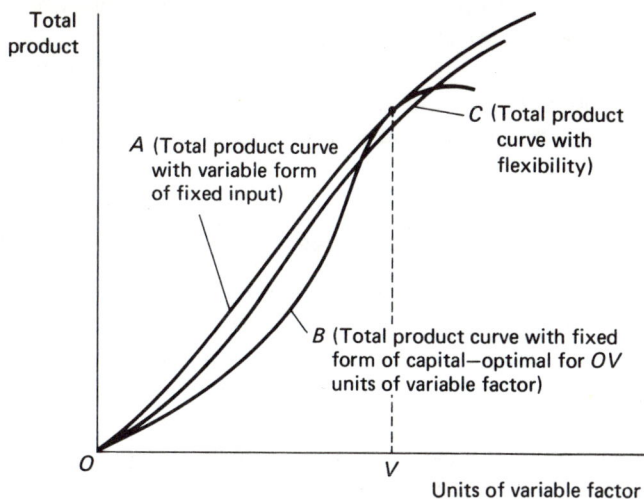

Figure 8.7 shows total product curves *A* and *B,* for each of which the quantity of capital is assumed constant as the quantity of labor is varied. (For the moment, ignore curve *C.*) Curve *A* is based on the assumption that the firm can vary optimally the *form* of the fixed quantity of capital available to it. At each point the firm is able to select its preferred form of capital, limited only to a fixed total quantity. For a trivial example, think of a firm that has a contract to pay $100 a month in rental fees to an office equipment concern. This is a fixed cost. When the firm employs ten typists, it will rent ten standard office typewriters. But when it needs only five typists, it exchanges the ten standard machines for five electric typewriters. The quantity of "capital" is constant, but the form is varied to fit the amount of the variable factor employed.

Total product curve *B* on Figure 8.7 shows total product as a function of the quantity of variable factor employed on the assumption that the form of the fixed quantity of capital cannot be changed. The existing form (ten standard typewriters) is optimal when *OV* units of the variable factor (ten typists) are employed, but is not the best form of capital to employ with quantities of labor greater or less than *OV.* Hence, curve *B* reaches the level of curve *A* only at that point at which the form of the capital is optimal; at all other points the fixed form of capital gives less total output than would be produced if the form of the constant quantity of capital were variable.

In practice, because a firm usually anticipates variations in its rate of output and hence in its employment of the variable factor, the firm is likely to choose a form of the fixed factor that is reasonably appropriate for a range of outputs, but is ideal for none. This gives the firm flexibility. Its productivity as shown by curve C in Figure 8.7 is never as high as that indicated by curve A, but does not lie as low as curve B for variations around OV.

The flexibility of curve C is thus purchased at a cost. The firm can lose by meeting unexpected and unplanned variations in the demand for its product, but it can also lose by planning for variations that do not develop.

THE SHAPES OF SHORT-RUN COST CURVES

The assumption that the form as well as the quantity of the fixed factor is constant affects importantly the likely shapes of the short-run cost curves. The shape of the average fixed cost curve will not be affected, but the average variable cost curve and hence marginal cost curve may now have almost any shape, depending on the particular characteristics of the specific factor that is assumed constant. One principle that is certain is that the short-run average variable, average total, and marginal cost curves will *eventually* rise. This is ensured by the principle of diminishing returns. It is also certain that the average total cost curve will have an initial decreasing phase; regardless of the behavior of variable costs there must be an initial range during which the decrease in average fixed costs dominates the average variable costs and causes average total cost to fall. At small outputs, average fixed cost rises toward infinity as output diminishes.

Which of the various possible shapes of the short-run cost curves is most characteristic of business firms is of course an empirical question. Many businessmen would hold that over a wide range of outputs average variable cost is fairly constant. This would imply that average total costs are decreasing over this range, being pulled down by falling average fixed costs. There is, moreover, general support for the proposition that in the short run, firms have an initial range of decreasing costs. As noted above, the firm will inevitably have rising average costs in the short run as its variable factors experience diminishing returns. With the adoption of these principles, the U-shaped average total cost curve of the earlier illustrations thus would be flattened into a slightly tipped saucer shape.

THE INTERRELATIONS OF SHORT-RUN AND
LONG-RUN COST CURVES

Although a firm's short-run cost curves may take many shapes, it is possible to make some generalizations about the relationships between short-run curves of whatever shape and the firm's long-run average and marginal cost curves.

First, it is clear that at no output can a firm's short-run average cost curve lie below its long-run average cost curve, for the latter represents the *minimum* average cost of producing each output when all factors can be varied. At best, short-run average cost may, for a given output or short range of outputs, be equal to long-run average cost.

Conversely, for any point on the long-run average cost curve, short-run plants or organizations will exist with a short-run average cost equal to long-run average cost. Because the short-run average cost curves rest on the long-run curve, the latter is often called an "envelope" of short-run average cost curves. It is misleading, however, to think of the long-run curve as being *derived* from the short-run curves for which it constitutes an envelope. While the long-run average cost curve is unique, the short-run is not, and many short-run average cost curves can be constructed, each of which is tangent to the long-run average cost curve at the same point.

The standard relationship between short- and long-run curves depends on whether the firm is in a phase of long-run constant, increasing, or decreasing costs.

Figure 8.8a shows the constant cost case. Assume that the firm with constant long-run average cost, line $LRAC$, chooses to produce output OX. It constructs the plant most suitable to producing this output, with a short-run average total cost curve $SRAC$. Short-run average total cost equals long-run average cost only at output OX; at all other points the short-run AC curve lies above the long-run AC curve.

At output OX short-run marginal cost passes through the minimum point of the short-run average cost curve. Long-run marginal cost for the constant cost firm is constant and equal to long-run average cost. Thus at point P all four costs (short- and long-run average and marginal costs) are equal.

Note that for outputs above OX, short-run marginal cost exceeds long run marginal cost, while at outputs less than OX the reverse is true.

Figure 8.8b illustrates the second case of a firm producing under conditions of long-run *increasing* costs. To produce the desired output, OX, the firm builds a plant or organization for which the short-run average and marginal cost curves are $SRAC_1$ and $SRMC_1$ respectively. The interesting point to note is that the firm producing *output OX* is *not* producing at the minimum point of its short-run average cost curve, but rather to the right of this minimum point.

For reasons explained later (see Chapter 9), a perfectly competitive firm would never produce under conditions of long-run increas-

Figure 8.8   Short- and Long-run Cost Curves

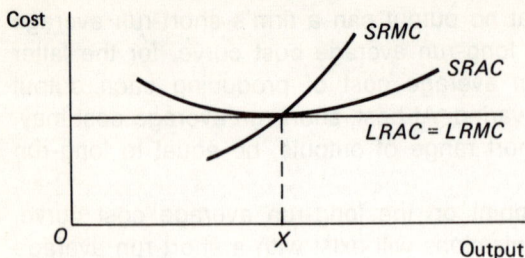

(a) Constant Costs

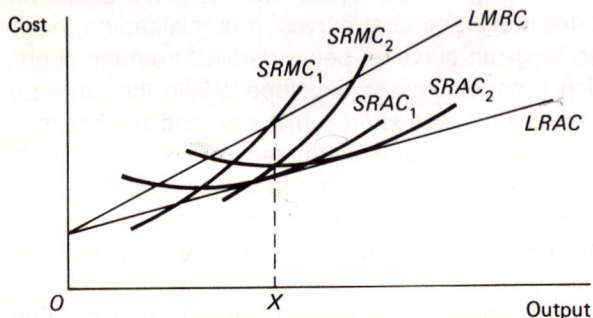

(b) Increasing Costs

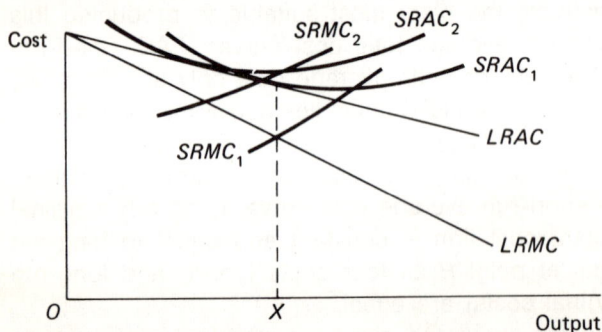

(c) Decreasing Costs

ing costs. But a monopoly or a firm in monopolistic competition could well do so.

Note that if the firm chose to construct the plant that reached its point of minimum average cost at output *OX*, its costs of producing that output (shown by *SRAC₂*) would be higher than if it built the smaller plant (*SRAC₁*) and operated the latter at a point beyond its minimum average cost.

If, as is often done in economics, the capacity of a plant is *defined* as the output the firm produces at the point of minimum average total cost, the rule appears that, when a firm has increasing costs, it will choose to operate a plant at an output greater than capacity.

Third, the firm with decreasing costs is illustrated in Figure 8.8c. The case is realistic not for the perfectly competitive firm but for the "natural monopoly" conditions often found in public utilities. The firm that wishes to produce output OX will construct a plant ($SRAC_1$ with the corresponding $SRMC_1$) with its average total cost tangent to the long-run average cost curve at output OX, but with its minimum average cost to the right, at greater outputs than OX. The plant that has its minimum average cost at output OX ($SRAC_2$ with $SRMC_2$) will not be used because its average cost at OX is higher than with the former plant size.

In short, the firm producing under conditions of decreasing costs will choose to operate with "excess capacity," which is both profitable and economically efficient.

One final point should be noted on Figure 8.8. On each graph, at the point of production (OX), the short-run average total cost curve is tangent to the long-run average cost curve. By geometry, when two average curves are tangent, the corresponding marginal values are equal. Thus long-run marginal cost equals short-run marginal cost at OX whether the firm's long-run costs are constant, increasing, or decreasing.

The raw materials for a study of the market behavior of firms—demand, production, and cost functions—have now been developed. Part IV analyzes the actions of firms and industries under varying market structures and conditions.

REVIEW QUESTIONS

1. Explain the following concepts:
    The principle of diminishing returns
    Market period
    Fixed and variable inputs
    Fixed and variable costs
    Short-run production function
    Average fixed cost; average variable cost; average total cost; marginal cost
    Flexibility
    "Capacity"
2. Explain and show graphically the relations between long- and short-run production functions for a firm, and between a firm's long- and short-run cost functions.
3. Compare the short-run production function of a firm with a factor which is fixed in quantity only, with that of an otherwise similar firm for which the same factor is fixed in a specific form.
4. If you know the shape of a firm's short-run average cost curve, what

if anything can you infer about the firm's long-run average cost curve?
5.   What range of shapes may a firm's short-run cost curves take?

FURTHER READING

Alchian, Armen, "Costs and Output," in Moses Abramovitz et al., The Allocation of Economic Resources. Stanford, Calif.: Stanford University Press (1959), 23–40.

Cassels, J. M., "On the Law of Variable Proportions," in Explorations in Economics. New York: McGraw-Hill (1936), pp. 223–236.

Stigler, George, "Production and Distribution in the Short Run." Journal of Political Economy 47 (1939), 305–327; reprinted in American Economic Association, Readings in the Theory of Income Distribution. New York: McGraw-Hill–Blakiston (1949), pp. 119–142.

Stigler, George, Production and Distribution Theories. New York: Macmillan (1941).

Viner, Jacob, "Cost Curves and Supply Curves." Zeitschrift für Nationalökonomie und Statistik 3 (1931), 23–46.

4 PRIVATE MARKETS

9

PERFECT COMPETITION: LONG RUN

THE CLASSIFICATION OF MARKETS

A market is a set of conditions in which one or more sellers meet one or more buyers for the purpose of exchange. Markets may be classified according to the number of firms in the market and by whether the products sold or the inputs purchased are homogeneous or differentiated.

A single seller of a product or factor that has no close substitutes is a monopolist; the cross elasticity of demand between his product and every other is low. A single buyer is a monopsonist. Oligopoly exists when firms are few enough that, in determining its own behavior, each firm takes into account the likely reaction by other firms to its actions. The corresponding term for buyers is oligopsony. When there are so many firms in a market that each firm acts in the belief that its actions will not directly affect the behavior of other firms, the market is called competitive.

Competitive and oligopolistic markets may be perfect or imperfect, depending on the homogeneity or differentiation of the products of the firms in the market. Products are differentiated (that is, heterogeneous) if buyers have a preference for the product of one firm over that of another. Differentiation may be based on the physical characteristic of the product, its location, its availability, or on any other real or imagined difference that causes the buyer to prefer one product to another. Conversely, two apparently dissimilar goods are economically homogeneous if buyers have no preference for one over the other.

No two products are ever perfectly homogeneous when one takes into account the fact that a product is defined to include all conditions of sale associated with the physical product. The crucial question is whether buyers will pay a higher price for the product of one firm than for that of another. If so, the products in that market are considered to be differentiated.

Markets with homogeneous products are called perfect markets; those with differentiated products are imperfect markets. Table 9.1 summarizes the terminology.

TABLE 9.1   Market Classification

	Homogeneous Products or Inputs	Differentiated Products or Inputs
Many Firms	Perfect competition	Imperfect competition (Sometimes termed "monopolistic competition"[1])
Few Firms	Perfect oligopoly or oligopsony	Imperfect oligopoly or oligopsony
One Firm	Monopoly or monopsony	——

The behavior of firms and industries with these varying characteristics is considered in successive chapters, beginning with perfect competition.

In analyzing markets, we ask in particular what determines the equilibrium price, output, and profit levels for the individual firms and for the industry, and the number of firms in the industry, and how these variables will change under assumed changes in the conditions under which the firms and industry operate. A further question is to what extent the behavior of the firms promotes the objectives of the economy, in particular whether the results are economically efficient and agree with the public's criteria of fairness.

[1]The phrase "monopolistic competition" was defined by its originator, E. H. Chamberlin, to cover all mixtures of competition and monopoly, including oligopoly. Today, use of this term is commonly restricted to the case of many firms selling differentiated products. To avoid any ambiguity, the phrase "Chamberlinian large group case" will often be used in this text for the market with many firms selling differentiated products. See E. H. Chamberlin, *The Theory of Monopolistic Competition* (Cambridge: Harvard University Press, 1933).

WHY STUDY PERFECT COMPETITION?

Students typically consider perfect competition as a grossly un-realistic case; paradoxically, it is the case used most often by economists. Why?

In part, the normative characteristics of perfect competition make it attractive to economists. It can be shown that under certain con-ditions perfect competition leads to perfect efficiency in the alloca-tion of resources. It also results in levels of prices and a pattern of income distribution which some individuals consider equitable but many others do not. Finally, perfect competition implies a de-centralization of decision making and of economic power, which has considerable appeal, especially in the United States, as an economic analogue to the political doctrine of the separation and decentralization of powers.

These normative aspects by themselves justify the study of per-fect competition. They do not justify using perfect competition as a positive description of the existing economy. Yet many economists often do just that.

Whether the theory of perfect competition provides a useful description of the actual operation of the economy is a question that is hotly debated in the economics literature.

Against its use it is argued that the theory is based on unrealistic assumptions—many firms, homogeneous products, perfect knowl-edge—which cannot, therefore, lead to correct conclusions.

In rebuttal, defenders of the use of the concept of perfect com-petition for purposes of prediction sometimes contend that the apparent realism or unrealism of assumptions is irrelevant. What matters is whether the theory leads to correct conclusions, that is, conclusions that agree with the facts of economic behavior. This, they argue, is the case with perfect competition. They further charge that there is no useful general alternative to the theory of perfect competition. Rarely, if ever, do the theories of imperfect or monop-olistic competition lead to correct or even determinate predictions, they assert.

All theory is simplification. Perfect competition theory is a par-ticular form of simplification which is relatively uncomplicated and easy to use, compared with the alternatives. When more complex and "realistic" theories give notably better results than the theory of perfect competition, that is, when they lead to predictions that are significantly different from those of perfect competition and when their predictions are substantially closer to actual results than are the predictions of perfect competition theory, it is unwise to use the theory of perfect competition. But if and when a more complex theory gives substantially the same answers as the simpler theory, it seems perverse to use the more complex theory just because it "looks" more realistic.

As even its defenders recognize, perfect competition cannot be used in all situations. In general, it does not do a good job in situations where personal variations are important. Perfect competition is a better predictor of the behavior of large groups than small and is more likely to be correct in predicting long-term behavior than short-run activity. It is used and useful in the analysis of international trade and in the generalized problems of the allocation of resources in an economy. It is less useful in analyzing the behavior of individual firms and of industries composed of few firms.

Clearly, the theory of perfect competition must be applied cautiously. For analyzing some situations the theory can be used in its general form; in other cases the theory of perfect competition can be useful if it is modified or extended in directions particularly relevant to the problem at hand. Many situations will exist, however, for which the concept of perfect competition is simply not relevant; here, the alternative theories of monopoly and imperfect competition may be applicable. Finally, when none of these appears satisfactory, the search for new theories must proceed.

THE ASSUMPTIONS OF LONG-RUN
PERFECT COMPETITION THEORY

The theory of the behavior of perfectly competitive firms and industries in the long run is developed in this chapter. Short-run competitive theory is analyzed in the following chapter. No attention is therefore paid here to the process by which long-run equilibrium is reached. Only the nature of the long-run equilibrium that will exist and the changes in the characteristics—prices, outputs, and number of firms in an industry—of the equilibrium resulting from changes in factors exogenous to the industry are considered here.

The results described by this long-run theory are best considered, not as a description of a state reached at any time, but rather as a description of the state to which the industry would *tend* if no unexpected change occurred in the fundamental conditions within which the industry operates (that is, the determinants of its demand and supply functions). In practice, before any state of long-run equilibrium would be reached, these factors would have changed, and the tendency of the industry would be redirected.

The basic assumptions of long-run competitive theory include the following:

A homogeneous product is produced by a group of firms, each

of which assumes its influence on the market is minimal. The demand curve for the individual firm is perfectly elastic at the level of industry price.

2/ All firms have access to the same technology. At any given time, the supply of every factor to each firm is perfectly elastic at the existing market price of the factor; the price a firm pays for a factor is not affected by a change in the quantity of a factor it employs.

NOTE It is *not* assumed that the demand for the product of the industry is perfectly elastic; nor is the supply of any particular factor to the industry necessarily perfectly elastic, although it may be.

3. Because all firms have access to the same technology, each firm has a perfectly elastic supply of every factor available to it at the market price of that factor, and—in the long run—each firm is able to choose whatever technical process of production it wishes, all firms will have identical long-run cost functions. These same costs are also available to any potential new firms that may wish to enter the industry.

The assumption of identical cost functions for all firms in a perfectly competitive industry is not as restrictive as it may appear. If any firm seems to have a cost advantage over the other (for example, because of its control of some superior factor of production not available to the other firms), the market value of that specialized factor would rise by the amount of its superior productivity. Other firms would be willing to buy the services of this factor at the higher price. This higher price, then, is a cost to the firm using the scarce factor. By this process the apparent lower costs of one firm are raised to the level of the other firms. The firm with a particularly advantageous location will find its rent rising; the unusually well qualified manager will be offered a higher salary by other firms.

It is irrelevant whether the firm rents or owns the scarce factor in question. In either case the cost of using it within the firm is equal to the opportunity earnings that factor could receive if used elsewhere.

A competitive industry is in long-run equilibrium when all firms in the industry are in equilibrium and no firm wishes to enter or leave the industry.

The decision of firms to enter or leave an industry is based on the profit level of the industry. If profits exceed the level that could be earned in other employments, new firms will wish to enter. If they are below this competitive level firms will leave. In long-run competitive equilibrium, therefore, all firms earn the same profit rate.

The rate of profits that induces neither entry nor exist is called "normal profits," the opportunity earnings of capital in alternative uses of similar risk. To the firm, normal profits represent a neces-

sary return to induce them to remain in the industry. They are therefore considered a cost of doing business, along with the prices of
all other inputs, and as such are included in the cost curves we
shall be drawing. The firm that has revenues just sufficient to cover
its cost (that is, a firm selling at a price that equals its average
cost) is making normal profits.

The facts that in long-run perfectly competitive equilibrium every
firm in an industry will be earning exactly normal profits and every
firm has a perfectly elastic, horizontal demand curve, simplify the
analysis of long-run equilibrium, for they mean that in equilibrium
every firm will be operating at its point of minimum average total
cost. The long-run equilibrium for the perfectly competitive firm is
shown in Figure 9.1, with the firm's long-run average total and
marginal cost curves (LRAC and LRMC) and its perfectly elastic
demand curve PD, which also constitutes an average revenue and
a marginal revenue curve. The firm can sell any quantity it wishes
at price OP. Its average revenue per unit of sale is therefore constant at the level of price OP, and its marginal revenue, the additional revenue from an extra unit of output, is also equal to the
price OP.

Figure 9.1   Long-run Equilibrium: Perfectly Competitive Firm

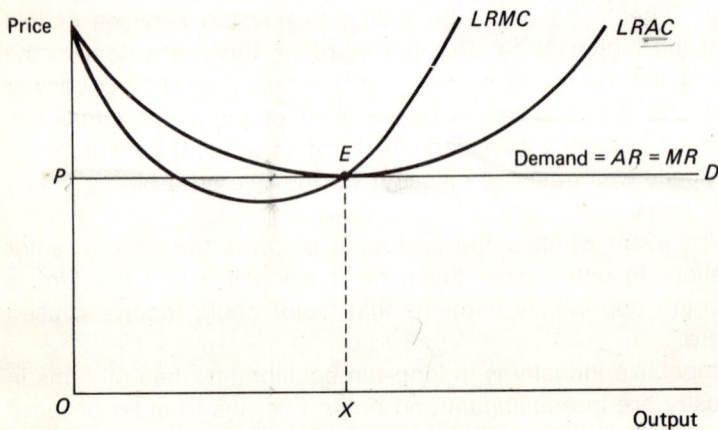

Any firm maximizes profit by producing the output at which its
marginal revenue equals its marginal cost. The competitive firm of
Figure 9.1, faced with a market price of OP, produces output OX.
For units greater than OX, marginal cost exceeds marginal revenue,
and hence the firm's profits would decrease. Similarly, a reduction
in output below OX would reduce the firm's revenues by more than
costs because to the left of output OX marginal revenue exceeds
marginal cost.

When the minimum average total cost of this firm, and by the uniformity assumption of all firms in the industry, is *EX*, the industry price must also equal *EX*. At any lower price, no firm would be able to cover its total costs, and hence would leave, or never enter, the industry. If price were higher than *EX*, firms would be able to make more than normal profits, and additional firms would be attracted into the industry, thus driving price down to the level (*EX* = *OP*) at which only normal profits are being made. Therefore, long-run equilibrium requires a price equal to the minimum average total cost of the firms.

CONSTANT, INCREASING, AND DECREASING COSTS

The costs of the firm depend on two factors: (1) the technological production possibilities available to the firm and (2) the prices of inputs, of factors of production, to the firm.

At any given time, the technology is assumed given and constant. For purposes of comparative analysis, we may wish to assume a change in technology, and consider its consequences. For the moment, assume that technology is constant.

The second factor determining the costs of the firm is the price of inputs. By assumption the prices of inputs do not change when any one firm in a competitive industry varies its production because the firm's demand for the factor is small, relative to total demand. But a shift in the production level of an entire competitive industry may well affect the prices of the factors of production employed in the industry. Three cases may be considered.

CASE 1   In the *constant cost competitive industry*, prices of inputs do not change as the size of the industry varies. Such could be the case if the inputs used in the competitive industry in question are standard types of factors used in many other industries, or if the inputs are themselves produced in a constant cost industry. The demand for them from the one competitive industry might then be small compared with the total market demand for them. Variations in the size of the competitive industry might have no effect on their price.

CASE 2   For the *increasing cost competitive industry*, the price of one or more of the factors of production it employs rises as the employing industry expands its production and hence its demand for the factor. The supply of the factor to the industry is less than perfectly elastic. To attract more units of this factor, the industry must pay a higher price for it. In many increasing cost industries some natural resource or particular type of land is an important input. Tobacco farming and mining are examples.

CASE 3   The price of some factor used by the *decreasing cost competitive industry* falls as the industry expands. This case is odd, and cannot occur unless the input is supplied by a noncompetitive industry, or is a factor whose supply to the employing competitive industry is backward sloping.

These three types of cost conditions and the behavior of competitive industries and firms that have them are discussed in turn.

THE CONSTANT COST COMPETITIVE INDUSTRY

If the technology available to firms is assumed constant and the prices of their inputs do not vary as the industry changes in size, the minimum average total cost of the competitive firm remains constant. The supply curve of such a constant cost competitive in-

Figure 9.2   Long-run   Equilibrium: Constant   Cost   Competitive Industry

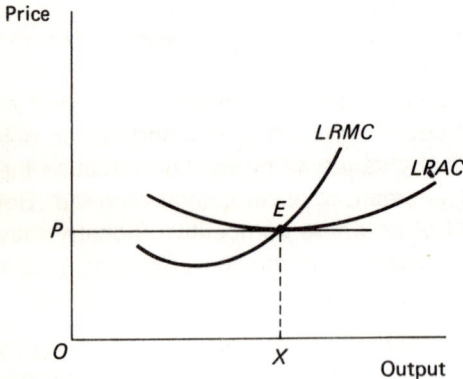

(a) Firm

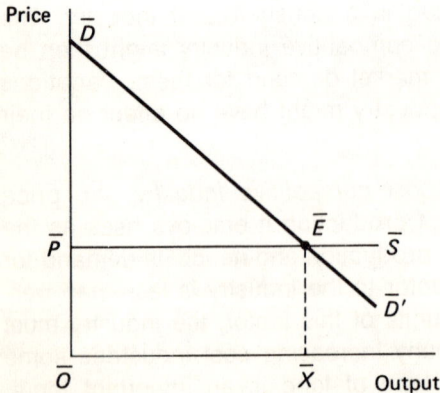

(b) Industry

dustry is then perfectly elastic at the level of the minimum average cost of the firm. Changes in the output of the industry would be accomplished, not by variations in the amount produced by the individual firm, but rather by changes in the number of firms in the industry, with each firm producing at its point of minimum average cost.

Long-run equilibrium for the perfectly competitive industry and representative firm is illustrated in Figure 9.2. The long-run average cost curve of the firm, as determined by the firm's production function and the given prices of inputs (as derived in Chapter 8) is curve *LRAC* of Figure 9.2a. The firm's minimum average cost is *EX*, reached at output *OX*. This minimum average cost then determines the level of the industry supply curve $\overline{PS}$.

The industry supply curve is perfectly elastic in the long run, at a height equal to $\overline{OP}$ (= *EX* of Figure 9.2a). Industry supply expands and contracts as firms enter and leave the industry.

A supply curve is often defined as the schedule of the amounts that would be supplied at various prices. For a perfectly elastic supply curve, as with the constant cost industry, it is preferable to define the supply curve as a schedule of the prices at which various quantities would be supplied. The perfectly elastic supply curve of the constant cost industry therefore means that any quantity would be supplied at the price $\overline{OP}$. This is induced by the entry or exit of firms if the price should be above or below $\overline{OP}$. In any long-run equilibrium the industry will be composed of a group of firms, each producing at the minimum point on its average cost curve. Through the entry and exit of firms, the industry is willing to produce *any* output at a price of $\overline{OP}$. The industry long run supply curve $\overline{PS}$ in Figure 9.2b results.

Combining this supply curve with an industry demand curve $\overline{DD'}$ in Figure 9.2b gives the equilibrium output ($\overline{OX}$) and price ($\overline{OP}$) for the industry.

This price then determines the level of the firm's demand curve, which is perfectly elastic at the level of industry price. Each firm in the industry will then produce at output *OX*, at a price of *OP*, and will be making normal profits.

THE EFFICIENCY OF COMPETITIVE EQUILIBRIUM

It is important to ask whether the situation represented by this long-run constant cost competitive equilibrium is efficient. Subject to some qualifications, the answer is yes.

Note that the industry output is being produced at the lowest possible cost at which output $\overline{OX}$ can be produced. If the same output were produced by more (or fewer) firms, each producing a smaller (or larger) output, the average costs of production for each firm and therefore for the industry would be higher.[2]

For the output of this industry to be efficient, two conditions must hold: First, the total value of the industry's production to the buyers must exceed the total value that the resources used here could contribute in their next best use. This may be called the total test of efficiency. If this test cannot be satisfied at any level of operation of the industry, the product should not be produced at all. The second test of efficiency is the marginal test: A good should be produced up to that unit of production for which the marginal value to the buyer is equal to the marginal value in alternative uses of the factors used to produce that unit.

If either the total or the marginal test of efficiency is violated, resources of production could be allocated more efficiently in such a way that net monetary gains would result; gainers from the reallocation would gain more than losers would lose.

It is impossible to assess the efficiency of one industry by itself in isolation from the rest of the economy, for the essence of efficiency is a comparison of alternatives.

When a competitive industry expands its output, it uses factors of production withdrawn from other uses. Efficiency asks whether this shift in factors creates net monetary gains.

Consider then the constant cost competitive industry operating as indicated in Figures 9.2a and 9.2b. We wish to compare the value of the industry's production with the value of the alternatives foregone as a consequence of this production. Measures of the two values in both total and marginal terms must be found and compared.

The industry demand curve, $\overline{DD}'$ of Figure 9.2b, gives the value of the output of this industry. Each point on it shows the value in money terms of an additional unit of the product to the buyer. Marginal value at output $\overline{OX}$ is thus $\overline{EX}$. The demand curve is thus a marginal value curve. Total value of output $\overline{OX}$, with the qualifications noted in Chapter 3, can then be measured by the summation of the marginal values (that is, the area under the demand curve up to the point $\overline{E}$, or area $\overline{DEXO}$).

The value of the alternatives foregone by producing this product is less easily determined. Under certain simplifying assumptions,

---

[2]The fact that each firm is operating at the minimum point of its average cost curve should be interpreted as a necessary condition for efficiency only for long-run equilibrium of a perfectly competitive industry. As we shall see later, there are many situations in economics (for example, single firm industries and even perfectly competitive firms in short-run situations) in which the most efficient point of production does not occur at the firm's minimum average cost.

however, the cost curves can be taken as measures of these foregone alternatives.

If the inputs used by this competitive industry are themselves being supplied competitively, the prices of the inputs are measures of the alternative values of these inputs in other uses. Industry A must pay, say, $3 an hour to hire a certain type of labor because that worker could earn $3 elsewhere. Other industries are willing to pay the worker $3 because that is the amount (on the margin) that his employment would add to the value of *their* output. Thus the price of a factor is a measure of the alternative value of that input. It follows, therefore, that the marginal cost of producing another unit in industry A is a measure of the value of output that will be foregone in other industries by having him shift to industry A.

Using the cost curves of Figures 9.2a and 9.2b as measures of alternatives foregone, the total alternatives foregone by producing $\overline{OX}$ units of the product of the constant cost competitive industry will be equal to the total costs of production, area $\overline{OPEX}$. This is clearly greater than the total value, area $\overline{DEXO}$. Hence the total test for efficiency is satisfied: Total value produced by these factors in producing product A exceeds the alternative value foregone in other possible uses of these factors.

The marginal test of efficiency requires production up to the point at which the marginal value of the good equals the marginal value of the opportunities foregone. At output $\overline{OX}$, the marginal value of good A as determined by the demand curve (which is a curve of marginal value) equals $\overline{EX}$. But $\overline{EX}$ also equals the marginal cost of producing good A. Therefore, the marginal test of efficiency is satisfied.

The important conclusion that the output of the long-run perfectly competitive constant cost industry is efficient, it should be noted, holds only under two important assumptions or qualifications:

(1) Factor prices must equal the marginal value of the factors if employed in alternative uses. This will not be true if those factors are not supplied under competitive conditions.

(2) The benefits of good A and the alternative value of the resources used to produce that good must be accurately measured by the market demand and cost curves. The conclusion must be modified if the behavior of the industry gives rise to external costs or benefits (that is, gains or losses to persons or firms other than those represented by the market demand and cost curves), for these costs and benefits must be included in any efficiency accounting.

The fairness of the long-run constant cost competitive equilibrium is a matter of subjective judgment. The fact that price is just equal to average cost, so that producers are making normal profits but not more, and that all consumers are paying the same price (that is, there is no price discrimination) lead some persons to consider the results equitable.

SOME EXAMPLES OF COMPARATIVE STATICS

The economist's model of perfect competition is often used to predict the effects of changes in the conditions facing an industry. For illustration, consider two cases: an increase in the demand for the industry's output and the imposition of a tax on the product.

The long-run equilibrium described here is a static equilibrium, which means it will continue to exist as long as no outside change occurs. If some outside change is then assumed to occur, the nature of the long-run equilibrium will also change. The concern here is not with the process or path by which the firms and industry move from the old to the new equilibrium, but only with a comparison of the new and the old static equilibrium situations. The method is called "comparative statics."

Assume first an increase in the demand for the industry's product, indicated in Figure 9.3b by a new industry demand curve $\overline{D'}\overline{D'}$ to the right of the original demand curve $\overline{DD}$.[3] The new equilibrium industry output is $\overline{OQ_2}$, compared with the former output $\overline{OQ_1}$. Note that for this constant cost industry the equilibrium price has not changed. The demand curve for the individual firm of Figure 9.3a therefore does not change, nor does the firm's profit-maximizing output.

The industry output has expanded, yet each firm is producing the same amount as before. This can happen only because the number of firms has increased.

The net long-run results of this increase in demand for the product of this industry are, then, (1) an increase in industry output and in the number of firms; and (2) no change in price or in the output of individual firms. Price is still equal to average cost (hence, normal profits are being made); price is also still equal to marginal cost. The situation is efficient.

As a second example, consider the effects of the imposition of a tax on the product per unit sold. The average and marginal costs of the firms rise by the amount of the tax, as does the firms' minimum supply price. The effect is to move vertically the industry supply curve, by the amount of the tax (see Figure 9.4). Equilibrium price rises by the amount of the tax, industry output declines. The

[3]The increase in demand for this product could be the result of a change in any of the demand determinants discussed in Chapter 3: a rise in buyers' incomes, a rise in the price of a substitute product, a fall in the price of a complementary product, or simply a change in buyers' tastes.

Figure 9.3 *Long-run Effects of an Increase in Demand*

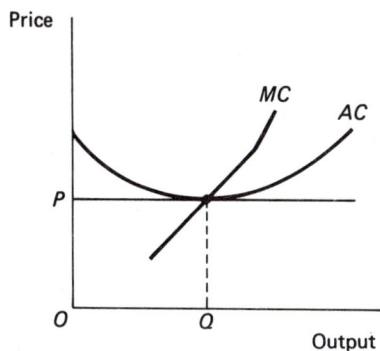

(a) Firm

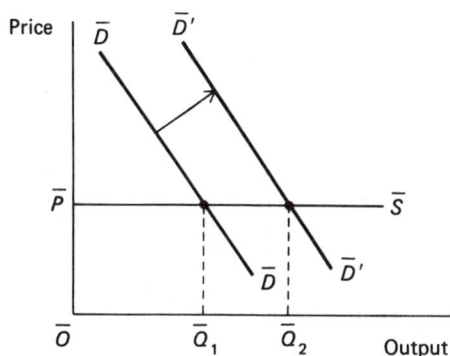

(b) Industry

output of the individual firm remains the same; therefore, the number of firms must decrease. Note that in this case the entire amount of the tax is passed on to the buyer. The effect of this and other types of taxes on economic efficiency is analyzed in Chapter 19.

THE INCREASING COST COMPETITIVE INDUSTRY

Turn now to the increasing cost competitive industry. As it expands production the price it pays for one or more of its inputs rises. An expansion in the tobacco-growing industry, for example, would mean a bidding up of the price of that land suitable for this crop. This rise in the price of an input has two effects. First, it tends to raise the costs of production. Second, firms will tend to vary their methods of production, using less of the now relatively more expensive land per unit of output, and more of other factors of production (men, machinery, fertilizers) the prices of which have not changed. The isocost curves of Chapter 7 will shift in response to

Figure 9.4   *Effects of an Excise Tax*

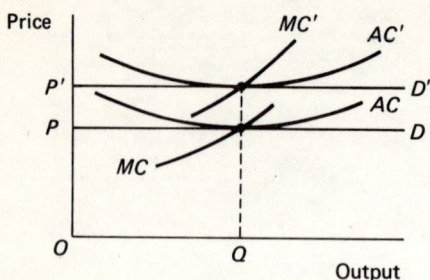

(a) Firm

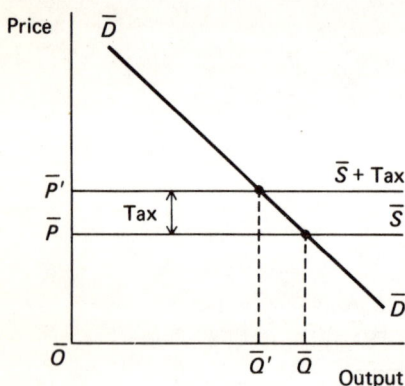

(b) Industry

this change in relative factor prices; the firm's expansion path will shift away from the factor the price of which has increased. And the minimum total cost of producing any particular output will rise.

The supply curve for the perfectly competitive industry is determined by the minimum average cost of the firms. The industry supply curve rises or falls as the average cost curves of the firms rise or fall.

As an increasing cost industry expands, the rise in the price of its scarce input causes the firms' costs to rise. This, in turn, raises the minimum price of the product at which firms will remain in the industry. Hence, at larger industry outputs, the point on the long-run industry supply curve will be higher. The result is an upward sloping long-run industry supply curve, curve $\overline{SS}$ of Figure 9.5b.

At the level of the firm, each expansion of the *industry* output raises the cost curves of the firms, as in Figure 9.5a. Higher industry prices of the product exactly match the higher minimum average cost of the firm because in any long-run competitive equilibrium the profits of the firm must be at the normal level.

Figure 9.5   *Increasing Cost Industry: Increase in Demand*

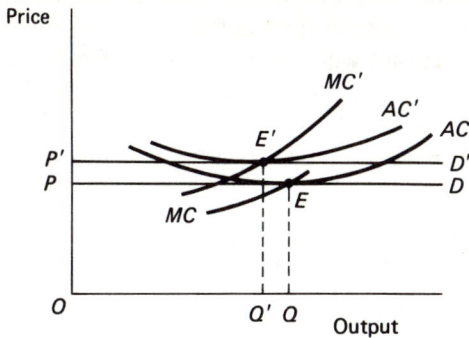

(a) Firm

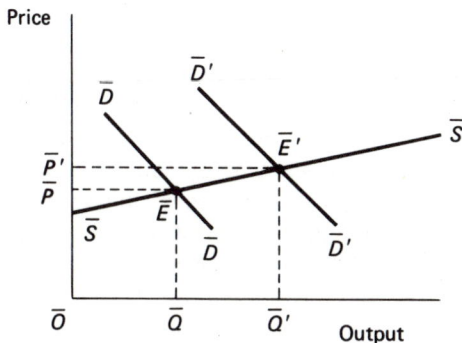

(b) Industry

In Figures 9.5a and 9.5b the effects of an increase in industry demand on an increasing cost competitive industry are illustrated. Originally, demand for the industry's product was $\overline{DD}$, in Figure 9.5b. Equilibrium price was $\overline{OP}$, and the industry output was $\overline{OQ}$. The firm's demand curve PD was tangent to the firm's average cost curve AC at the minimum point E, at which it intersected the firm's original marginal cost curve MC. Firm output was EQ, price was OP, and the firm was making normal profits.

With the increase in industry demand to $\overline{D'D'}$, the industry equilibrium shifts to point $\overline{E}'$ with industry output $\overline{OQ'}$, and price $\overline{OP'}$.

The firm's new cost curves will be above the old. The firm's new minimum average cost may occur at a smaller, larger, or the same output compared with the minimum point of the average cost curve before the shift in demand for the industry's product. When the price of one input rises, the firm will adjust its method of production in the light of the new price relationships among inputs. As noted, it will tend to substitute other factors for the input with the rising price. This substitution is likely to cause a horizontal shift in the minimum point of the firm's average cost curve.

Whether firms expand or contract will affect the number of firms in the industry. In the case illustrated in Figure 9.5, industry output rises from $\overline{OQ}$ to $\overline{OQ}'$ while the output of the individual firm falls from OQ to OQ'. In this case, the number of firms will rise from $\overline{OQ}/OQ$ to $\overline{OQ}'/OQ'$.

EFFICIENCY AND THE INCREASING COST INDUSTRY

The long-run market behavior of the perfectly competitive increasing cost industry leads to an equilibrium price and output that are efficient, subject to the same qualifications noted for the constant cost case above.

The argument is somewhat complex—in fact, it was not understood by economists for many years.[4] It involves economic rent and the distinction between real and money costs of production.[5] *Economic rent* is a payment to a factor of production in excess of the amount needed to keep it in its present employment. It is completely analogous to consumer surplus, the excess of the value of a product to a consumer over the amount paid for it. Rents paid to factors of production constitute part of the money cost of production, but do not constitute a real cost of production.

Consider a simple example. A man wishes to hire one or two boys for yard work. One will work for $5 a day; the second, of equal ability, requires $7. If both boys are hired, fairness requires each be paid $7. But the boy who would work for $5 receives $2 in economic rent. This rent is not a real cost to society and is a surplus to the boy, but it is a money cost to the employer.

The real cost of expanding the output of the increasing cost industry is the cost of attracting additional units of the factor into the industry. The money cost of expansion includes, in addition to these real costs, any increase in rent payments to existing factors.

For efficiency, output should be produced up to the point at which the marginal value of the product, as measured by the demand curve, is equal to the marginal *real* cost of production. Rent payments should not be included in the marginal cost used in determination of efficiency.

[4]See Alfred Marshall, *Principles of Economics,* 8th ed., (London: Macmillan, 1920), bk. V, chap. 12; Howard S. Ellis and William Fellner, "External Economies and Diseconomies," *American Economic Review 33* (1943), 493–511, reprinted in George J. Stigler and Kenneth E. Boulding, eds., *Readings in Price Theory* (Homewood, Ill.: Irwin, 1952), pp. 242–263.

[5]See the more extended discussion of economic rent in Chapter 16.

The long-run supply curve of the increasing cost competitive industry shows both the average cost of production including rent payments to the scarce factor of production and the real *marginal* cost (excluding rents) of producing an additional unit of output at each scale of production. Since under competitive behavior the industry will expand to the point at which the demand curve for the product of the industry intersects this supply curve, at the point of equilibrium the marginal value of the product is equal to the real marginal cost, and the marginal test of efficiency is satisfied.

The total test of efficiency, that total value exceed total real cost, is also clearly satisfied because up to the point of equilibrium the demand curve (which measures marginal value) lies above the supply curve (which measures marginal real cost).

One could construct, on the industry diagram, curves representing marginal revenue and marginal money cost to the industry as it expands, but these curves are irrelevant both to the behavior of the industry and to the determination of the economic efficiency of that behavior.

COMPARATIVE STATICS AND THE INCREASING COST COMPETITIVE INDUSTRY

Some cases of comparative statics for the long-run increasing cost industry are now considered. The nature of the industry equilibrium after some exogenous change in the determinants of its behavior is compared with the equilibrium before the change. The comparison of these results with similar changes in the constant cost industry case should be noted.

CASE 1   **An increase in demand**   This case has been illustrated in Figures 9.5a and 9.5b. Price rises in the increasing cost industry, whereas in the constant cost industry price is stable. In both cases, industry output increases but, for a given increase in demand, output expands more in the constant cost industry than in the increasing cost industry. In both cases profits remain at the normal level. In the increasing cost industry rents to the scarce input increase.

CASE 2   **A unit tax on the product**   In effect, a unit tax adds a uniform amount to the costs of the firm. All cost curves rise by the amount of the tax, as does the industry supply curve. The price to the buyer will rise also.

In the constant cost industry, price rises by the full amount of the tax; industry output declines. Because each firm retains the old rate of output, fewer firms are required to produce the smaller industry output.

The effects of a unit tax on the increasing cost industry are somewhat different, as Figures 9.6a and 9.6b indicate. As in the constant cost case, the industry supply curve will move up vertically by the amount of the tax. The new equilibrium gives a smaller industry output and a higher price than before the tax. But the price does not rise by the full amount of the tax.

Figure 9.6   Effects of Excise Tax: Increasing Cost Competitive Industry

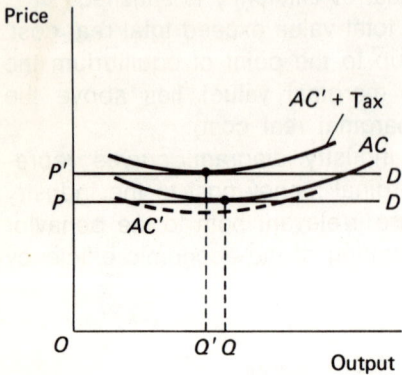

(a) Firm

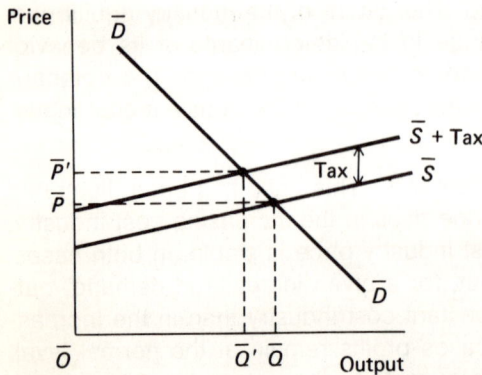

(b) Industry

Who pays the rest of the tax? Not the individual firms, for they will not continue to produce if their returns fall below the level of normal profits.

The difference between the amount of the tax and the rise in industry price must be accounted for by a fall in the costs of the firms. This is in fact what will occur. The smaller output of the industry after the tax has been imposed means the industry is purchasing fewer factors of production. At least one of these factors, for which the demand has dropped, will be faced with a lower price for its services; the industry supply curve has an upward slope because some factor becomes more expensive as the industry expands; therefore, as the industry contracts the price of this factor falls, lowering the cost curves of all firms.

Part of the impact of the tax, therefore, falls on the scarce factor of production, which is less scarce now relative to demand, and hence must accept a lower price.

The lumber industry provides an example of an increasing cost industry in which a unit tax would lower the price of an input. The supply of logs is not perfectly elastic, but can be expanded only at increasing costs. A unit tax on lumber would thus fall partly on the users of lumber, and partly on the suppliers of logs.

As noted earlier, increasing cost industries typically use some agricultural product or natural resource as an input; the supplies of most man-made inputs can, at least in the long run, be increased without significant increases in costs.

THE DECREASING COST COMPETITIVE INDUSTRY

A long-run decreasing cost competitive industry is one in which the price of one or more inputs decreases as the industry expands, dropping the cost curves of the firms. This is a rather odd situation. Why should input prices drop when the demand for them increases? Only if the inputs are not supplied under competitive conditions is it possible, and even then it would not be common.

For example, a monopoly that supplies an essential input to the competitive industry may have strongly increasing returns to scale and decreasing costs. When the competitive industry increases its demand for the monopolized product, the lower costs associated with the larger monopoly output may (but only may) induce the monopoly to reduce its price. This would give the purchasing competitive industry decreasing costs.

Competitive decreasing costs may also arise from the purchase of an input from a supplier, such as a government agency or a company whose prices are regulated, which itself has decreasing costs, and which sets prices on an average cost basis. Transportation provides an example. A competitive wheat industry, for example, may find that, as it grows in a given geographical area, its freight rates for shipping wheat to mills decline because the railroads have decreasing costs and charge lower rates as their traffic expands.

The long-run industry supply curve of the decreasing cost industry slopes downward, reflecting the fact that as industry output expands the firms' cost curves drop.

An increase in demand would cause industry price to fall. The

effects of a unit tax on the product are illustrated in Figure 9.7. Note
that the price and the minimum average cost of the firms rise *more*
than the amount of the tax.

**Figure 9.7   *Effects of an Excise Tax: Decreasing Cost Competitive
Industry***

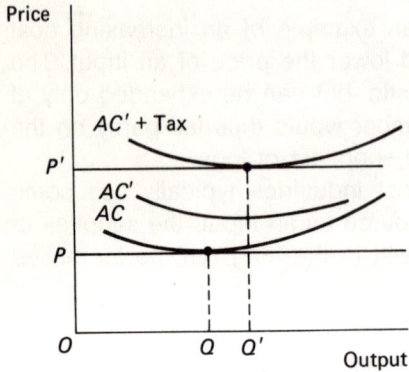

(a) Firm

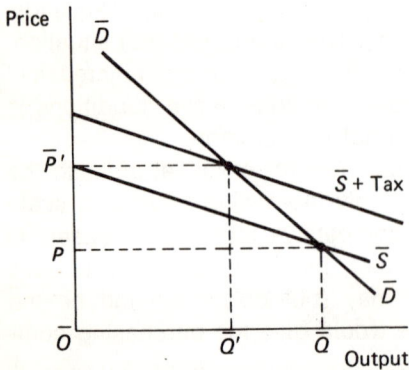

(b) Industry

The efficiency analysis of the decreasing cost case is not analogous to that of the increasing cost industry. The efficient output for
the decreasing cost industry occurs where the industry demand
curve cuts the industry *marginal* cost curve (output $\overline{OQ'}$ in Figure
9.8), *not* at the point of competitive equilibrium (output $\overline{OQ}$), where
demand cuts the industry supply curve, which measures average
cost. Here the industry marginal cost curve lies below the industry
supply curve. The industry marginal cost curve (*LRMC* in Figure
9.8) represents the *real* costs of producing this good, in contrast to
the increasing cost case, because no economic rents are involved.

Figure 9.8   *Efficiency and the Decreasing Cost Competitive Industry*

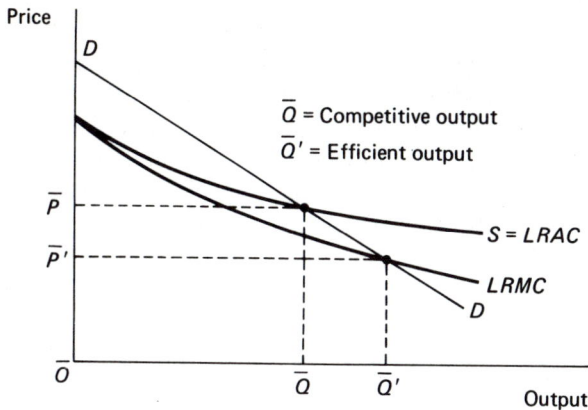

This case represents a major qualification to the principle that the behavior of a perfectly competitive industry is efficient. A decreasing cost competitive industry is not: it produces too little and at too high a price for efficiency.

DOES PERFECT COMPETITION EXIST?

How close does the world come to the model of perfect competition analyzed in this chapter?

The decreasing cost competitive industry is little more than a theoretical curiosity. Increasing cost industries do appear to exist, particularly those dependent on natural resources, land, or specialized resources. It is likely that most manufacturing industries have reasonably constant costs.

The perfect knowledge assumed in the theory obviously does not exist, and undoubtedly many of the discrepancies between the theoretical description of business behavior and actual behavior in practice are caused by imperfect knowledge.

The assumption of homogeneous products is clearly invalid for many sectors of the economy, although it is more reasonable in some areas (for example, agriculture) than in others. In later chapters cases involving product differentiation are analyzed.

The assumption that firms have U-shaped long-run average cost curves has provoked a good deal of criticism of the theory and, as has been noted, there is considerable empirical evidence that for many firms initial decreasing costs are followed by fairly constant costs over a wide span of plant sizes. It is instructive, therefore, to ask how the conclusions of the analysis of this chapter would differ if instead of U-shaped average cost curves the analysis is revised to incorporate an assumption that firms have the L-shaped long-run average cost curve found so often in practice.

Very few of the previous results would be affected. Prices, profits, and industry output would behave as indicated earlier in this chapter. The one significant difference is that using the alternative assumption about the the shape of firms' cost curves, the equilibrium size of the firm would be indeterminate. It is only certain that in long-run equilibrium the size of any one firm would be somewhere along the flat stretch of its average cost curve. Firms of different sizes would coexist. Because of this ambiguity of the size of individual firms, the number of firms in the industry would also be indeterminate. When conditions call for expansion in the output of the industry, the increase could come either from the entry of new firms or from the expansion of existing firms.

Because both forms of expansion would be provided at the same costs in terms of resources, it would not matter from the viewpoint of economic efficiency which way the expansion took place.

More generally, with reference to efficiency, the adoption of the L-shaped cost curve assumption would not affect any of the conclusions about the efficiency of the perfectly competitive industry reached earlier in this chapter.

A POSTSCRIPT

Perhaps the strongest justification for perfect competition as a description of economic behavior is that it is descriptive of the natural tendency of a society of utility maximizing individuals. At any one time there will be monopolies, discrimination, and inefficiencies of all kinds. But over time, it can be argued, the invisible hand of Adam Smith will tend to operate. Information will spread; mistakes will not be repeated; alternatives will develop to erode the power of monopolies; capital will flow from less to more profitable areas, thus tending to equalize the profit rate throughout the economy; analogously, prices of individual factors and products will tend to equalize throughout the society. All this would occur not through plan but simply from the self-centered behavior of individuals seeking their own advantage.

This view is simplistic, of course, for it fails to take into account the persistence of imperfect knowledge, technological barriers to competition, and, perhaps most important, the recognition by individuals that they may gain mutually from joint political behavior that affects the economic functioning of a society.

But it would be equally misleading to ignore the natural force of individuals pursuing their own self-interest. The long-run theory of perfect competition provides recognition of this force.

REVIEW QUESTIONS

1. Explain the following concepts:
   A market
   Homogeneous products
   Heterogeneous or differentiated products
   Monopoly
   Monopsony
   Oligopoly
   Oligopsony
   Perfect competition
   Imperfect competition
   Monopolistic competition
   Normal profits
   Long-run equilibrium price and output for the perfectly competitive firm
   Long-run equilibrium price and output for the perfectly competitive industry
   The efficiency of long-run competitive equilibrium: firm and industry
2. In the long run, what determines the number of firms in a perfectly competitive industry?
3. What justification is there for the assumption that all firms in a competitive industry have identical cost functions?
4. For constant, increasing, and decreasing cost competitive industries, show graphically the long-run effects on the industry price, output, and number of firms, and on the firm's price and output of each of the following:
   (a) An increase (or decrease) in industry demand
   (b) An increase (or decrease) in the price of one factor employed in the industry
   (c) An improvement in technology
   (d) The imposition of a unit tax on the product

FURTHER READING

Ellis, Howard S., and William Fellner, "External Economies and Diseconomies." *American Economic Review 33* (1943), 493–511; reprinted in George J. Stigler and Kenneth E. Boulding, eds., *Readings in Price Theory.* Homewood, Ill.: Irwin (1952), pp. 242–263.

Henderson, James M., and Richard E. Quandt, *Microeconomic Theory: A Mathematical Approach.* New York: McGraw-Hill (1958), chap. 4.

Knight, Frank H., *Risk, Uncertainty, and Profit.* Boston: Houghton Mifflin (1921).

Marshall, Alfred, *Principles of Economics.* 8th ed., London: Macmillan (1920), bk. V.

Stigler, George, "Perfect Competition, Historically Contemplated." *Journal of Political Economy 65* (1957), 1–17.

10

PERFECT COMPETITION: SHORT RUN

SHORT-RUN COSTS

In the short run, the number of firms in a competitive industry cannot change. An existing firm may discontinue production if it chooses, but in doing so would incur losses equal to its total fixed costs. The characteristics of the firm's short-run production and cost functions were described in Chapter 8. Because the firm has some constraining commitments in the short run, some inelasticities in the supplies of some factors of production, the firm will inevitably run into diminishing returns to the variable factors it employs. Some of the firm's costs are fixed and will not vary as the output of the firm changes. Diminishing returns to the variable factors, on the other hand, necessarily mean that the firm's short-run marginal, average variable, and average total costs will eventually rise. The U-shaped average total cost curve is therefore a characteristic of the short run.

Fixed costs do not influence the behavior of the firm in the short run. Since by definition they do not change with output and cannot be escaped even if the firm abandons production, the profit-maximizing firm ignores them. These same costs, of course, become variable over the long run, when they do influence the behavior of the firm.

The determination of the nature of a particular firm's short-run costs is extremely subtle and difficult, a fact masked by the simplicity of the graphs of those cost curves and the casual manner in which they are manipulated in theory textbooks and classes.

First, the firm has difficulty obtaining accurate and useful information about costs from its accounting records, and has uncertainties about future costs and revenues.[1]

Second, there are many short runs. The firm must identify those costs that are relevant to the planning decisions it makes and to the length of time any particular policy is expected to remain in effect. The costs relevant to a rise in demand that is expected to be permanent, for example, may be quite different from those related to a temporary increase.

Third, many short-run costs are opportunity costs internal to the firm. This means that the best alternative use of a resource may lie within the firm itself. The cost to a multiproduct firm of producing one product with one of its factors of production—a machine, or for that matter the managerial staff of the firm—may in the short run have nothing to do with the accounting cost of that input. The cost of the factor relevant to the firm's decision making may instead be determined by the reduction in profits the firm would incur by not using the same input for a different purpose within the firm (for example, to produce another product). In addition, insofar as present use of a factor reduces the future value or productivity of that input, the reduction in future value constitutes a cost of using the factor currently, and is part of the marginal cost of production.

In the short run, the cost to a retailer or wholesaler of using shelf or warehouse space for one product may include the profit that would be earned on another product requiring the same storage space. In a crowded restaurant, the cost of serving the customer who orders only coffee may include the opportunity earnings from a dinner customer.

The short-run cost curves employed in economic theory are shorthand devices intended to represent the influence of all the factors discussed here. They summarize the views the firm has of its costs when it is considering how to react to changes in external factors.

---

[1]Economic theory includes an essential inconsistency with respect to the assumption of perfect knowledge. While perfect knowledge is usually included as a basic assumption of the theory of perfect competition (as was, in fact, done in earlier chapters of this book), the very existence of the short run as an analytical concept requires some imperfection in knowledge. With perfect knowledge of all present and future economic conditions facing it, the firm would be in continuous long-run equilibrium, and the concept of the short run would be unnecessary.

The exact behavior of an individual firm or industry cannot be predicted with accuracy. The analysis gives some generalized conclusions and describes tendencies of the direction if not the speed of the changes in crucial variables such as prices, quantities supplied, and profit levels that will result from the impact of exogenous change.

THE SHORT-RUN SUPPLY FUNCTION OF THE COMPETITIVE FIRM

Equilibrium occurs in the perfectly competitive industry when the quantity demanded equals the amount supplied. The industry supply function is in the short run simply a summation of the short-run supply functions of the individual firms.

The competitive firm faces a perfectly elastic demand curve at the level of industry price. The firm's demand curve also constitutes an average revenue and a marginal revenue curve for the firm. The firm maximizes its profits or minimizes its losses by producing that output at which the price of the product (that is, its marginal revenue) is equal to the marginal cost of the firm. The major qualification to this general profit-maximizing proposition is that unless the firm's total revenues cover its total variable costs the firm will discontinue production. This means that the price of the product (which equals average revenue) cannot be less than average variable cost.

From these behavior propositions the short-run supply function of the competitive firm can be derived. To anticipate, the marginal cost curve of the firm at all points to the right of its intersection with the average variable cost curve constitutes the supply curve of the competitive firm.

Figure 10.1 shows the short-run cost curves of a firm. At no price below OP will the firm produce. It would withdraw from production even though it would then lose an amount equal to its total fixed costs because its losses would be even greater if it engaged in production.

At price OP', the firm's profit-maximizing output is OX' at which price (= marginal revenue) equals marginal cost. In this situation the firm is losing money, but its losses are less than the firm would lose by shutting down. Losses, area $P'C'JE'$, are equal to total cost, area $OC'JX'$, minus total revenues, area $OP'E'X'$.

Similarly, at a price of OP'' the firm would produce OX'' units of the product. Here the firm is making more than normal profits.

By continually varying the assumed price of the product and hence the height of the firm's demand curve, the amounts the firm would supply at each price are determined. It is obvious that the marginal cost curve from point C to the right constitutes such a supply curve for the firm.[2]

Figure 10.1   *The Short-run Supply Curve of the Competitive Firm*

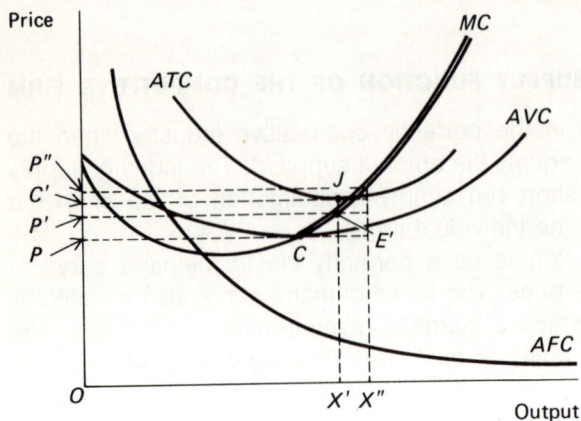

Note that in short-run equilibrium the firm will never operate to the left of the minimum point of its average variable cost curve.

SHORT-RUN EQUILIBRIUM FOR THE PERFECTLY COMPETITIVE INDUSTRY AND FIRM

Short-run equilibrium for the perfectly competitive industry requires that industry supply equal industry demand, and that each of the existing firms in the industry be in equilibrium (that is, be producing the output which, at the existing industry price, maximizes its profits or minimizes its losses).

The short-run industry supply curve is simply a horizontal summation of the supply curves of the firms in the industry. The amount the industry would supply at any given price is the sum of the amounts which each of the existing firms in the industry would be willing to supply at that price. Because each firm's supply curve is necessarily upward sloping, the combined industry supply curve also has the same upward slope in the short run. Curve $\overline{SS'}$ of Fig-

[2]The proposition that the supply curve of the perfectly competitive firm is the firm's marginal cost curve for all points to the right of its minimum average variable cost is as correct in long-run analysis as in the short run. In long-run theory, however, the point is not useful because the competitive firm will never in the long run have occasion to operate at any output other than that represented by the minimum point on its average total cost curve. (Recall that in the long run all costs are variable, and the firm's long-run average total cost curve is identical with its average variable cost curve.)

Figure 10.2   Short-run Equilibrium: Firm and Industry in Perfect Competition

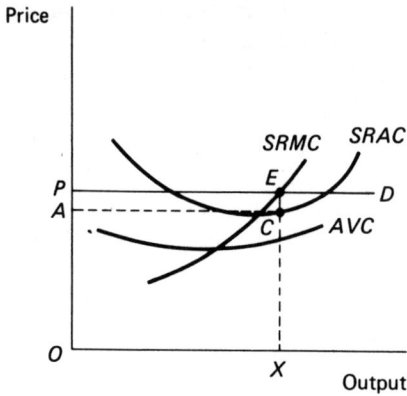

(a) Firm

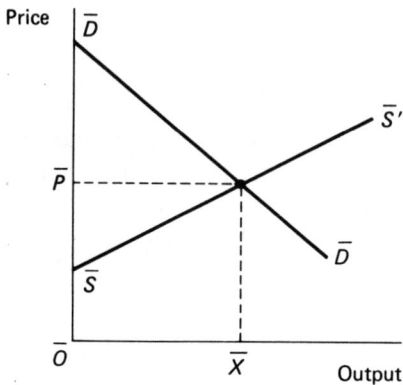

(b) Industry

ure 10.2b shows the combined amounts that the existing firms in the industry would be willing to supply at each price.

When cost differences exist between firms in the industry, the industry supply curve will not be a simple magnification of the supply curve of any firm. But it is certain that the industry curve will be upward sloping. Its lowest point (point $\bar{S}$ of Figure 10.2b) will be at the level of the minimum average variable cost of the firm with the lowest average variable cost curve. This is the lowest price at which any of the firms will be willing to supply any of the product.

To determine the equilibrium industry price, the industry supply curve is combined with the demand curve for the industry's product, as in Figure 10.2b. Short-run equilibrium price is $\overline{OP}$, and industry output is $\overline{OX}$. Each firm in the industry then faces a perfectly elastic demand curve, *PD* in Figure 10.2a, at the level of the industry equilibrium price. The firm then produces quantity *OX,* at which point the price equals the firm's marginal cost. Because the industry supply curve is simply a summation of the supply curves of the firms, the summation of the amounts the firms produce at the equilibrium price will equal the industry output $\overline{OX}$.

In the case illustrated, the firm is making excess profits of *EC* per unit produced, or a total of *ECAP.*

In the short run, firms may be making excess profits or losses. When excess profits are earned, additional capital will be attracted into the industry, thus increasing the industry supply, and lowering price. This process continues until the industry and all the firms in it reach a position of long-run equilibrium, with each firm making only normal profits.

Conversely, if in short-run industry equilibrium the existing firms are making losses, capital will over time be withdrawn from the industry, industry supply will decline, and price will rise. When the price has once again reached its long-run equilibrium level, normal profits are attained and the process of withdrawal of capital ceases.

In the market period in a perfectly competitive equilibrium, the amounts supplied by the industry and by each firm are fixed. An increase in industry demand will cause the price of the product to rise, but the quantity supplied will not change. Profits of all firms will rise. Gradually, as firms are able to adjust their production programs, outputs will rise, industry price will fall, and a new long-run equilibrium will be approached.

THE EFFICIENCY OF SHORT-RUN COMPETITIVE EQUILIBRIUM

Is the short-run equilibrium of the perfectly competitive industry efficient? Firms may not be producing at that output that would give them the minimum average cost. But price does equal short-run marginal cost for each firm and for the industry.

Subject to the qualifications noted in Chapter 9, that no external costs and benefits arise from the operation of the industry, and that the firm's costs do in fact represent the value of the alternative uses of the factors of production, the short-run competitive equilibrium is efficient.

In this short-run case one can wish that the firms and industry could move to a long-run equilibrium. But this is not possible given the short-run constraints within which the industry is operating. Efficiency asks, what is the best that can be done given the existing situation and the constraints present. In the short-run situation an answer lies in the competitive equilibrium. The reason is familiar: price is equal to marginal cost; hence, the marginal value of the output of the competitive industry, represented by the price buyers pay for it, equals its marginal cost, which is a measure of the marginal value of the alternative product that could be produced if factors were transferred from this industry to other uses. By definition, the fixed factors cannot be transferred. Therefore, only the variable factors are relevant in assessing short-run efficiency. If output were increased, the value of the added product would be less than the value foregone in other industries by shifting factors from them; if output here were reduced, more value would be lost here than would be gained elsewhere.

Note also that the existing output of the industry is being produced at the lowest cost at which that output could be produced given the existing short-run constraints. The marginal costs of all firms are the same at their points of production, for each is equal to the industry price. If one firm should expand while another contracted (keeping industry output constant) the total industry costs of production would increase. The cost savings of the contracting firm are less than the extra costs incurred by the expanding firm. Nor could industry costs be reduced if some firms shut down and other firms expanded outputs. This obviously would raise the average variable cost per unit of output. A rule for production at minimum cost for an industry is thus that all firms be producing at the same level of marginal cost.

It is tempting to think that industry costs might be reduced if the number of firms were increased so each could produce at its point of minimum average cost. But by definition, the number of firms in an industry cannot increase in the short run. This option is therefore not available.

Situations such as those described, with firms and industry in short-run but not long-run equilibrium, can only arise if firms earlier had made some miscalculation about future markets. Whenever the future is anticipated with perfect foresight, firms and industries will be in continuous long-run equilibrium.

COMPARISON OF SHORT- AND LONG-RUN COMPETITIVE EQUILIBRIUM

A competitive industry and firms that are in long-run equilibrium are also in short-run equilibrium. The converse is not necessarily true. The industry and firms in short-run equilibrium may not be in long-run equilibrium, in which case the entry or exit of firms will occur over time to bring the industry into a simultaneous long- and short-run equilibrium.

Figures 10.3 illustrates these points, as well as the short- and long-run effects of an increase in the demand for the product of a long-run constant cost competitive industry. In Figure 10.3a, the short- and long-run average total and marginal cost curves of the competitive firm are shown. In addition to initial industry demand of $\overline{DD}$, Figure 10.3b shows the long-run (LRIS) and short-run (SRIS) industry supply curves.

Figure 10.3   *Short- and Long-run Effects of an Increase in Demand*

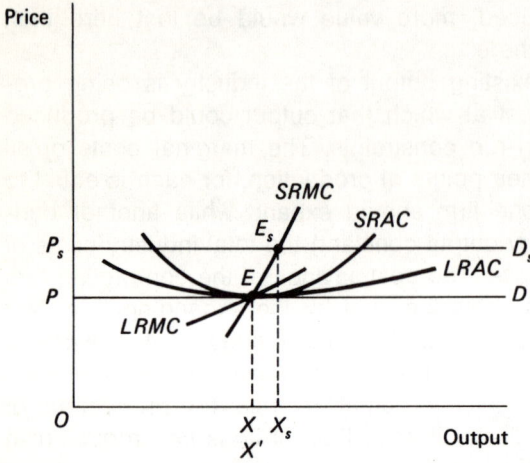

(a) Firm

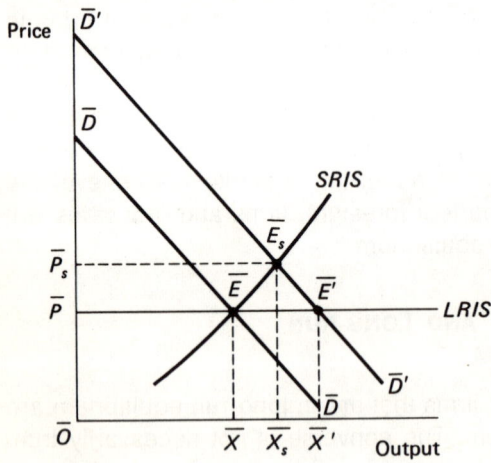

(b) Industry

With the initial industry demand of $\overline{DD}$, the industry and firms are in both long- and short-run equilibrium at a price of $\overline{OP}$. Industry output is $\overline{OX}$, and the firm produces OX, making normal profits.

Industry demand is then assumed to increase to the level indicated by $\overline{D'D'}$ of Figure 10.3b. The short-run response to this increase in demand is a rise in industry price to $\overline{OP_s}$ and an increase in industry output to $\overline{OX_s}$. With the firm's new short-run demand curve raised to P_sD_s, the firm expands output to OX_s. The firm is making excess profits. Note that at this moment the industry and firms are in short-run but not long-run equilibrium.

Over time, the industry would move to a new long-run equilibrium at point $\overline{E'}$, with industry output $\overline{OX'}$. For this constant cost industry, price in the new long-run equilibrium would return to $\overline{OP}$, the same level from which it began.

In the long run the individual firm's demand curve (PD) would drop to its original level, as would the price (OP), and the firm's output (OX); profits would return to the normal level. Once again the industry and the firm are in simultaneous long- and short-run equilibrium.

THE SHORT-RUN EFFECTS OF A SALES TAX

The apparatus of short-run demand, cost, and supply functions can be used to illustrate many problems in comparative statics (for example, the effects of changes in demand, factor prices, technology, and taxes in the short run). As an example, consider the short-run impact of a sales tax on the product of a competitive industry. In practice, such a tax would no doubt be placed on many products at the same time, therefore affecting many of the conditions facing the one industry we examine. The following is therefore better considered as an exercise in economic theory rather than a serious prediction of actual behavior.

A sales or excise tax levied as a percentage of the firm's price is best represented as a reduction in the revenue (demand) curve, rather than an increase in the firm's costs because the amount of the tax depends on the price of the product, not on the firm's costs or output. In Figure 10.4 $\overline{DD'}$ represents industry demand. The pretax equilibrium price is $\overline{OP_1}$ and industry output is $\overline{OQ_1}$.

The percentage excise tax creates a differential between the amount buyers pay for the product and what sellers receive. With a 50 percent tax, and an industry demand curve of $\overline{DD'}$, the industry's net revenues will be represented by curve $\overline{RD'}$. It coincides with the industry demand curve at point $\overline{D'}$, where the price is zero and hence the tax is zero. At any positive price, the net revenue curve lies the same percentage below the demand curve. When the tax rate is 50 percent, the revenue curve is two thirds the height of the demand curve.

The new short-run equilibrium for the taxed industry is at output

Figure 10.4 *Short-run Effects of a Sales Tax on a Competitive In-dustry*

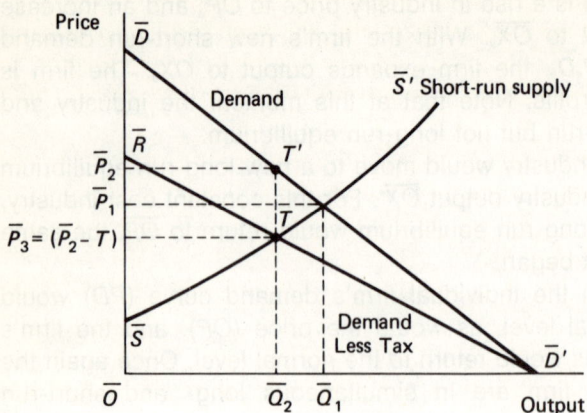

$\overline{OQ}_2$. The price to the buyer, including the tax of TT', is $\overline{OP}_2$. Net proceeds to the sellers per unit of sale have, however, fallen to $\overline{OP}_3$. In the case illustrated, buyers and sellers share about equally in the tax. The firms' profits (not illustrated) have of course been reduced. The slopes of the supply and demand curves determine how much of the tax will fall on each group. The steeper the slope of one curve relative to the other, the larger a share of a tax falls on that group.

In the long run, in response to a sales tax, industry output would be further reduced, price would rise still higher, and the number of firms in the industry would decline until, in long-run equilibrium, firms would again be making normal profits. In the constant cost competitive industry the entire burden of the tax would in the long run fall on buyers. If the industry has increasing costs, however, the burden will be shared between buyers and the scarce factor of production responsible for the industry's increasing costs.

REVIEW QUESTIONS

1. Explain the following concepts:
   Short-run supply for the perfectly competitive firm
   Short-run supply for the perfectly competitive industry
   Short-run equilibrium price and output for the perfectly competitive firm
   Short-run equilibrium price and output for the perfectly competitive industry
   The efficiency of short-run competitive equilibrium: firm and industry

2. Compare the effects on short-run competitive price and output of a

lump-sum tax, a unit tax, and a sales tax, all yielding the same tax revenue.

3. If the taxes of question 2 were placed only on one firm in a perfectly competitive industry, what short-run and long-run consequences would follow?

4. Under what conditions will a firm close down temporarily? Permanently?

FURTHER READING

Arrow, Kenneth J., "Toward a Theory of Price Adjustment," in Moses Abramovitz *et al., The Allocation of Economic Resources.* Stanford, Calif.: Stanford University Press (1959), pp. 41–51.

Gordon, Donald F., and Allan Hynes, "On the Theory of Price Dynamics," in E. S. Phelps *et al., Microeconomic Foundations of Employment and Inflation Theory.* New York: Norton (1970), pp. 369–393.

Hicks, J. R., *Capital and Growth.* New York: Oxford University Press (1965), chap. V, "The Method of Marshall."

Hicks, J. R., *Value and Capital.* 2nd ed., London: Oxford University Press (1946), esp. chaps. 9, 10, 15, 16, 18.

11

MONOPOLY

THE BASES OF MONOPOLY POSITION

The world is not perfectly competitive.[1] In Chapter 9, markets were classified by the number of firms in the market and by homogeneity or differentiation of the product.

Perfect competition requires many firms producing homogeneous products. In Chapters 11 through 14, the behavior of firms under conditions other than perfectly competitive is analyzed along with the factors bringing about these conditions. We begin with monopoly.

A monopoly is a single seller of a product without close substitutes. The cross elasticity of demand between the monopolist's product and no other good has the high negative value characterizing close substitutes.

Every good has substitutes of some degree, and every firm is subject to some degree of competition. The tele-

[1]It is interesting and curious that many of the most persistent critics of the use of perfect competition by economists (for example, businessmen) are simultaneously among the most faithful users of the theory. The usual defense of "free enterprise" is in fact based on the standard conclusions of the theory of perfect competition; efficiency in production, fairness of prices in the sense that they provide competitive profits and incomes based on the marginal productivity of factors, and absence of market power. These critics seem to assert that the conclusions but not the assumptions of the theory of perfect competition are realistic.

phone company has some competition from the postal service; electricity competes with oil or gas for the space-heating customer; railroads may compete with barge lines for bulk traffic. Further, substitutes may develop over time for monopolistically supplied goods.[2] Such potential competition may play an important role in restraining monopoly behavior.

A monopsony is a single buyer of a good or service that has no close substitutes. The U.S. government is a monopsonist in the purchase of gold; the coal-mining firm in an isolated company town may be a monopsonist in the hiring of labor and property. The good or service purchased by the monopsonist may be *supplied* on competitive or noncompetitive terms. When a monopolist sells to a monopsonist, the situation is called *bilateral monopoly.*

Monopoly position implies: (1) the demand curve for the seller will be downward sloping (the firm *is* the industry), (2) the firm need not take into account, in establishing its own policies, the possible reactions by other firms, and (3) by definition, the monopolist's market will not be affected by the entry or exit of other firms.

How would a firm find itself in such an enviable position? Why do other firms not enter to compete?

The firm may have had a legal monopoly status conferred upon it by legislation. But this is begging the question, for we then should ask why the public would choose to grant this privilege. Two reasons are common. First, the government may give public recognition to contributions to the advancement of knowledge through patent grants. Second, monopoly status may by law be conferred on a firm with strongly decreasing costs. Such firms are called natural monopolies and are protected because a single firm can supply the good or service at a significantly lower cost than could two or more firms. The presence of competing firms would be likely to lead either to collusion and excessive costs and prices, or to crippling competition leading to deterioration of product quality. Typically, however, such natural monopolies are subject to price regulation. This aspect of natural monopolies will be considered in Chapter 19 on government regulation of private business. The case of the unregulated monopoly is analyzed here in some detail, not because it is commonly found in practice, but because its characteristics of costs, demand, and behavior and the economic problems arising from them exist in lesser degrees throughout the economy. In particular, long-run decreasing costs, which are so prevalent with monopolists, also strongly influence the behavior of firms in more competitive positions.

[2]See Joseph A. Schumpeter, *Capitalism, Socialism, and Democracy* (New York: Harper & Row, 1942), especially chaps. 6–8, for a classic statement of this argument.

PROFIT MAXIMIZATION BY A MONOPOLIST

The demand curve facing a monopoly is in effect an industry demand curve with the typical downward slope. As with competitive analysis, the demand curve represents the marginal value to the buyers of successive units of the product. For the monopolist who does not engage in price discrimination (analyzed in Chapter 12), and who, therefore, charges the same price to all buyers, the demand curve represents an average revenue curve. Because it is downward sloping, the monopolist can sell greater outputs only by reducing his price. His marginal revenue from an additional unit of output is less than its price. In cutting price to sell more, the seller simultaneously receives less from the customers buying the current output.

The relationship[3] among average revenue or price, marginal revenue, and elasticity of demand is

$$\text{Marginal Revenue} = \text{Price} \ (1 - 1/e)$$

For profit maximization, the monopolist produces the output at which marginal revenue equals marginal cost. Because price exceeds marginal revenue, this necessarily means that the price he charges will exceed his marginal cost of production. Herein lie the seeds of inefficiency in the allocation of resources. For if the marginal cost of production measures the value of the resources in their next best use, the monopolist will fail to produce some units of his product for which the value to the buyers exceeds the alternative cost of production.

Figure 11.1 illustrates the long long equilibrium for a monopolist. The demand curve is *DD,* the marginal revenue curve is *MR.* The profit maximizing output is *OQ,* where marginal revenue equals marginal cost. Equilibrium price is shown not at the intersection of the *MC* and *MR* curves, but on the demand curve at this profit-maximizing output, that is, at point *E(= OP).*

Assuming competitive conditions prevail elsewhere, the efficient output for the monopoly is *OQ'*. By expanding from *OQ* to *OQ'* the total value of the product to buyers increases by the area under the demand curve between these two outputs, area *QEl'Q'*. Total costs would rise by the area under the marginal cost curve between *OQ* and *OQ'* (that is, area *QII'Q'*). The net gain in surplus by producing *OQ'* rather than *OQ* units of output is thus represented by the area *EII'*, the difference between the increase in total value and the rise

[3]Total revenue $(TR) = PQ$. Differentiating with respect to Q, $MR = dTR/dQ = P + Q(dP/dQ)$ and $MR = P[1 + (Qdp/PdQ)]$. But elasticity, with its conventional change of sign, is $- Pdq/QdP$. Therefore, $MR = P[1 - (1/e)]$.

Figure 11.1 *Equilibrium Price and Output for the Monopoly*

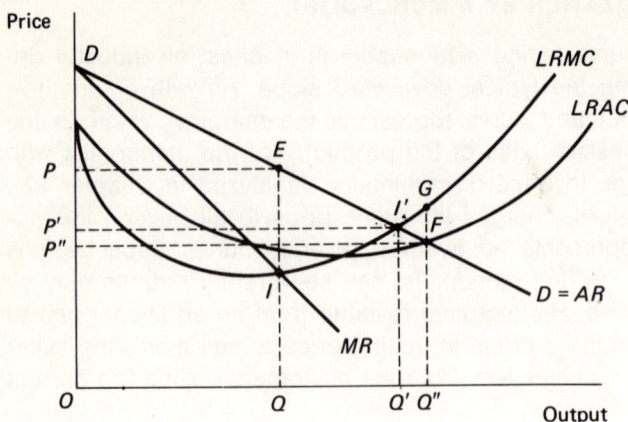

in total costs. Conversely, the loss in efficiency due to monopoly operation at output *OQ* rather than *OQ'* is area *EII'*.

An increase in output from *OQ* to *OQ'*, with a drop in price from *OP* to *OP'*, would make the seller worse off, but the consumers' gain in money terms would exceed the seller's loss by area *EII'*.

Note that the point of efficient output does not in this case coincide with the minimum point of the firm's average cost curve. Only under perfect competition (and only then in the long run) does the minimum *ATC* necessarily represent the efficiency maximum. Under perfect competition, industry output can be expanded at lowest cost by adding extra firms, each producing at this minimum cost point. In the analysis of monopoly this procedure is by definition not available; the monopolist's point of maximum efficiency is therefore not likely to be located at the minimum point of his *ATC* curve.

Operation by the firm in Figure 11.1 at either the profit-maximizing price *OP* or the efficiency price *OP'* gives the firm excess profits. When such profit levels are considered inequitable, a conflict arises between the objectives of efficiency and equity.

When, as in many instances of government regulation of prices,[4] it is argued that fairness requires a price that provides normal profits—no more and no less—a similar conflict between equity and efficiency arises. At a price of *OP"* and an output of *OQ"* (Figure 11.1), the firm is just making normal profits. But the output is too

[4]The doctrine of a "fair return on a fair value of their investment" in public utility regulation illustrates this criterion of equity. See, for example, the discussion in Charles F. Phillips, Jr., *The Economics of Regulation*, rev. ed. (Homewood, Ill.: Irwin, 1969), chaps. 3, 5, and 9.

great for efficiency. The efficiency loss at output OQ", as compared with the efficient output of OQ', is measured by area I'FG. From the point of view of efficiency it is not correct to say a firm should produce as much as it can while still covering its total costs from customer revenues.

PROFIT MAXIMIZATION FOR A NATURAL MONOPOLY

The firm in Figure 11.1 would have been able to operate at the efficient output and still cover its costs. Probably the more common case is the natural monopoly illustrated in Figure 11.2, with long-run decreasing costs and a marginal cost below average cost at all outputs. Profit-maximizing output for the monopolist who does not practice price discrimination is OQ, at a price of OP.

Figure 11.2   *The Decreasing Cost Natural Monopoly*

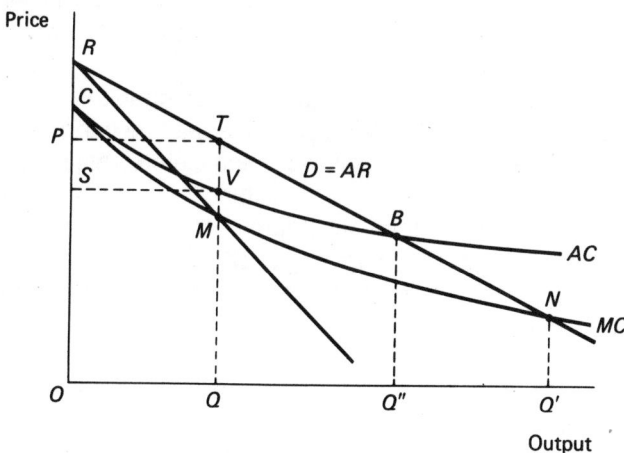

The efficient output, at which the demand (marginal value) curve intersects the marginal cost curve is OQ'. To sell this output at a single uniform price to all buyers, however, would require a price of Q'N, which is less than average costs. Total revenues would then be less than total costs.

Maintaining output OQ' would require either some form of subsidization of the firm or product, or permitting the firm to discriminate in price. Subsidization can be done fairly easily if a government agency is supplying the good, but not if the supplier is a private firm.

The impossibility of finding an output at which price equals both average cost (to cover total costs) and marginal cost (for efficiency) is not restricted to monopolies with decreasing costs. It is very general and accounts for many problems of public policy. This difficulty may occur (1) in the long run, with any market structure except perfect competition, if the firm does not have constant costs, and (2) in the short run everywhere, including perfectly competitive firms.

A compromise solution, which is often used by regulatory agencies in setting the prices of public utilities, is to require the firm to set a price equal to average cost. The output would then be OQ'', and price would be $Q''B$. The firm is then receiving normal profits. The regulated price and output are less inefficient than those of an unregulated profit-maximizing monopoly, but are also less efficient than output OQ', the point at which marginal value (= price) equals marginal cost.

The primary advantage of the regulatory solution over the $P = MC$ solution is that setting price equal to average cost avoids the subsidization problem without creating excess profits. The argument for the regulatory price is based more on equity than on efficiency grounds. This is characteristic of the laws regulating public utilities in which "fairness" is a common element and efficiency is rarely mentioned.

There is, however, an efficiency argument for the regulatory principle of setting price equal to average cost, which may be important. One rule for efficiency is $P = MC$. But, as noted before, efficiency also requires what may be called the "total test." The total value of the output must exceed the total (avoidable) costs of supplying it. If, when price is set equal to marginal cost, total revenues fall short of total costs, as they will when marginal cost is less than average cost, it is not known whether the total test is being satisfied.

Consider the firm illustrated in Figure 11.3. Following instructions to set a price equal to marginal cost, it sets price OP and produces output OQ. Total revenues equal the rectangle $OPRQ$. Total costs, however, are area $OCFQ$, in excess of total revenues.

The total test for efficiency asks, however, not whether revenues exceed costs, but whether the total value of the product exceeds the total cost. To determine the total value to buyers of output OQ, one must know the location of the demand curve, for the total value is equal to the area under that curve.

All the producer knows for certain is that at a price of OP, OQ units of the good will be purchased. If, in fact, the demand curve follows the path of curve D_1D, total costs exceed total value at any output, and the good should not be produced at all. If, on the other hand, the true demand curve is D_3D, total value exceeds total costs, and production at output OQ is efficient.

The advantage of setting a price equal to cost (if any price exists at which average cost would be covered) is this: revenues equal to

Figure 11.3   *The Total Test of Efficiency and Marginal Cost Pricing*

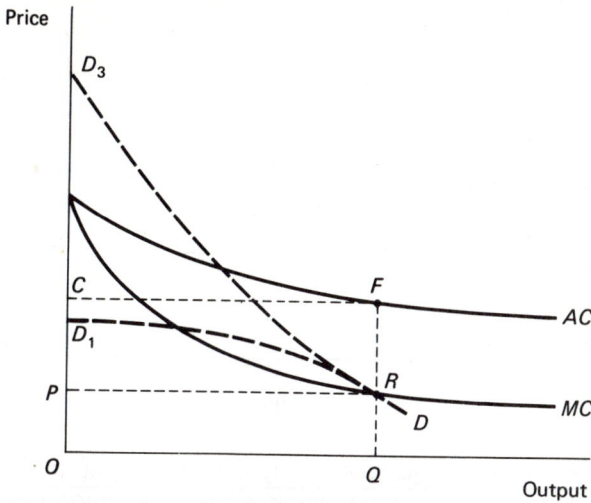

or greater than total costs is a sufficient although not necessary condition for satisfying the total test of efficiency. Since total value inevitably exceeds total revenues for the monopolist, when total revenues cover costs, so also must total value.

The adequacy of total revenues to cover total costs is a sufficient but not necessary condition for satisfying the total test for efficiency. The total value of a product may exceed its total costs even if total revenues (under nondiscriminatory prices) do not cover total costs. Consider, for example, a classic case of a bridge,[5] on which the marginal cost of an additional vehicle is zero. Such a situation is illustrated in Figure 11.4. Marginal cost pricing here requires a zero price with which *OQ* vehicles per day would use the bridge. Note that here the demand curve lies below the average cost curve at all service levels. There is no single price that would provide revenues sufficient to cover total costs. Nevertheless, the bridge services should be supplied at a zero price because total value, which is measured by the area under the demand curve, exceeds total cost over a wide range of outputs.

This is more easily seen if an average value curve is included in the figure. The demand curve is a marginal value curve. A curve of average value lies above the demand curve. The total test for efficiency then can be phrased in terms of averages and is satisfied

[5]The case dates back to Jules Dupuit, "On the Measurement of the Utility of Public Works," *Annales des Ponts et Chaussées,* 2nd series (1844), vol. 8. A translation of this article, originally published in French, appears in *International Economic Papers,* no. 2 (New York: Macmillan, 1952), pp. 83–110.

Figure 11.4 *Efficiency and the Bridge*

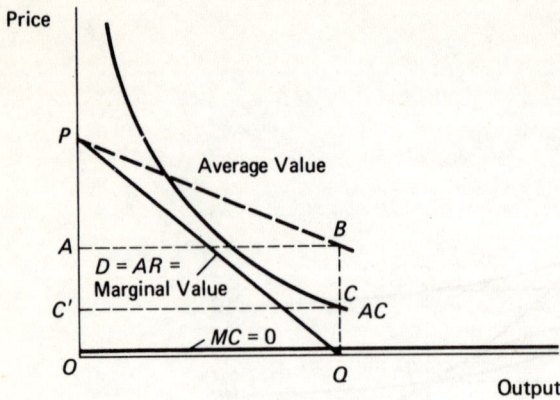

if average value exceeds average cost at any level of output. In the case illustrated in Figure 11.4, average value exceeds average cost (and hence total value exceeds total cost) over a wide range. The total test is therefore satisfied: for efficiency the good should be produced. The efficient quantity of the good (or, as here, service) is then determined by the marginal test. Setting marginal value equal to marginal cost maximizes the excess of total value over total cost and gives efficiency—here at a zero price, with *OQ* quantity of the service supplied.

Urban and commuter transportation services may also be examples of this type of situation where the desirability of having a service seems clear even though it cannot be self-supporting through revenues from customers. Public operation of such services, often subsidized from general tax revenues, is not uncommon.

LONG-RUN BEHAVIOR OF THE MONOPOLIST

Consider now the effects on the monopolist of changes in exogenous factors affecting him. The monopolist does not have a supply curve as such. Unlike the perfectly competitive firm, the amount the monopoly will produce depends not only on its marginal cost curve, but also on the elasticity of its demand curve. An increase in the monopolist's demand, for example, will lead to an increase in *either* price *or* quantity or *both*. It is possible for an increase in demand, if accompanied by an increase in elasticity of demand, to result in a lower price or, if accompanied by a decrease in elasticity, to lead to a decrease in output. Compare these possibilities with the case of a perfectly competitive industry in which an increase in demand inevitably induces an increase in output and in which price will fall only in the long-run decreasing cost industry, a case that rarely exists.

The effects of the imposition of a unit tax on a monopolist are illustrated in Figure 11.5. The tax raises the long-run average and marginal cost curves by the amount of the tax. Output will be cut back from OQ to OQ'. Price will be raised from OP to OP', by less than the amount of the tax. Part of the tax is shifted to the buyer and part falls on the monopolist, reducing his profits.[6]

Figure 11.5 *Effect of a Unit Tax on a Monopolist*

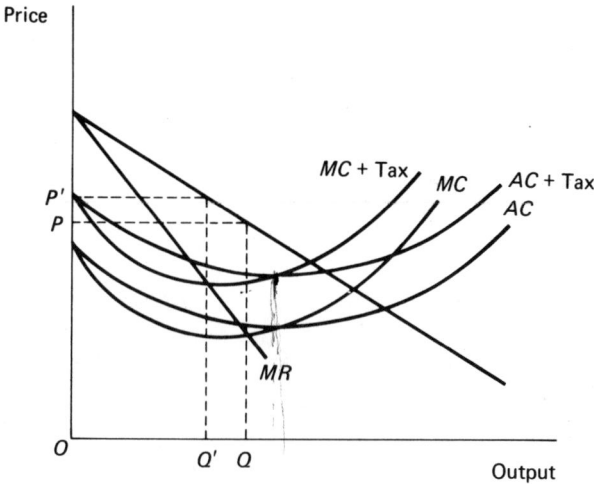

A lump-sum tax comes completely out of the monopolist's profits. He can escape it in the long run only by withdrawing from production, which he will do only if the lump-sum tax exceeds his excess profits.

SHORT RUN AND LONG RUN

As an illustration of the short-run and long-run behavior of the non-discriminating monopolist, consider the increase in demand illustrated in Figure 11.6. Initially, the firm is in both long- and short-run equilibrium at output OQ_1 with price OP_1.

Demand then increases to D', shifting with it the firm's marginal revenue curve.

In a short run, the firm can expand output somewhat within its existing fixed commitments. It equates the new marginal revenue

[6]See the more extended discussion of the effects of taxes in Chapter 18.

Figure 11.6   *Increase in Demand for a Monopolist: Short- and Long-run Effects*

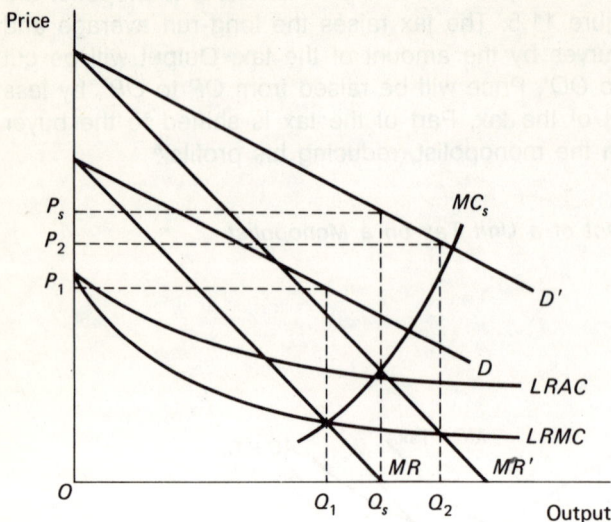

(MR') to the short-run marginal cost (MC$_s$). Its profit-maximizing short-run output is OQ$_s$; price as shown by the new demand curve at this output is OP$_s$. Output has increased, price has increased over its original level, and the firm's excess profits are greater than in the original equilibrium.

In the long run, the firm expands to a new long-run equilibrium at OQ$_2$, with price OP$_2$. Its profits are higher here than in either of the previous situations.

It is more difficult to generalize about the behavior of the monopolist and his responses to changes in the exogenous factors affecting him than to describe perfectly competitive behavior. The monopolist's actions depend on slopes or elasticities of demand and cost curves in ways that are irrelevant to competitive behavior. Perhaps only two generalizations about the unregulated nondiscriminating monopolist are possible: his output will fall short of the efficient level and his profits will usually exceed the level of normal profits.[7] It is tempting but dangerous to attempt to compare the behavior of a monopoly with a perfectly competitive industry. The conclusions would be valid only if the two industries faced identical cost and demand conditions, a situation that would rarely occur in practice. The fact that cost and demand conditions in practice do not satisfy the assumptions of perfect competition is what usually gives rise to the noncompetitive market forms.

---

[7]In the short run, even a monopolist may be making losses.

REVIEW QUESTIONS

1. Explain the following concepts:
    Bilateral monopoly
    Monopoly
    Monopsony
    Natural monopoly
    Average value
2. Discuss the advantages and disadvantages of each of the following pricing rules for a natural monopoly:
    (a) The profit-maximizing price
    (b) $P = AC$
    (c) $P = MC$
3. Explain and compare the marginal and the total tests of determining efficiency in the operation of a monopoly.
4. Is price = marginal cost a necessary condition for efficiency? a sufficient condition? Explain.
5. Compare the effects on a monopolist's price, output, and profits of a lump-sum tax, a unit tax, and a sales tax of equal tax yields, in the long run and in the short run.
6. The competitive firm has a supply curve; the monopoly does not. Why not?

FURTHER READING

Harberger, Arnold C., "Monopoly and Resource Allocation." *American Economic Review Papers and Proceedings 44* (1954), 77–87.

Marshall, Alfred, *Principles of Economics.* 8th ed., London: Macmillan (1920), bk. V, chap. 14.

Robinson, Joan, *The Economics of Imperfect Competition.* London: Macmillan (1933).

Schumpeter, Joseph A., *Capitalism, Socialism, and Democracy.* New York: Harper & Row (1942), esp. chaps. 7–8.

12 PRICE DISCRIMINATION

THE NATURE OF PRICE DISCRIMINATION

Price discrimination exists when a firm charges different prices for the same good or the same price for two products with different costs, or when the price differential between two related products is not equal to the difference in their costs of production. Charging different prices for the same product is extremely common, but probably not as prevalent as discriminating by failing to charge different prices for products with different costs.[1]

The economist often views discrimination differently from the man in the street. To the latter, two goods often appear to be identical when to the economist it is clear that significant cost differences exist between them. In such cases discrimination exists if the firm *fails* to charge differential prices.

Problems of price discrimination are particularly likely to arise for the firm with regularly fluctuating demand for its product, for example, daily, weekly, or seasonal variations. The firm will create capacity to supply the peak demands, and at other periods will have excess capacity. The marginal cost of supplying an additional customer at times of peak demand includes the

---

[1]As J. M. Clark has said, "The most common form of discrimination is the failure to discriminate."

marginal capital cost of expanding the facilities, whereas the marginal cost of serving an off-peak customer includes only the expenses of variable factors. A failure to charge different prices at peak and off-peak periods constitutes price discrimination.

Thus price discrimination exists when the same price is charged, for example, for electric power in the daytime as at night, afternoon and evening performances of a play or movie, or for selling to a retail customer who requires more of the salesman's time as for selling to a buyer who decides quickly. The firm that provides free extra services for some customers (for example, delivery or credit facilities) without charging for them is discriminating against the customers who do not use the special services.

Firms also often practice price discrimination when the difference in the prices charged for two goods related in production (for example, the standard and the deluxe model of a good) is greater than the difference in the costs of producing the two.

Finally, many times firms are able to charge different prices for the same good, either discriminating among different groups of customers or using quantity discounts that do not mirror the differences in the costs of supplying different quantities.

No firm can make its prices conform exactly to the costs of supplying various customers, nor would it wish to. For one thing, customers resent differential prices. Second, the costs to the seller of making an accurate determination of his costs are often too high to justify the effort. Hence, the firm will price for groups of customers or transactions, basing its price on the average of the costs of the group. This results in price discrimination. It also makes businessmen more anxious to serve certain types of customers than others (for example, the steady customer gets more service than the transient).

Two types of price discrimination—perfect and imperfect price discrimination—will be distinguished.[2] Perfect price discrimination exists when the seller charges each customer the maximum amount he will pay for each unit of the product. The seller thus appropriates all of the consumers' surplus. The buyer is made no better off by the transaction; all the gains of trade accrue to the seller. Conversely, a perfectly discriminating buyer pays the seller the minimum amount the seller will accept for each unit of the good or service sold. The buyer takes all the gains of trade, leaving the seller no better off from the exchange.

As shown in Chapter 5, the effects of perfect price discrimination can also be achieved when the seller (or buyer) sets an all-or-none offer for the product for each individual buyer (or seller); the seller

[2]These correspond to Pigou's first and third degree discrimination, respectively. See A. C. Pigou, *The Economics of Welfare,* 4th ed. (London: Macmillan, 1932), chap. 17.

or buyer sets a total price for a specified quantity of the product, rather than selling or buying it unit by unit. The quantity sold and the total amount paid for it will be the same whether perfect price discrimination or the all-or-none technique is used.

Imperfect price discrimination, on the other hand, exists when the seller (or, conversely, the buyer) separates his market into two or more segments and charges different prices in each market. In contrast to perfect price discrimination, no discrimination is practiced between individuals in a single group, nor does the price per unit vary with the quantity sold.

Imperfect price discrimination is of course found in practice more often than perfect price discrimination. The latter represents a limiting case. Perfect discrimination is emphasized here, not because of its practical importance, but for its important and interesting efficiency implications.

PERFECT PRICE DISCRIMINATION— S TP

When the seller can collect the maximum amount the buyer is willing to pay for each unit of sale, the firm's demand curve becomes its marginal revenue curve. One can then construct an average revenue curve lying above the demand curve, the chief use of which is to determine the firm's excess profits. The new *AR* curve is not a demand curve, it should be remembered, and does not show the prices at which output is sold. It does show the average amount received by the seller for each output, but the actual range of prices charged will lie along the regular demand curve. The average revenue curve under perfect price discrimination is the same as an average value curve, which was found to be useful in Chapter 11.

The firm's profit-maximizing output now occurs where the *demand* curve cuts the marginal cost curve (output *OQ* in Figure 12.1). The

Figure 12.1 *Perfect Price Discrimination*

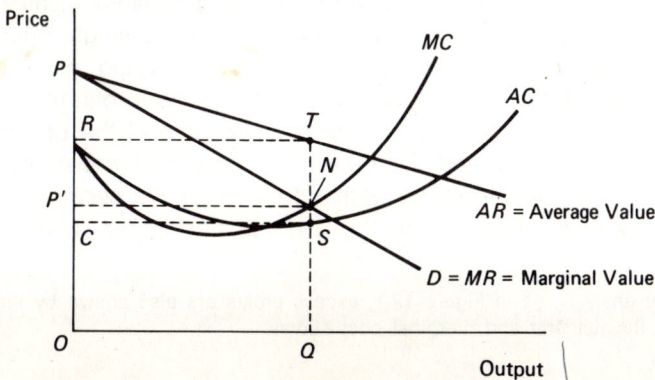

prices charged by the firm will range from a high of *OP* at the beginning of the demand curve, to a low price of *OP'*, charged for the marginal unit of sale. The marginal price *OP'* equals marginal cost.

Perfect price discrimination may be grossly inequitable, for the seller appropriates all potential consumers' surplus and leaves the buyers no better off from the transaction. But the output produced under perfect price discrimination does satisfy the tests of efficiency. The value of the marginal unit of the product to the buyer (measured on the demand curve, which, as usual, is a marginal *value* curve), is just equal to the value of the resources used to produce it if they were employed in an alternative use (as measured by the marginal cost curve). Every customer is supplied who is willing to pay a price equal to marginal cost.

The equilibrium of the perfectly discriminating monopolist is efficient by the marginal test (by which marginal value equals marginal cost), and by the total test. For this perfectly discriminating firm, total revenues equal the total value of the product to the buyers. The firm will not produce at all if revenues fall short of costs. Thus profit maximization by a perfectly discriminating monopolist leads to maximization of efficiency.

The *average* revenue received per unit of output is *QT*. Excess profits are shown by area *RTSC*.[3]

Inevitably, perfect price discrimination leads to greater output than does simple monopoly for two firms with identical demand and cost functions. The perfectly discriminating firm produces to the output at which the demand curve intersects the marginal cost curve; the simple nondiscriminating monopolist stops short at the point at which the marginal cost curve is cut by the *nondiscriminating* marginal revenue curve. The latter inevitably lies below and to the left of the demand curve. With a linear demand curve and constant marginal costs, for example, the output of the perfectly discriminating monopolist will be twice that of the simple monopolist.

The use of discriminatory prices may make possible the production of a good or service that would not be produced at all if the firm were not able to discriminate. There may be no single price that the nondiscriminating seller can charge that would provide revenues sufficient to cover costs. Yet it could be profitable to produce it under discriminatory conditions. The case of the bridge discussed in Chapter 11 and illustrated in Figure 11.4 constitutes an example of this situation. The demand curve for the services of the bridge lay everywhere below the average cost curve, and no

---

[3]In long-run analysis, as in Figure 12.1, excess profits are also shown by the area between the demand and marginal cost curves.

single price existed by which revenues would cover total cost. With perfect price discrimination, however, the average revenue curve of the firm or agency providing the bridge would lie above the demand curve, and, in the case illustrated, also above average cost. A perfectly discriminating profit maximizing firm would produce output OQ, and charge prices ranging from a high of OP to a low of zero. (The zero price is equal to marginal cost.) The firm's excess profits would equal area ABCC'.

A further example of a case in which a good or service might not be supplied at all if a seller were unable to practice price discrimination might be a doctor in a small town. If he did not charge discriminatory fees, he might not receive sufficient income to persuade him to remain in the town. Discrimination raises his income and may induce him to remain.

In this case, discriminatory pricing definitely increases efficiency, for the total value of the good or service exceeds its total costs and the good should be produced. The good would not be produced by a nondiscriminatory seller because the revenues of the seller (measured by the area under the nondiscriminating marginal revenue curve) would be less than his costs, even though the total value of the product (shown by the area under the demand curve) exceeds total costs.[4]

IMPERFECT PRICE DISCRIMINATION

In practice, a firm cannot discriminate perfectly. The ability to discriminate depends on the firm's opportunities to classify its customers in a meaningful and identifiable way, and to keep its markets separate, so that customers in the low-price market cannot pass the product on to customers in the high-price market. Markets are sometimes separate by nature (appendectomies are the prime example); other markets are separated by distance, transportation costs, and sometimes tariffs, which prevent supplies of the lower priced market from invading the other. It is not uncommon for a U.S. manufacturer to sell at a lower price abroad than in the United States. Markets may be classified by sex—Ladies Night at the ball game—and by age—movies, transportation. Magazines attempt to differentiate between old and new subscribers.

Ignorance helps the discriminator. Many virtually identical items

[4]The reader may wish to amuse himself by trying to think of goods or services that are *not* being currently offered in markets only because the potential suppliers are unable to practice price discrimination. See Joan Robinson, "An Inherent Defect in Laissez-Faire," *Economic Journal 45* (1935), 580–582; reprinted in Joan Robinson, *Collected Economic Papers*, (Oxford: Blackwell, 1951), pp. 49–51.

are sold under two trade names and two prices. Ignorance is assisted by slight product differentiation—the standard and the deluxe models, where the extra price of the latter more than covers its extra cost to the seller.

The seller will want to discriminate when it is profitable. Differences in the costs of supplying groups of customers, or in the elasticities of demand for his product by different groups will give rise to discrimination.

For simplicity only the case of identical products being sold to two groups of customers is considered here. The products sold in the two markets have a common marginal cost curve.

If the two groups have the same elasticity of demand at any price, price discrimination will not add to profits. As shown earlier at the profit-maximizing output the following relation holds: $MC = P(1 - 1/e)$. This can conveniently be rewritten: $P = MC[e/(e - 1)]$. Thus, if two or more markets have the same marginal cost function (as is assumed in our example), the profit maximizing prices will vary inversely with the elasticities of demand in those markets. If two or more markets have the same elasticity of demand at any given price, profit maximization requires equal prices in the two markets. It is therefore pointless for a firm to attempt to divide its market into two segments and price separately in each unless the demand characteristics differ between them.

A lower price will be charged in the market with the higher elasticity of demand. Elasticity will be higher the more substitutes there are for a product. Therefore, a seller who faces competition in one market but not in another will naturally charge a lower price in the competitive market. Thus world market prices for some products are lower than the prices within one nation. A company often charges a lower price on sales to a firm that could, if it desired, produce the product itself, than to another firm without this capability.

The profit-maximizing price-setting technique for the discriminating firm with two or more separable markets is to set a price in each market so that marginal revenue in each market is equal to the marginal cost of producing the composite output. Because marginal revenue in each market is equal to the same composite marginal cost, the marginal revenues are equal to each other at the respective profit-maximizing outputs. Using subscripts for separate markets and MC_c for composite marginal cost, profits are maximized when outputs are adjusted so that $MR_1 = MR_2 = MC_c$. At these outputs, an increase or decrease in the amount supplied in either market would reduce profits.

Figure 12.2 illustrates the procedure for determining the profit-maximizing prices and quantities in two markets. In Figure 12.2 are

Figure 12.2 *Two-market Price Discrimination*

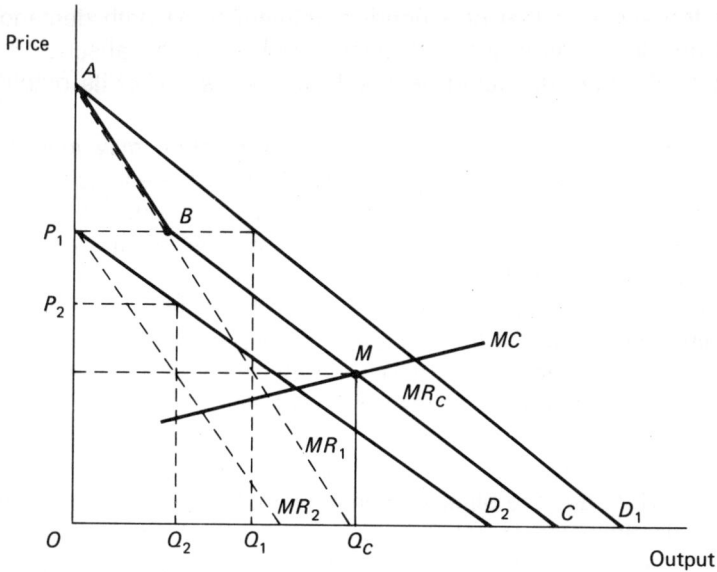

the demand curves facing the seller in two markets, the separate marginal revenue curves derived from each of these demand curves, and the seller's marginal cost curve. The seller is interested in finding those outputs in the two markets at which the marginal revenues in the two markets would be equal. He does this by adding horizontally the marginal revenue curves of the two markets. The kinked line ABC in Figure 12.2 is the summation of the marginal revenue curves of the two markets.

The joint output that maximizes profits is found at the intersection of the composite marginal revenue curve (ABC) and the marginal cost curve, at output OQ_c.

This point of intersection does not, however, show the profit-maximizing price. To determine the prices charged in the two markets, we must locate the point on each individual marginal revenue curve at which the marginal revenue for that market equals the common marginal cost (Q_cM). These points determine the outputs for the separate markets, output OQ_1 for the first market, and OQ_2 for the second. The prices charged in each market are located in the usual way (that is, by the point on the demand curve for that market at the profit-maximizing quantity). This gives prices of OP_1 and OP_2 for the two markets.

Note that no composite demand curve was constructed because it would have no meaning for the discriminator. It might be used, however, to compare the output of the discriminating firm with the output the firm would have sold if the seller had not practiced price discrimination. It can be shown that the output of the discriminator will be the same as that of a nondiscriminator if (1) both demand curves are linear (as in the illustration), and (2) in the absence of discrimination the firm would have sold at least some of its output in each market.

In the absence of these conditions, discrimination may lead to an increase or decrease in output, depending on the elasticities of demand in the two markets.[5] The most likely conditions for output to increase come when the seller, with discrimination, moves into a new market not supplied before.

The case of linear demand curves gives the same output under discrimination as without it. Profits are, however, higher under discrimination. What can be said about the efficiency of this particular case of discrimination? The answer is not difficult. For concreteness, assume the price charged by a nondiscriminating firm would be $1, and that under discrimination one group would be charged a price of $1.20 and the other 80 cents. Output is the same whether the firm discriminates or not. Therefore, when discriminatory prices are instituted, assuming for convenience that each buyer purchases one unit of the product, the number of buyers added in the low-price markets must equal the number of purchasers excluded from the high-price market (that is, individuals who would have bought at a price of $1, but who will not pay the $1.20 now required of them). Each of the excluded customers priced out of the higher price market by the rise in price from the nondiscriminatory $1 to the discriminatory $1.20 (group A) values the product at amounts from $1.20 to $1; the buyers added by the drop in price from $1 to 80 cents (group B) place a value on the product between $1 and 80 cents. Clearly, this type of discrimination reduces efficiency, for the customers added by discriminatory pricing place a lower monetary value on the product than do those excluded.

In this situation a little "black-marketing" would increase efficiency: Each member of group B could resell the product to a member of group A. No one would be worse off, and at least half of the traders would be better off.

REVIEW QUESTIONS

1. Explain the following concepts:
   Price discrimination vs. price differentials
   Perfect price discrimination

[5]See Joan Robinson, *The Economics of Imperfect Competition* (London: Macmillan, 1933), chap. 15.

Imperfect price discrimination
All-or-none offer

2. Under what conditions should price discrimination be permitted? be encouraged?

3. In comparison with a single price system, what effect does price discrimination have on
    (a) average price?
    (b) output?
    (c) profits?
    (d) efficiency?

    Distinguish between perfect and imperfect price discrimination, and between an increasing and a decreasing cost firm.

4. Assume two markets for a good which has a constant marginal cost of $1. Elasticity of demand in market A is a constant 2; in market B elasticity of demand is 2.5. What are the profit-maximizing prices in the two markets?

5. A firm produces a standard and a deluxe model of its product, at constant average costs of $1 and $1.50 respectively. The elasticity of demand for each product is a constant 2. What price will be charged for each model? Will price discrimination exist? If the market demand for the deluxe model had, instead, a constant elasticity of 1.5, what prices would result?

FURTHER READING

Phillips, Charles F., Jr., *The Economics of Regulation.* rev. ed., Homewood, Ill.: Irwin (1969), chaps. 10–11.

Pigou, A. C., *The Economics of Welfare.* 4th ed., London: Macmillan (1932), chap. 17.

Robinson, Joan, *The Economics of Imperfect Competition.* London: Macmillan (1933), bk. V.

13

IMPERFECT COMPETITION IN THE LONG RUN

- ☐ fewness and product differentiation
- ☐ barrier pricing
- ☐ Chamberlin's large group model
- ☐ the efficiency of the tangency equilibrium
- ☐ fixed price with the large group

FEWNESS AND PRODUCT DIFFERENTIATION

Monopoly and perfect competition represent limiting cases that rarely, if ever, occur in practice. The overwhelming majority of actual markets are imperfectly competitive. It is therefore important to develop theoretical generalizations describing such situations. The task is difficult. Instead of a broad general theory adequately describing most of such markets, economics has developed a group of models, each applicable to a particular type of market or market behavior. Because of the number and variety of these models, only a sampling can be presented here.

Where competition is not perfect, three questions arise:

(1) Are the products of different firms homogeneous or differentiated? If products are differentiated, demand curves will be downward sloping.

(2) On what terms can new firms enter the industry? If a new firm is free to enter on essentially the same terms as the existing firms, that is, with comparable cost and demand functions, and the size of the new firm is small relative to the total market, in the long run profits in the industry will tend to be normal; if not, excess profits may persist in the industry.

(3) Do firms take competitors' possible reactions into account when determining their price and output be-

havior? It is in this area that theories have proliferated, each based on some special assumption about competitive interdependence, about how competitors will react to actions of one firm.

The discussion of the models of imperfect competition is divided into two parts. The present chapter considers the essentially long-run problem of the determinants of the number of firms in a market, both for oligopolies and for the Chamberlinian case of a large number of firms producing differentiated products. The following chapter develops some models of the short-run behavior of oligopolistic firms and industries.

BARRIER PRICING

In the long run, firms will enter an industry (here loosely defined as a group of firms producing similar but not necessarily identical products) if they expect to be able to make excess profits in the industry. Under perfect competition (as described in Chapter 9) the entry of new firms continues until the level of profits for all firms is forced down to normal levels, and each firm must produce at its minimum average total cost in order to survive.

In practice, entry of new firms attracted by excess profits may be effectively halted before the profit level of existing firms is reduced to the level of normal profits. As a model—or, rather, a group of models—associated with the name of Joe Bain[1] shows, this situation can occur particularly when the firms' cost functions show strongly decreasing costs and if only a few firms are sufficient to satiate the market demand for the product. Even though existing firms are making more than normal profits, a new firm may be unwilling to enter if the addition of its output to industry supply would drive industry profit rates below the level of normal profits. The theory describing this situation is sometimes called the "barrier-pricing model."

As noted in Chapter 7, considerable empirical evidence exists to show that firms typically have an initial stage of decreasing costs followed by a range of sizes over which average costs are fairly constant. The size at which the firm's average cost curve becomes substantially constant can be termed its *minimum efficient size* (noted as *MES*). If the total market demand for a product can be supplied by a single firm of the minimum efficient size or smaller, a natural monopoly exists. If the market is very large relative to the *MES* of any single firm, conditions approximating those of perfect competition can obtain and any excess profits will be competed

[1]See Joe S. Bain, *Barriers to New Competition* (Cambridge: Harvard University Press, 1956), and Franco Modigliani, "New Developments on the Oligopoly Front," *Journal of Political Economy* 66 (1958), 215–232.

away by new entrants. An interesting case arises, however, when market conditions require a "few" firms—too few for perfect competition, too many for the natural monopoly situation. The theory of barrier pricing deals with this case.

Assume an industry of two or more existing firms with cost curves of the type described. If the existing firms compete effectively, the price of the product will be driven down to the level of the horizontal section of the firms' AC curves. No additional firms will enter, but the production is efficient, for the existing firms will be producing at an output at which price equals marginal cost. The size of the individual firms, however, is in this case indeterminate. Each will be operating somewhere along the flat section of its average cost curve.

The particular variation of the barrier-pricing model which we shall explain assumes, however, that the existing firms do not compete effectively with each other. They maximize their joint profits in the long run by discouraging entry of new firms. One question Bain poses is this: How high a price above the competitive level, that is, above the level of the firms' minimum ATC, can the existing firms maintain without encouraging new firms to enter? In other words, how large a *barrier premium* can the existing firms extract?

The answer depends on the particular behavior assumptions made. As one example, assume that when a new firm contemplates entry it expects that the existing firms will continue to maintain their existing level of production. If so, the effective demand curve for a new firm consists of the industry demand curve at all outputs greater than the existing production level of the old firms. This is the market the new firm expects to be available to it. The potential entrant compares this residual market demand with his estimated cost curve in order to determine whether entry would be profitable.

For example, if industry demand is represented by line DD' in Figure 13.1, when the existing firms set a price of OP_1, their combined output would be OQ_1. The market demand then facing a potential new entrant would be represented by segment D_1D', with the origin located not at point O, but at point Q_1, which represents the output level which the existing firms are expected to maintain in the face of competition from a new firm. If existing firms set a price of OP_2, the residual demand for a new firm would be D_2D', with origin at point Q_2.

The new firm will enter if it expects to make more than normal profits. The maximum price the existing firms can set without inducing entry by a new firm is found by superimposing the cost curve (AC) of the new firm over the demand curve of Figure 13.1 and then sliding that cost curve to the right (carrying its vertical axis along with it) until the cost curve is just tangent to the industry

Figure 13.1 *Residual Demand*

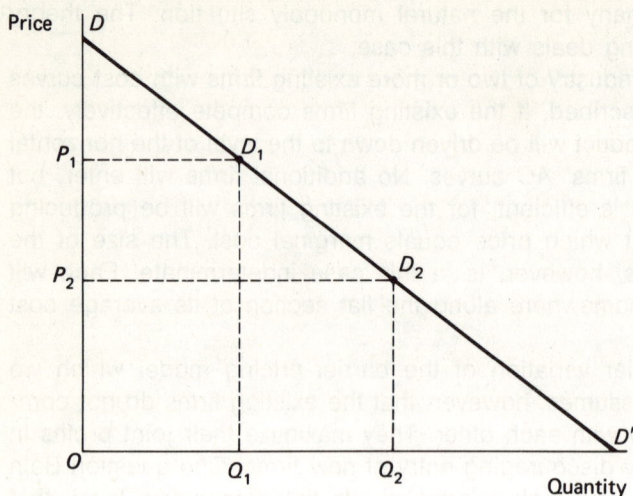

demand curve, position AC' of Figure 13.2. The critical price is now found at the intersection of the industry demand curve and the transplanted vertical axis of the cost curve, $O'P_b$. (Note that the critical price is *not* determined by the point of tangency of the demand and average cost curve.)

If the existing firms set any price higher than $O'P_b$, the residual demand available to a new firm would exceed the residual demand curve (P_bQ) resulting from a price of $O'P_b$, the residual demand curve would lie above the new firm's average cost curve at some points, and the new firm would be attracted into the industry by the promise of excess profits. Conversely, if the existing firms set a price

Figure 13.2 *Barrier Pricing*

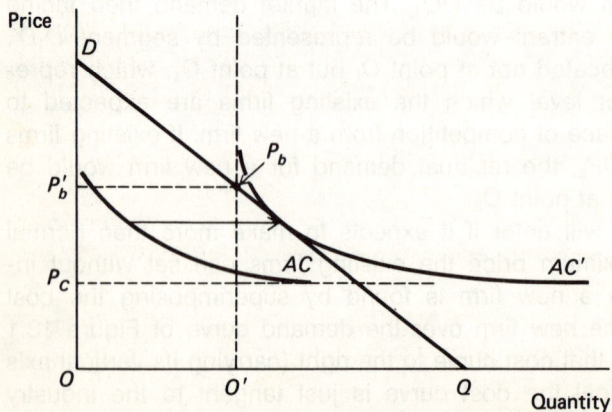

lower than $O'P_b$, no new firm would be induced to enter, for the residual demand curve left to it would be insufficient at every possible output for the firm to cover its costs and make normal profits.

When the existing firms charge price $O'P_b$, the residual demand curve available to a new entrant is just sufficient to allow the new firm to make normal profits at the point at which the residual demand curve is tangent to the average cost curve. It is therefore the critical price.

The so-called *barrier premium* is defined as the difference between the barrier or critical price and the competitive price level, OP_o; the latter is determined by the height of the flat stretch of the firms' average cost curves.

If the existing firms are operating on the flat portions of their *AC* curves, the barrier premium equals their excess profits per unit produced. This premium will be larger, the less elastic is the industry demand for the product, and the larger a share of the market would be supplied by a firm of the minimum efficient size.

This barrier-pricing model can be applied to a monopolist who fears the entry of rivals. It shows that potential competition, as well as actual competition, can restrain the exercise of monopoly power.

The existence of firms setting barrier prices in an otherwise competitive world would lead to inefficiency in the allocation of resources, for the price of the product will be higher than the marginal cost of supplying it. Some buyers willing to pay marginal cost will be excluded from the market.

CHAMBERLIN'S LARGE GROUP MODEL

If economies of scale are not strong and the products of different firms are only slightly differentiated, no significant barrier premium can exist. In 1933, in *The Theory of Monopolistic Competition,* E. H. Chamberlin introduced a model of this case in which many firms produce somewhat differentiated products.[2] The theory attracted an unusual amount of attention when introduced, perhaps because it seemed to fit the situation of the 1930s. In more recent years, while the case lives on in the textbooks, many economists have become disenchanted with it, chiefly because they believe a theory which leaves out oligopolistic interrelations is unrealistic.

Chamberlin's large group case is best considered as a long-run theory. In the long run, oligopolistic interrelationships are probably less important than in the short run, and the behavior of individual firms is perhaps more determined by fundamental demand and cost

[2] E. H. Chamberlin, *The Theory of Monopolistic Competition,* 8th ed. (Cambridge: Harvard University Press, 1962).

considerations than by the personal reaction pattern of one's competitors.

Chamberlin's large group case is based on the following assumptions:

(1) The products of each firm are differentiated from those of other firms in the group. The firm's demand curve is therefore not perfectly elastic, but is downward sloping. The products of the different firms are thus close but not perfect substitutes, and the demand for the product of any one firm is strongly influenced by the prices charged by other firms in the group (but not by the price of any single competing firm).

(2) Firms can and will enter or leave if profits of existing firms are above or below normal. This implies that new firms have the same cost and demand functions as existing firms.[3]

(3) The number of firms is so large that no single firm will have sufficient impact on the market to cause other firms to respond oligopolistically to any of its actions.

The case is thus comparable to perfect competition, except that the firms produce differentiated products.

Because the products are differentiated, some economists are reluctant to talk about an "industry" and substitute the word "group." The argument seems trivial, and the two terms will be used interchangeably here.

The assumptions of the model require that each firm have a downward sloping demand curve and long-run normal profits. These conditions can *only* exist in the situation illustrated in Figure 13.3, with the demand curve tangent to the firm's average cost curve at a point to the left of its minimum point. At this output, marginal cost will equal marginal revenue.[4]

Firms move in and out of the industry in response to the profit levels of existing firms. In the short run, if the number of firms is less than that required for long-run group equilibrium, existing firms will have demand curves to the right of that shown in Figure 13.3, with the appropriate price and output levels; excess profits will be received. Additional firms will then in the long run be attracted into the industry. Conversely, if the number of firms is excessive compared with long-run group equilibrium, existing firms

---

[3]The assumption of uniform costs may be dropped without serious consequences. When firms have different cost functions, the low cost firms earn differential rents. Incorporation of these rents into the costs of the firms has the effect of raising their costs to the level of the other firms. The assumption of uniform costs can therefore be extended to cover the existence of cost functions that differ among firms.

[4]Recall that when two average curves are tangent, their respective marginals are equal.

Figure 13.3 *Long-run Equilibrium: the Chamberlinian Large-Group Case*

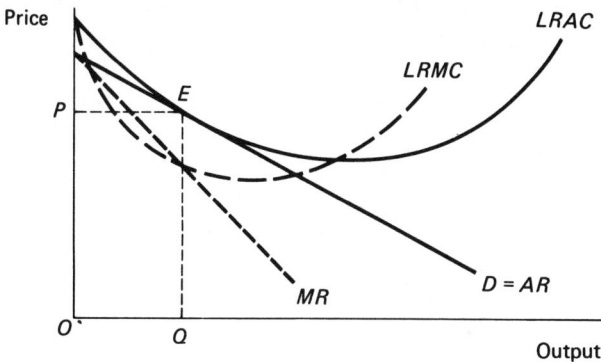

will be making less than normal profits, and firms will leave until profits climb to the normal level.

As Chamberlin points out, the case is a blend of perfect competition and monopoly. The product differentiation, downward sloping demand curve, and equilibrium price in excess of marginal cost are monopoly elements; the freedom of entry, the tangency of the demand and average cost curves, and the long-run normal profit level are characteristics of perfect competition.

THE EFFICIENCY OF THE TANGENCY EQUILIBRIUM

In the long-run Chamberlinian equilibrium each firm produces a smaller output than that at which its average total cost reaches a minimum and sets a price higher than that minimum average cost. These characteristics attracted considerable attention in the 1930s. The theory seemed to explain what many thought was waste in the economy: too many firms each producing too little at too high a price. If there were fewer firms, it was sometimes argued, costs and prices might be lowered, and increased efficiency achieved. The proliferation of gasoline stations to serve the rapidly increasing number of automobiles was—and still is—commonly cited as an example of this apparent waste.

Chamberlin himself definitely did not make these judgments.[5] A reduction in the number of firms might expand the size of the remaining firms, reduce the average cost at which the representative firm produced and hence lower the price of the product, but, he

[5]See in particular, E. H. Chamberlin, "Product Heterogeneity and Public Policy," *American Economic Review* 40 (1950), 85–92, reprinted in E. H. Chamberlin, *Towards a More General Theory of Value* (New York: Oxford University Press, 1957), pp. 92–102.

pointed out, it would also reduce the variety of products available to the public. No evaluation of the large group case should fail to take into account the apparent preferences of the public for variety, for the option of choosing among alternatives.

The question of the efficiency of the tangency equilibrium will be analyzed with the usual tools.[6] Inefficiency exists when price exceeds marginal cost, for this means some consumers who are willing and able to pay marginal cost are not being supplied. In these terms, the inefficiency of the tangency equilibrium is clear.

The argument is, however, incomplete. It is true that if only one firm were being considered it could be argued that for maximum efficiency the firm should expand output to a point at which its demand curve intersected its marginal cost curve. But in considering a large group, it is inappropriate to apply the *ceteris paribus* assumption to each firm. It is necessary here to describe the efficient output for *all* firms in the group, not just for one.

The interrelationships of the demand functions of all the firms in the group must be considered, for the demand curve of each firm is strongly influenced by the price and output policies of the other firms.

The description of an efficiency optimum for the large group case that follows answers the question: What price and output policy for each of the firms in a Chamberlinian large group of firms producing similar but differentiated products would satisfy the requirements for economic efficiency? The description of the efficiency maximum (denoted as *EM*) will be compared with the Chamberlinian tangency equilibrium (*CE*) already described in order to determine to what extent the latter constitutes a pattern of efficient behavior.

It must be emphasized that no claim is made that the pattern described in the efficiency maximization discussion could be achieved in practice. The analysis does illustrate the difficulties in identifying the conditions for maximum efficiency where interrelationships among firms are more complicated than with perfect competition or monopoly.

Imagine for a moment that some all-powerful and efficiency oriented authority could set the price and output policy for all the firms in an industry with differentiated products, an industry in an otherwise competitive economy. If as a first step in the pursuit of efficiency the price of each of the existing firms in the industry is lowered to equal marginal cost, the demand curve of each firm would drop, for the demand of each firm depends on the prices being charged by the other firms in the group.

---

[6]The analysis here is similar in results but not in method to that of Robert L. Bishop, "Monopolistic Competition and Welfare Economics," in Robert E. Kuenne, ed., *Monopolistic Competition Theory: Studies in Impact* (New York: Wiley, 1967), chap. 12.

Imagine, then, a situation in which all firms have set prices equal to marginal costs. Their demand curves would be significantly lower than in the original tangency situation. The new situation is illustrated in Figure 13.4b. It may be compared with the standard tangency equilibrium of Figure 13.4a. In this first step toward a description of efficient behavior, the number of firms in the group is assumed to have remained constant.

Figure 13.4   *Short-run Efficiency Maximization: the Large-Group Case*

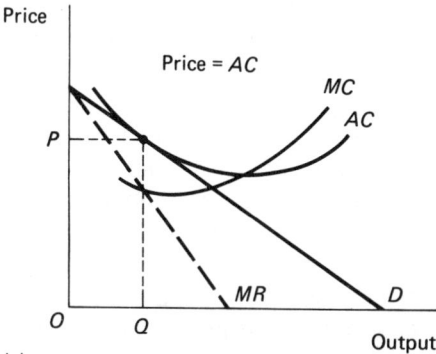

(a)

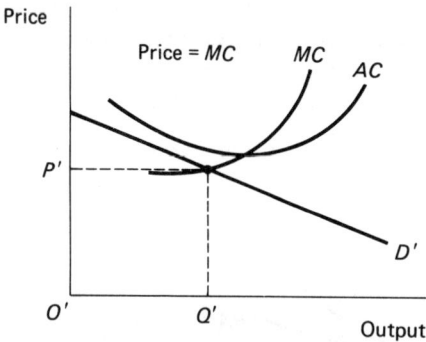

(b)

The situation shown in Figure 13.4b satisfies the short-run marginal test for efficiency, for price equals marginal cost. The firm's revenues would not cover its total costs, but, as noted before, this does not necessarily mean the firm should not be in the industry.

The output policy of the representative firm shown in Figure 13.4b represents a short-run maximization of efficiency: given the existing number of firms in the group, the situation is efficient.

Efficiency, however, also requires the "correct" number of firms. The efficiency test for the number of firms asks whether the addition of one more firm would add more to the value received by buyers of its output than the output would cost. Cost is a measure of the value of the resources in the next best alternative employment. The total value contributed by a firm and its total costs can be determined and compared from the respective areas under the demand curve and the long-run marginal cost curve. Alternately, an average value curve for the firm can be constructed. Average value can then be compared with average total cost at any output.

If the average value of the product of a representative firm in the industry is less than average cost at every level of output, and hence the total value the firm contributes is less than the total costs, there are too many firms in the industry for efficiency. Conversely, if at any output total value exceeds total cost for existing firms, new firms should enter. Long-run efficiency for the industry is therefore achieved when for the representative firm total value is exactly equal to total cost. This situation, illustrated in Figure 13.5, exists when the average *value* curve is just tangent to the average cost curve.[7] The demand curve, which is a curve of marginal value, lies below the average value curve. The firm produces output *OQ,* at which level of production the average value curve is tangent to the average cost curve, and hence the marginal value equals marginal cost. The price that would induce buyers to purchase this output is *OP* (which does not cover average cost).

Note that in the efficiency result firms are still not producing at their minimum average cost points, a further demonstration that production at this point is not required for efficiency.

Figure 13.5   *Long-run Efficiency Maximization: the Large-Group Case*

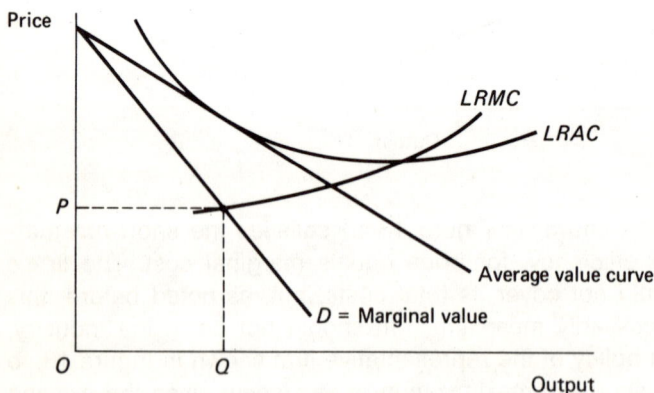

[7]Note that this test for the efficient number of firms—that the total value contributed by a firm just equals its total costs—is also satisfied by the perfectly competitive firm in long-run equilibrium.

The long-run efficient results (*EM*) of Figure 13.5 can be compared with the original Chamberlinian equilibrium (*CE*) of Figure 13.4a. The central questions are these:

(1) Is industry output more or less in *EM* than in *CE*?

(2) Are there more firms with *EM* than *CE*?

The first question can be answered easily. Industry price is lower with *EM* than in *CE;* therefore, industry output is greater with *EM* tnan in *CE*. An industry with differentiated products composed of profit maximizing firms produces too little for efficiency.

The second question, whether too few or too many firms exist in the Chamberlinian equilibrium, is more difficult. The greater industry output may be produced by a larger number of firms, by expansion in the levels of output of existing firms, or even by a still greater expansion in the output of a smaller number of firms. The question of the number of firms in the efficiency maximization situation thus depends on what happens to the output level of the individual firm as compared with the original Chamberlinian equilibrium situation. This in turn depends on relative slopes of the new demand curve of Figure 13.5 as compared with the old demand curve of Figure 13.4a.

It is certain that the new demand curves of *EM* will lie below the old curves of *CE*. If new and old demand curves have the same slopes, each firm in *EM* will produce more than the representative firm in *CE* because the average *value* curve of *EM* will then be less steep than the average *revenue* curve of *CE*, and will therefore be tangent to the firm's average cost curve at a greater output than the tangency of the average revenue curve of *CE* with the average cost curve. Since the industry with *EM* will be producing more than the industry within Chamberlinian equilibrium, in this case we cannot say whether *EM* requires more or fewer firms than *CE*.

If, on the other hand, the effect of *EM* is to swing a linear demand curve down (elasticities of demand at each price remaining the same on the old and new demand curves), the representative firm in *EM* will produce the same output as the firm·in *CE*. The average *value* curve of *EM* would coincide with the average *revenue* or demand curve of *CE*. Hence, the higher industry output of *EM* must come from the entry of additional firms. In this plausible case the Chamberlinian equilibrium results in too few firms for the efficient allocation of resources.

These results can be compared with the standard criticisms of the behavior of the industry and firms in the large group case, that is, too many firms, each producing too little. Our new results are that the profit maximization case results in too little being produced by the industry, and the likelihood (but not certainty) that each of the existing firms is producing too little. On the other hand, it cannot be said, in general, that profit maximization leads to too many firms. The apparent waste of four gas stations at a single intersection thus cannot be explained by the large group theory.

FIXED PRICE WITH THE LARGE GROUP

An interesting and quite possibly realistic variation on the large group case is based on an assumption that the price for the group is somehow fixed at a level above the tangency equilibrium price. The price may be maintained by law (to "protect" the industry), by collusion among the firms, or perhaps by a gentlemen's agreement operating through a trade association or labor union. Free entry of new firms is also assumed.

The case is illustrated in Figure 13.6 in which the curve labeled DD' is the firm's demand curve drawn on the assumption that whatever price this firm charges all other firms will also charge this price. It is thus a representation of one firm's share of total industry demand. This demand curve of the firm will be less elastic than the demand curve of the earlier analysis, which was based on the assumption that the prices of all other firms were constant.

Figure 13.6 *Free Entry with Fixed Price*

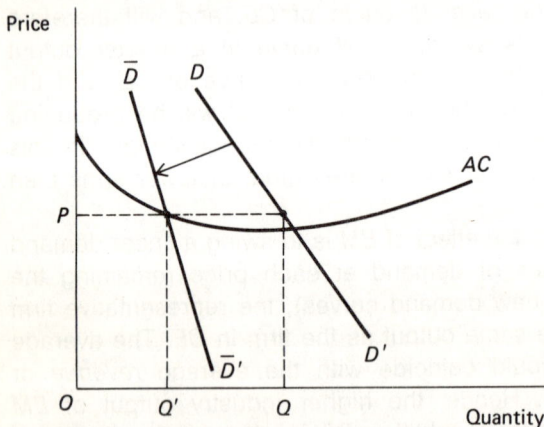

With the DD' curve, consider that the price is fixed by some outside agency at the level OP. By law or custom the firm is not permitted to charge a lower price. It sells output OQ and makes substantial excess profits.

These excess profits will attract additional firms into the industry. As they enter, they obtain a share of the total market, and the demand curve for each of the existing firms moves to the left as its share of the market contracts.

The process of entry by new firms will continue until the firms are making no more than normal profits. The long-run equilibrium is then represented by demand curve $\overline{DD}'$, output OQ', with price still at OP. As the existing firm's output contracts from OQ to OQ', its average cost rises until the excess profits are eliminated and price equals average cost.

The result is grossly inefficient. There are too many firms, each producing too little. Free entry in this fixed price case eliminates excess profits, but only at the expense of creating excess capacity. The fixed price ends up failing to protect the profits of the firms and inflicting unnecessarily high costs on the customers.

Real estate and life insurance selling may be examples of this case, considering each salesman as a "firm." One might also suggest barber shops, the legal profession, and retail stores in "fair trade" states.

Laws regulating minimum prices are often passed in an attempt to protect the incomes of the sellers. The fixed price case shows that to maintain incomes of a group above a competitive level entry as well as prices must be controlled. It also demonstrates that free entry by itself is insufficient to ensure efficient allocation of economic resources.

REVIEW QUESTIONS

1. Explain the following concepts:
    Product differentiation
    Barrier pricing
    Minimum efficient size (MES)
    Barrier premium
    Chamberlin's large group case
2. What determines the size of the barrier premium in the Bain barrier-pricing model?
3. Does free entry guarantee efficiency in the allocation of resources? Discuss with reference to Chamberlin's large group case and to the fixed price-free entry case.
4. In the Bain model, what will be the effect of an increase in industry demand on
    (a) the equilibrium price?
    (b) the size of the barrier premium?
    (c) the number of firms in the industry?
    Do your answers depend on whether the elasticity of demand has also changed? Explain.
5. Do you think any of the models in this chapter are helpful in explaining the proliferation of gasoline service stations? If so, in what respect? If not, can you devise a more useful alternative model?

FURTHER READING

Bain, Joe S., *Barriers to New Competition.* Cambridge: Harvard University Press (1956).

Bishop, Robert L., "Monopolistic Competition and Welfare Economics," in Robert E. Kuenne, ed., *Monopolistic Competition Theory: Studies in Impact.* New York: Wiley (1967), chap. 12.

Chamberlin, E. H., *The Theory of Monopolistic Competition.* Cambridge: Harvard University Press (1st ed., 1933: 8th ed., 1962).

Chamberlin, E. H., *Towards a More General Theory of Value.* New York: Oxford University Press (1957).

Modigliani, Franco, "New Developments on the Oligopoly Front." *Journal of Political Economy* 66 (1958), 215–232.

14

OLIGOPOLISTIC BEHAVIOR IN THE SHORT RUN

THE STATE OF OLIGOPOLY THEORY

The long-run behavior of firms is easier to describe than is their short-run behavior. In the long-run, under conditions of monopoly or of perfect competition certainly, and even imperfectly competitive areas including oligopolies, the behavior of firms is dominated by real factors—production functions and preferences of individuals as represented through demand and supply functions—factors that are relatively sure. But in the short run, uncertainty prevails. An individual firm is often unsure how other firms will behave, and in particular how other firms will react to its own behavior.

Oligopolistic conditions exist when a firm anticipates the reaction of other firms to its own behavior, and modifies that behavior in accordance with its expectations of how other firms will react. In this it contrasts sharply with perfect competition and the large group case—in which no one firm had a significant effect on any other firm in the industry—and with monopoly—in which no other firm produces a similar product.

The mark of a good theory is its generality. The more a theory explains, the better it is. An ideal oligopoly theory would explain all or at least most oligopoly behavior. Unfortunately, no such theory exists. Oligopoly behavior depends on the *expectations* one firm has of other firms' behavior patterns.

So far, economists have found it difficult to generalize about these expectations. Instead, a group of theories has been developed, each based on a particular set of assumptions about the reaction patterns of firms.

Critics of the theories of oligopoly can argue that in the long run expectations will not be maintained if they are inconsistent with more fundamental underlying determinants of behavior such as production possibilities, consumer preferences, and the urge of firms to exploit any opportunity that offers profits above the competitive level. Expectations inconsistent with these factors can only exist in the short run; otherwise they are soon recognized as erroneous. Oligopoly theory then is seen as short-run theory, which gives way in the long run to less speculative theories.

The path toward a general solution to a problem often lies through the step-by-step solution of partial more tractable problems. If one can't solve the big one, one tries solving a smaller more restricted problem which, if solved, may help lead one to a solution of the larger problem. The smaller problems may not be intended as realistic or even important, except insofar as they assist in the solution of the more general problem. The results of the smaller problem are then not intended to be applied to policy areas. A study of them is more a study of the methods of economics and of economists than of actual behavior. Many oligopoly models are of this type.

A sampling of the many oligopoly theories found in the literature of economic theory is presented here. Some models are selected because of their importance in the history of economic analysis; others are selected because they promise a useful way of looking at oligopoly behavior and may help in understanding this important sector of the economy.

THE COURNOT DUOPOLY MODEL

Early oligopoly theories concentrated on homogeneous duopoly (that is, two sellers with identical products). Each seller has a price–output policy; each is concerned with how his rival will react to his policy. The earliest duopoly model was devised by Augustin Cournot in 1838. It is a simple model, but one upon which many oligopoly theorists still build variations, of which the Bain barrier-pricing model described in Chapter 13 is just one example.

Cournot made the following assumptions: (1) the two firms have zero costs (his example was a spring, the waters of which presumably had medicinal or at least invigorating properties); (2) the products of the two firms are homogeneous; (3) each seller sets a price on the expectation that his rival will not change his *output* in response to any move of the initiating firm. Given these assumptions and a market demand for the products of the two firms, a solution follows, which can perhaps best be understood by considering a sequence of actions by the two firms. For simplicity, assume the market demand curve for the product is linear. Under perfect competition, with zero marginal costs, quantity OQ_c of Figure 14.1 would be demanded at a competitive price of zero.

Figure 14.1 *Cournot Duopoly Theory*

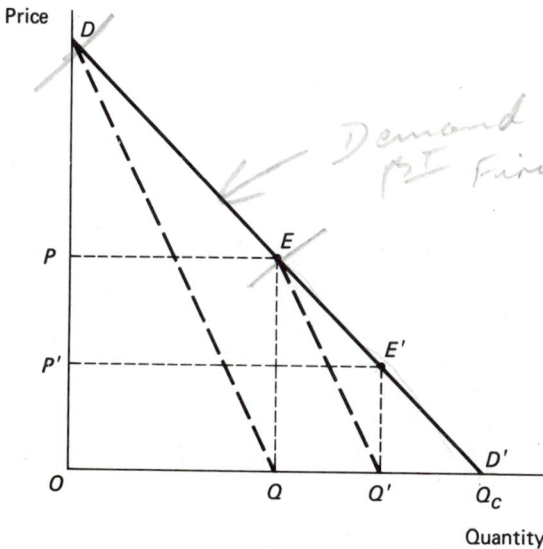

Begin by assuming that only one firm exists. It sets a profit-maximizing price. Since its marginal costs are zero, it maximizes profits by maximizing total revenues, setting a price such that marginal revenue is zero. With a linear demand curve, the profit maximizing output is OQ, which is half of the competitive output OQ_c.

A second firm enters. By assumption, the second firm (firm B) believes that firm A will continue to sell output OQ, no matter what firm B does. The residual demand curve for the product of the second firm is therefore the lower part of the industry demand curve, beyond point E. Its demand curve is then ED' (in relation to an origin at point Q). With zero marginal costs, firm B maximizes its profits by charging price OP', selling output QQ' which, in the linear demand case, represents 1/4 of the quantity that would be consumed at a competitive price of zero.

Firm A then reassesses its policy. With firm B now supplying 1/4 of the competitive market, the residual demand for the output of firm A, it believes, is the lower 3/4 of the industry demand curve. Firm A will maximize its profits by producing half of that amount. And so the process goes. Each firm in turn supplies 1/2 of the total market left to it after the other firm's output is subtracted from total industry demand.

The process of readjustment of outputs by the two firms can end only if each is supplying 1/3 of the total industry demand, which means each is supplying 1/2 of the market remaining after the other firm has supplied its 1/3 of the market. This represents a stable equilibrium for the industry.

The results can be generalized to any number of firms. Where n is the number of firms, and Q_c is the competitive output (OD' in Figure 14.1) the output of each firm in equilibrium will be $Q_c[1/(1 + n)]$, and the total industry output will be $Q_c[n/(1 + n)]$. Clearly, the more firms in the industry, the closer actual output will approach competitive output.

Similarly, equilibrium price approaches competitive price as the number of firms increases. Denoting P_m as the monopoly price and P_c as competitive price, the *excess* of equilibrium price over competitive price is $(P_m - P_c) 2/(1 + n)$. As n becomes very large, this premium becomes insignificant, and equilibrium price approaches competitive price. These numerical results apply only to the case of a linear demand curve, but the general principle—the more firms, the closer price and output are to competitive levels—remains valid for other cases.

As with many oligopoly models, the chief weakness of the Cournot duopoly theory is the implausibility of its assumptions. More specifically, it assumes that firms will persist in expectations that experience shows are incorrect. A further weakness is that no provision for entry of additional competitors is incorporated in the model.

THE BERTRAND–EDGEWORTH DUOPOLY MODEL

Joseph Bertrand developed a duopoly model in which each of two firms supplying a homogeneous product assumes that if it should change its price, its rival would continue to maintain its existing price. This is even less plausible than Cournot's assumption that the rival will maintain its existing output, for the results are much more drastic. Starting again with one firm setting a monopoly price, the second firm simply undercuts that price by a fraction, and thus takes the entire market away from the first firm. The first firm retaliates by undercutting the second firm, and so the process continues until a competitive price has been reached: the two firms charge the same price and share the market.

Francis Y. Edgeworth (he of the box diagram) modified the Bertrand model and made it more interesting and perhaps more realistic. Edgeworth pointed out that if the firms had limited productive capacity and could not completely satisfy the total market demand at a competitive price equal to marginal cost, a point would arrive in the process of successive undercutting of prices at which one firm would find it more profitable to *raise* its price, rather than lower it. This would occur at a price at which neither firm would have sufficient productive capacity to satisfy the entire competitive market.. Therefore, even if one firm charged a lower price than did the second, the first could not satisfy all willing buyers, some of whom would be forced to seek a supply from the second firm even if the second firm set a higher price. As the Bertrand process of successive undercutting of price continued, a point would be reached at which the responding firm could make more profits by *raising* price and not fully utilizing its capacity, than by undercutting its competitor and producing capacity output.

The Edgeworth story is not yet finished. For as soon as one firm finds it profitable to raise its price rather than lower it, the second firm will then find it profitable to raise its price to a level just under that of the first firm. This initiates another round of successive price cutting, which again continues until one firm finds it more profitable to raise its price. And so the process goes on: successive undercutting, followed by a price jump by one firm, which leads into yet another round of successive undercutting. No equilibrium exists.

Perhaps we should not be too hasty in discarding this theory with its indeterminacy and the apparently unrealistic behavior of the firms based on erroneous expectations retained even after they have been shown to be wrong. There is some similarity between the Edgeworth model and price wars in retailing, gasoline in particular. If one store claims to undersell any other by 5 percent, and the second says, "Nobody, but nobody, undersells us," the stage is set for Edgeworth-like behavior.

The analogy—and it is no more than an analogy—should not be overdone. But theory and practice suggest that for short periods of time firms do behave in a manner that can only result from erroneous expectations of competitors' reactions.

GAME THEORY

In 1944, John von Neumann and Oscar Morgenstern published the *Theory of Games and Economic Behavior,* which many economists hoped and expected would be the long awaited general theory of oligopoly.[1] While subsequent extensions of the theory continue to be interesting and provocative, the theory has not fulfilled these ambitious expectations. The theory is quite complex. We deal here only with an extremely simplified version. The theory is applicable to two or more firms, but only the so-called two-person game is determinate. When three or more persons are participating, the possibilities of side deals between any subgroup become enormous and the results are often indeterminate.

Games in the von Neumann–Morgenstern context include a wide variety of possible activities, each involving conflict—poker, military combat, business competition. A game is called a *zero-sum* game if one player's gains are another person's losses. In a *constant-sum* game, the sum of the gains or losses of the two participants is constant, whatever their behavior; any increase in the gains of one party is matched by a decline in the gains of the other. For purposes of exposition, any constant-sum game can be converted into a zero-sum game by subtracting the constant sum from the gains of each party. In a zero-sum game, then, the gains of one party must equal the losses of the other. Two-person constant- or zero-sum games always have a determinate solution; unfortunately the same is not true for variable-sum games.

A zero-sum game will be used to illustrate the theory. It may be assumed that the gains and losses shown are relative to some con-

Figure 14.2 *Game Theory*

B's strategies

A's strategies		B₁	B₂	B₃	Row minima (gains of A)
	A₁	0	-3	4	-3
	A₂	1*	5	3	← 1 A's maximin
	A₃	-1	7	-2	-2
Column maxima (losses of B)		↑ 1	7	4	

B's minimax

[1]John von Neumann and Oskar Morgenstern, *Theory of Games and Economic Behavior* (Princeton: Princeton University Press, 1944). Less demanding expositions of the theory are found in Leonid Hurwicz, "The Theory of Economic Behavior," *American Economic Review* 35 (1945), 909–925, and the entertaining account of John McDonald, *Strategy in Poker, Business and War* (New York: Norton, 1950).

stant sum of gains for the two parties. Only the numerical calculation will be affected by this transformation from a constant-sum to
a zero-sum game.

Assume a duopoly situation. Each firm has several possible
"strategies" it can follow (for example, pricing policies or output
policies). Each firm is assumed to know how much it would gain or
lose for each *combination* of strategies used by the two firms. But
neither firm knows which strategy the other firm will employ. Hence
the uncertainty.

The possible results of the game or rivalry can be summarized in
a "pay-off matrix." Assume that each firm has three possible
strategies available to it (for example, three output or price levels).
Identifying the firms as A and B, the matrix in Figure 14.2 shows the
gains firm A would receive for each combination of strategies by
A and B. Because this is a zero-sum game, any gains by firm A
are equal to the losses of firm B. No separate table of firm B's returns is necessary.

Consider firm A. Its returns can run a gain of $7 to a loss of $3.
If firm A chooses a strategy that gives it the highest average gain,
it would choose strategy A_2. But the crucial assumption made by
von Neumann and Morgenstern is that a firm expects the worst; it
chooses the strategy that gives it the greatest profit *when the other
firms pursues the strategy least favorable to the first firm.* If firm A
chooses strategy A_1, it could lose $3; with A_2, the worst it would do
is gain $1; with A_3, its worst would be a loss of $2. Firm A therefore chooses strategy A_2. The last column shows firm A's minimum
gains for each of its strategies; it chooses the greatest of these.
Firm A seeks the maximin: it maximizes its minimum gains.

Firm B, following comparable thinking, determines (as in the last
row of Figure 14.2) the worst it would do with each of its strategies
on the assumption that for each strategy it chooses, its competitor
firm A follows that strategy least favorable to firm B. With strategy
B_1 the worst firm B would do would be to lose $1. (Remember the
signs on the table should be reversed to show B's returns; when A
gains B loses, and vice versa). With B's strategy B_2, it could lose
$7; with B_3, it could lose $4. The last row of Figure 14.2 shows
these column maxima, the greatest amount B would lose by choosing each strategy. B is assumed to seek the minimax, which minimizes its maximum losses. B chooses strategy B_1 for which the
maximum loss, $1, is the least of the three maximum losses.

With firm A choosing its strategy A_2 and firm B choosing its
strategy B_1, the results are in the starred cell: A gains $1, and B
loses $1. This is an equilibrium.

But is it a stable equilibrium? When each firm sees how the other
is behaving, will it desire to change its strategy? The answer in

this case is no. A's best response to B's strategy B_1 is A_2, and B's best response to A_2 is B_1. Neither firm can improve on the situation. The result is thus stable.

This stability of the equilibrium will only result, however, under certain conditions. Specifically, the matrix of gains must have what is called a "saddle-point," a cell that is simultaneously the minimum of the column maxima and the maximum of the row minima. The starred box in Figure 14.2 satisfies this requirement.

Figure 14.3 ***Mixed Strategies***

		B's strategies		
		B_1	B_2	Row minima
A's strategies	A_1	1	4	1
	A_2	5	3*	← 3
Column maxima		5	↑ 4	

Consider, however, the results of Figure 14.3 where for added simplicity only two strategies are open to each firm. Firm A would choose strategy A_2, which guarantees it a gain of \$3. Firm B selects strategy B_2, which guarantees it will not lose more than \$4. This is a solution (the starred box), but it is not a saddle point. If both choose strategy 2, will either then want to change? The answer is yes. Firm A, seeing firm B choose its strategy B_2, will want to shift to strategy A_1, raising its gains from \$3 to \$4.

But if it does so, firm B would then want to shift its own strategy from B_2 to B_1 thus cutting its losses from \$4 to \$1. In response, firm A would want to shift back to its strategy A_2. So the process would continue, never reaching a stable equilibrium.

This result sounds like Edgeworth's, a continuous oscillating process. At this point, von Neumann and Morgenstern introduce the concept of *mixed strategies,* that is, the possibility that a firm will choose not one strategy, but a mixture of strategies, sometimes using one and sometimes another. But to prevent a competitor from observing and anticipating the variation in strategies, they are varied in a random way. (It is like poker; it is best to mix bluffing and nonbluffing, but in a way that the opponents cannot anticipate.)

When no saddle point exists, the problem for a firm is determining its optimum mix of strategies, that is, how often (what percent of the time) each strategy should be employed. The optimum mixed strategy will give a firm the same overall return *regardless* of what strategy or combination of strategies the competing firm employs.[2]

Von Neumann and Morgenstern proved that with mixed strategies a stable equilibrium will *always* exist.

They thus succeeded in building a model that avoids major weaknesses of many other oligopoly models—indeterminacy and instability. But the assumptions necessary to achieve their results are so restrictive that their model has not been widely accepted as a good description of oligopoly behavior. It has, however, inspired a huge volume of further research in the area.

PRICE INFLEXIBILITY

None of the models studied so far suggest why prices of goods should be stable or inflexible in the face of shifts in market conditions. Price flexibility is as characteristic of our oligopoly and monopoly models as it is of perfect competition. But in the popular literature and in Congressional hearings, monopolists, and oligopolists are commonly accused of fostering price stability, of "administering" their prices with subsequent enrichment of themselves at the expense of the public—both consumers and factors of production whose employment is said to take up the shock.

This section considers a well-known and rather controversial theory in which price inflexibility exists, after which some other conditions under which price inflexibility (1) might be possible, and (2) may be advantageous to producers, are considered less formally.

---

[2]To find its optimum mixed strategy in the two strategy situation, as in Figure 14.3, firm A seeks the percentage (p) of the time it should choose its strategy A_1. Then $(1 - p)$ is the percent of the time it should choose strategy A_2. Firm A chooses a (p) such that its gains are the same regardless of which strategy firm B uses.

Denote A's gains as $_AG_{ab}$, where (a) and (b) refer to the strategies employed by the two firms respectively. If B employs its first strategy, A's gains are $_AG_{b=1} = p(G_{11}) + (1 - p)(G_{21})$. If B employs its second strategy, A's gains are $_AG_{b=2} = p(G_{12}) + (1 - p)(G_{22})$. For A's optimum mixed strategy, $_AG_{b=1} = {_AG_{b=2}}$, that is, $p(G_{11}) + (1 - p)(G_{21}) = p(G_{12}) + (1 - p)(G_{22})$. Substituting the values of Figure 14.3, $p(1) + (1 - p)(5) = p(4) + (1 - p)(3)$.

Solving for (p) gives $p = .4$, which means that A should use its first strategy 40 percent of the time and its second strategy the remaining 60 percent of the time. A's gains will then be 3.4, no matter what strategy or mixture of strategies firm B employs.

The mathematical complexities arise when more than two strategies exist. But the basic conclusion will still stand: A two-person, zero-sum game will always have a stable equilibrium.

╷he Kinked Demand Curve [3]

The theory of the kinked demand curve describes an oligopolist who believes his competitors will match any price cut he makes, but will not follow him if he raises prices. The demand curve facing him, then, is essentially composed of two sections (see Figure 14.4).

Figure 14.4   *The Kinked Demand Curve*

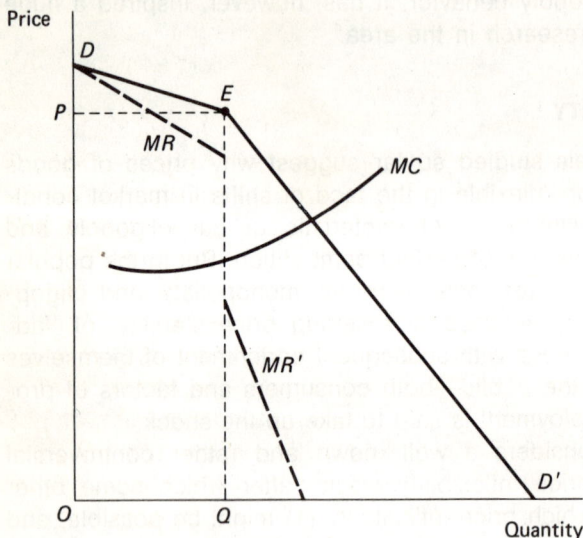

The upper segment (*DE*), for prices above the existing price *OP*, has considerable elasticity of demand, indicating the drop in demand for his product when he raises his price but his competitors maintain their existing price. His competitors follow his price decreases, however, and the lower section of his demand curve (*ED'*) simply reflects his share of the total industry market. The firm's marginal revenue curve is discontinuous, with a gap at the output at which the demand curve has the kink.

The firm's profit-maximizing price and output are then determined by its marginal cost and marginal revenue curves. If, as in the illustration, the marginal cost curve passes through the gap in the

[3]See Paul M. Sweezy, "Demand Under Conditions of Oligopoly," *Journal of Political Economy 48* (1939), 568–573, and George J. Stigler, "The Kinky Oligopoly Demand Curve and Rigid Prices," *Journal of Political Economy 55* (1947), 432–449. Both articles are reprinted in George J. Stigler and Kenneth E. Boulding, eds., *Readings in Price Theory* (Homewood, Ill.: Irwin, 1952).

marginal revenue curve, the profitable policy is simply to maintain existing price and output.[4]

Because the location of the kink is determined by the prevailing *price,* an increase in the demand for the firm's product has the effect of shifting the location of the kink to the right, at the same price level; the gap in the marginal revenue curve also shifts to the right. Should the firm's marginal cost curve continue to pass through the gap in the marginal revenue curve, the firm will expand output in response to the increase in demand, but will maintain its previous price.

Analogously, should the firm's cost function rise or fall, no change in price or output would be called for so long as the marginal cost curve remained within the gap in the marginal revenue curve. Thus the model "explains" price stability.

Variations on the theme are possible. For example, the size of the gap depends on the difference in slopes of the two sections of the demand curve. The slope of the upper segment depends on the degree of differentiation of the one firm's product, compared with that of other firms. The more differentiated its product is, the fewer customers it will lose when it raises its price and the steeper the slope of the upper segment. For perfectly homogeneous competing products, the upper segment of one firm's demand curve would be perfectly elastic, and it would lose all buyers by setting a price above that of its competitors.

The gap exists only in the minds of the seller. The important question here is whether an entrepreneur *believes* other firms will behave in the manner described. It is difficult to find empirical evidence of a state of mind; it is therefore difficult to refute or support the theory with empirical findings.

A major weakness of the theory is that at most it explains why prices do not change; it does not explain how the existing price originated. The theory thus may constitute an element in a theory of oligopoly, but it cannot be a complete theory.

The Desire to Maintain Inflexible Prices

There are perhaps two fundamental reasons why firms should wish to maintain stable prices. The more defensible is simply that

---

[4]Note that the rule that profits are maximized when marginal revenue equals marginal cost does not apply to discontinuous curves. It is replaced by the statement that for profits to be maximized at an output, marginal cost must exceed marginal revenue for increases in output, and marginal revenue must exceed marginal cost for smaller outputs. The awkwardness of this statement suggests one reason economists (and others) much prefer to work with continuous functions.

changing prices is costly, to buyers as well as sellers. Individuals and firms make their consumption and production plans on the basis of prices—existing and expected future prices. In a complex economy of millions of different goods—and even many thousands entering the plans of a single individual—changes in prices require recasting of plans. If a price is higher than expected the buyer is irritated and may change his plans; if it is lower than expected he has the pleasure of added consumer (or producer) surplus but still may change his plans to take advantage of the new situation. Changing plans involves costs of time and money. For the firm, a change in its price may involve significant expenses: new price lists, reeducating salesmen, repersuading buyers, and so on. In many cases these costs are not trivial. They are real costs. Price stability is, in fact, efficient if the gains from price flexibility are more than offset by these costs of change.

Price flexibility also adds to uncertainty, which for most individuals is undesirable. Individuals appear to prefer stable prices and stable incomes to fluctuating patterns of prices or incomes which are on the average the same as the stable levels. But it is difficult for individuals to express their desires for stability through the market.

Less justification exists for a second reason firms may wish to maintain stable prices: to avoid competition. Firms may compete in quality of product, service, and advertising, as well as in price. Nonprice competition is in fact easier and more comfortable than price competition. Prices are so obvious to buyers that it is often difficult for a firm to maintain a price differential on its competitors. Price agreement is then an effective way to reduce competitive pressures. The difficulty lies in achieving agreement among firms on the price to be charged. To avoid disagreements on price, the simplest method is simply to maintain the existing price—hence, price inflexibility.

Insofar as price inflexibility is based on a desire to avoid competition, its efficiency results are likely to be harmful. Not only is the price level likely to be higher than it otherwise would be, but the gains of flexibility in the allocation of resources will be lost. Price will not be fulfilling its allocative function efficiently.

The Power to Maintain Inflexible Prices

Stable prices will be maintained only by those firms *able* and *desirous* of doing so. When will firms be able to do so? Any firm can set any price it desires, of course, if it is willing to accept the consequences. The significant question, then, is when a firm can maintain prices without serious consequences. There are two obvious answers. First, a firm can do so if its product is significantly differentiated, that is, if its demand curve is not too elastic. Here is the monopoly influence. Monopolists do have a power over prices in this sense that competitive firms do not have. What of oligopolists? Here, product differentiation is also important. A firm may find itself with an adequate market and more than adequate profits by catering to special tastes, even though its price differs from those set by its closest competitors.

There is, however, yet another method by which an oligopolist may sometimes build inelasticity into his demand curve and hence avoid serious consequences of price changes. That is if he can persuade his competitors to follow his own price policy. *Price leadership* is such a situation. A firm's leading position may result simply from its size relative to the market (as shown in a price leadership model in the following section). Alternately, it may be based on fear of other firms of retaliation from the leader should they fail to play the role of faithful followers. The antitrust literature is full of such cases.

In sum, a firm may be able to maintain stable prices if (1) its product is significantly differentiated or (2) it can persuade other firms to follow its policy of price inflexibility.

PRICE LEADERSHIP

The analysis of oligopoly requires not only a theory of what price will be established, but also how the output of the industry will be distributed among the constituent firms. Many an oligopoly agreement (a cartel—domestic or international) has foundered on this problem. All firms want high prices, but they also want to sell large volumes, for their profits depend on outputs as well as on prices. An effort by one or more firms to increase volume by undercutting the industry price is common, and strict agreements allocating output among firms are difficult to arrive at and equally difficult and often illegal to enforce.

A price leadership model probably found more often in textbooks than in practice is illustrated in Figure 14.5. The theory describes what might be called a limiting case: The leader sets the price, but all other firms may sell all they wish to at this price. The problem: What price will the leader choose?

In practice, this case would be represented by an industry composed of one very large firm and a group of small firms; perhaps it should be called "monopoly with a competitive fringe."

The output policy of the small firms in the industry is strictly competitive. Given the price set by the leader, each small firm produces up to the point at which this price equals its marginal cost. The small firms thus have the standard competitive supply curves. In

Figure 14.5 *Price Leadership*

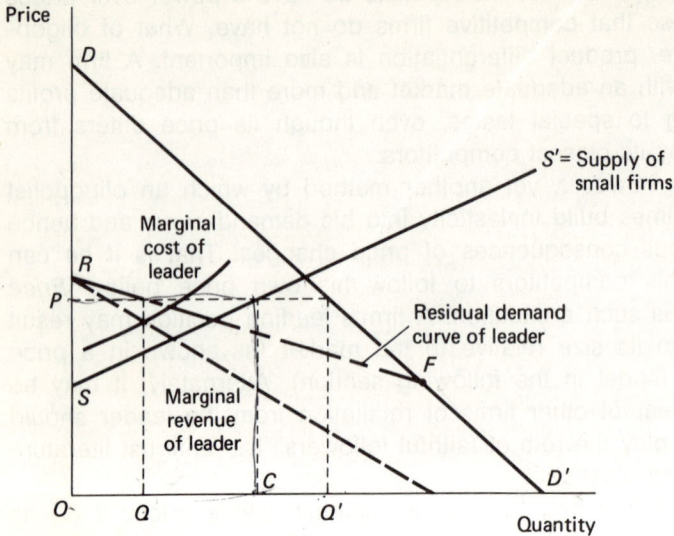

Figure 14.5, these supply functions of the small firms are aggregated into curve *SS'*, which is the industry supply curve excluding the supply of the dominant firm.

Curve *DD'* is the demand curve for the entire industry. The effective demand curve for the dominant firm is then found by subtracting from the industry demand curve, at each price, the amount which the small firms would be willing to supply at that price. The resultant residual demand curve for the product of the leading firm is labeled *RFD'* in Figure 14.5. It coincides with the industry demand curve to the right of point *F*, at prices so low that the competitive firms would be unwilling to supply any output. Note that at any price above *OR*, the small firms are more than willing to supply the entire industry demand, leaving no market for the dominant firm.

The dominant firm then chooses its profit-maximizing price at the intersection of its marginal cost curve and the marginal revenue curve derived from its residual demand curve. It sets price *OP*, supplying *OQ* of the good itself. The remainder of the industry demand at this price (*QQ'* = *OC*) is supplied by the smaller firms.

The result is not efficient. The output is less than the competitive output. In addition, too much of the output is supplied by the small firms, and too little by the dominant firm. The same industry output could be produced at lower cost by a shift in production from small to large firms, because at the margin of production the marginal cost of the small firms exceeds that of the large firm.

This price leadership model may have some applicability to the short run when the number of firms is given. It seems likely that in the long run entry of additional firms would erode the power of the price leader.

THE FUTURE OF OLIGOPOLY THEORY

The oligopoly models presented in this chapter are but a few of an incredibly large number that have been developed, so many and diverse that no adequate survey of the field has ever been published. Almost anyone can devise a new model simply by introducing a slight variation in the behavior patterns that firms are assumed to follow.

The critical problem is describing the behavior of individuals and firms under conditions of uncertainty. Until some major advance is made in explaining and predicting how people behave when their knowledge is incomplete and partially erroneous, oligopoly theory is likely to remain fragmented—a set of separate models crying out for a unifying framework.

REVIEW QUESTIONS

1. Explain the following concepts:
   Cournot's duopoly model
   The Bertrand duopoly model
   The Edgeworth duopoly model
   Duopoly
   Game theory
   Saddle point
   Zero-sum game
   Constant-sum game
   Maximin
   Minimax
   Mixed strategies
   Price inflexibility
   Kinked demand curve
   Price leadership
2. Develop an oligopoly model of your own: Specify the assumptions carefully and show the implications of those assumptions for the price and output behavior of the industry. (A suggestion: Begin with an existing model and vary its assumptions slightly.)
3. Which of the oligopoly models discussed in this chapter seems most useful? For what purposes? Can you suggest applications of the models?

FURTHER READING

Fellner, William, *Competition Among the Few.* New York: Knopf (1949).
Hurwicz, Leonid, "The Theory of Economic Behavior." *American Economic Review 35* (1945), 909–925.

Phelps, E. S., *et al.*, *Microeconomic Foundations of Employment and Inflation Theory.* New York: Norton (1970), especially pt. II.

Stigler, George J., "The Kinky Oligopoly Demand Curve and Rigid Prices." *Journal of Political Economy 55* (1947), 432–449.

Sweezy, Paul M., "Demand Under Conditions of Oligopoly." *Journal of Political Economy 47* (1939), 568–573.

5 INCOME DISTRIBUTION IN PRIVATE MARKETS

15

FACTOR PRICES AND MARGINAL PRODUCTIVITY

☐ marginal productivity
☐ the competitive case: demand for a single factor by a firm
☐ market equilibrium for a single factor
☐ the efficiency of the competitive factor equilibrium
☐ two or more variable inputs
☐ monopoly and monopsony in factor markets

The theory of the determination of the distribution of income in private markets is simply the theory of price applied to factors of production. It is straightforward supply-and-demand analysis, differing from the theory of product pricing chiefly in that business firms are basically sellers in product markets and buyers in factor markets. The sellers of the services of factors of production are typically individuals (workers, savers) and the supply of such services is determined by their personal preferences. Business firms, the demanders of these services, desire these inputs not for the utility they provide, but for their contribution to production and profit maximization. The theory of factor pricing is based on the supply theory of Chapter 4 and the production theory of Chapters 7 and 8.

For convenience in exposition, product and factor markets are unusually described separately. Actually, the equilibrium prices and quantities of products produced are determined simultaneously with the prices and quantities of factors employed. The connecting link is a production function, relating quantities of inputs to amounts of output.

The theory of the determination of factor prices is also generally applicable to intermediate goods and services purchased by business firms from other firms. As with the original factors of production hired from individuals, these intermediate goods are demanded for their productivity, not their utility. The supply of these goods is based on the cost functions of the supplying firms, whereas the supply of original factors like labor is based on individual preferences.

In this chapter the general theory of factor price determination for both competitive and noncompetitive markets is presented. The following chapter considers some characteristics of particular types of factors.

MARGINAL PRODUCTIVITY

The *marginal revenue product* (*MRP*) of a factor of production is the change in the total revenue of a firm when one additional unit of that factor is employed. *Marginal factor cost* (*MFC*) is the increase in a firm's total costs when one extra unit of the factor is used. These two terms should be carefully distinguished from marginal cost and marginal revenue. Marginal revenue product and marginal factor cost refer to the effects of a one-unit change in the *factor* employed; marginal revenue and marginal cost are the changes when one additional unit of the *product* is produced. Thus,

$$\text{Marginal revenue product} = \frac{\Delta R}{\Delta F} \qquad \text{Marginal revenue} = \frac{\Delta R}{\Delta Q}$$

$$\text{Marginal factor cost} = \frac{\Delta C}{\Delta F} \qquad \text{Marginal cost} = \frac{\Delta C}{\Delta Q}$$

(where R = revenue, C = cost, Q = output, and F = quantity of factor).

A firm will maximize profits by employing each factor up to the point at which the factor's marginal revenue product equals marginal factor cost. This rule is exactly equivalent to the familiar principle that firms maximize profits by producing up to the point at which marginal revenue equals marginal cost.

That equivalence is shown by the following transformation of MR = MC into MRP = MFC: Marginal revenue equals marginal cost or

$$\frac{\Delta R}{\Delta Q} = \frac{\Delta C}{\Delta Q} \tag{1}$$

By definition, the marginal physical product of a factor (*MPP*) equals $\Delta Q/\Delta F$. If both sides of equation (1) are multiplied by MPP we have

$$\frac{\Delta R}{\Delta Q} \cdot \frac{\Delta Q}{\Delta F} = \frac{\Delta C}{\Delta Q} \cdot \frac{\Delta Q}{\Delta F} \tag{2}$$

Thus,

$$\frac{\Delta R}{\Delta F} = \frac{\Delta C}{\Delta F} \tag{3}$$

or *MRP* equals *MFC*.

Note further that, as equations (2) and (3) clearly show, marginal revenue product equals marginal revenue times the marginal physical product of the factor.

These relationships hold in both competitive and noncompetitive markets. Our analysis of the determination of the equilibrium price of a factor and the quantity of the factor employed will begin with the competitive case.

The presence or absence of competition affects factor markets in three distinct ways.

First, the factor may be *supplied* under competitive or noncompetitive conditions. If a factor is supplied competitively, individual suppliers are price-takers and cannot affect the price. Each supplier will then offer that quantity of factor services at which the prevailing market price of the factor is equal to his marginal supply price, the price at which he is just willing to supply the last unit. The marginal supply price for a worker, for example, will be the monetary equivalent of the marginal disutility of the last unit of labor supplied. When the factor of production being supplied is an intermediate good produced by competitive firms, the marginal supply price will be the marginal cost of producing the good.

The factor supply curve of the individual and also the aggregate supply curve of all individuals and firms supplying the factor will under these competitive conditions show the marginal real cost of supply.

The *demand* for a factor may be competitive in either of two senses. First, the firms employing the factor may compete in their demands for it, with each employer acting as a price-taker with respect to the factor. The equilibrium price of the factor will not be affected by changes in the amount of the factor employed by any individual firm.

In the corresponding noncompetitive case, an individual employer has some monopsonistic influence; the price he pays for a factor will be affected by changes in the quantity he employs.

Second, the firms demanding the services of a factor may produce products which they sell in competitive or noncompetitive markets. Their demand for the factor will of course be influenced by the nature of the demand for their products.

In factor analysis, therefore, one must specify whether or not competition exists in each of three ways: Is the factor supplied competitively? Do the employing firms buy competitively? Do the employing firms sell their products competitively?

The analysis begins with the case in which competition prevails in all three ways.

THE COMPETITIVE CASE: DEMAND FOR A
SINGLE FACTOR BY A FIRM

In the competitive case, demand for a single factor comes from a group of firms that hire the factor and sell products competitively. The market is the factor market, not a product market. Demand comes from all firms using a particular type of factor (for example, typists). The firms employing a particular type of factor may be in many different product industries.

In the simplest possible case, consider a perfectly competitive firm in the short run that is able to vary the quantity of only one factor (call it labor). The analysis applies to any and all factors; labor is simply used for illustrative purposes. For the moment, all other factors are assumed fixed.

The firm's production function gives the relationship between quantities of labor employed and the physical output of the firm, which can be represented with total, average, and marginal physical product curves.[1]

For the firm selling in a perfectly competitive market, the physical product curves can easily be transformed into total, average, and marginal value curves. For this competitive firm, the price of its product is constant no matter how much it produces, and marginal revenue equals the price of the product. The physical product curves are therefore simply multiplied by the product price in order to convert them to curves showing the total revenue, the average value of the product per unit of the variable factor employed, and the important value of the marginal product curve. The last shows the market value of the marginal physical product produced when one additional unit of the factor is employed.

The relationship between the value of the marginal product (VMP) and the marginal revenue product (MRP) should be carefully noted.

Value of the marginal product equals the marginal physical product of a factor multiplied by the price of the product: $VMP = MPP \times P_p$ (where MPP is marginal physical product, and P_p is the price of the product, to be distinguished from the price of the factor P_f). Value of the marginal product is the value buyers place

[1]See Chapter 8.

on the additional output resulting from a one unit increase in the amount of the factor employed.

Marginal revenue product, on the other hand, equals marginal physical product times the firm's marginal revenue: $MRP = MPP \times MR$. MRP is the change in the revenues of the firm from selling the marginal physical product of the factor.

MRP will equal VMP if and only if the price of the product equals marginal revenue so that with each term MPP is multiplied by the same figure. This is a characteristic of perfect competition. If the firm employing the factor sells its product in a noncompetitive market, the MRP of a factor will be less than its VMP.

A divergence between MRP and VMP has, as noted below, important efficiency implications. For profit-maximizing behavior in the factor market, the firm compares the cost of a factor with its MRP, the additional revenues the firm receives. Efficiency, on the other hand, depends on a comparison of the cost of the factor with the VMP (that is, the value of the marginal product to its buyers). Efficiency is not likely to be achieved, therefore, unless VMP equals MRP.

The competitive firm's average product and value of the marginal product curves are illustrated in Figure 15.1. The competitive firm maximizes its profits by employing the factor up to the point at which the marginal factor cost equals the value of the marginal product of the factor. When the factor market is competitive, the marginal factor cost is simply the price of the factor. Using labor as the example, the firm then hires workers up to the point at which the prevailing wage rate equals the firm's value of the marginal product of the factor subject to the qualification that if the wage rate exceeds the maximum average value of product per worker, the firm will not hire any workers.

Figure 15.1 *Factor Demand of the Competitive Firm*

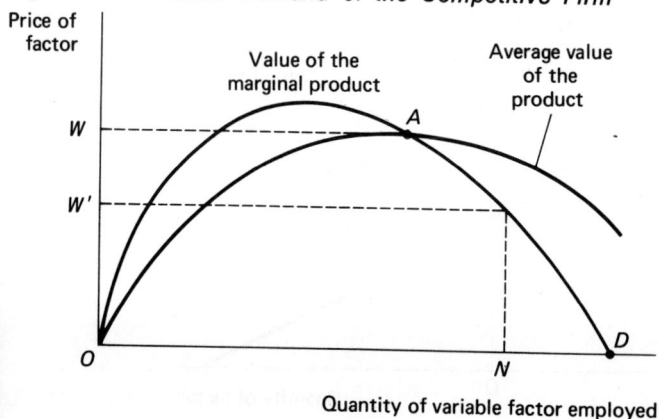

Quantity of variable factor employed

The firm's value of the marginal product curve below its intersection with the average product curve thus constitutes the firm's demand curve for the factor under competitive conditions.

For example, if the price of labor is OW' per worker, the firm will hire ON workers. Beyond that point, the added cost of a worker exceeds his contribution to the firm's revenues. If the firm hires fewer than ON workers it is not maximizing profits, for to the left of that point the added revenue exceeds the cost of a worker.

At any wage rate above OW, however, the firm would not hire any workers, for its wage costs would exceed the total value of its output.

It is clear, therefore, that the value of the marginal product curve, from point A to point D, constitutes the demand curve of the firm for this factor.

MARKET EQUILIBRIUM FOR A SINGLE FACTOR

Just as the supply curves of competitive firms are added to find the market supply curve, so the demand curves of individual firms for any particular factor of production are aggregated to form the market demand curve for the input.

To this market demand curve for the factor is added the market supply curve of the factor derived (as in Chapter 4) by aggregating the supply functions of individual units of the factor. Competitive factor market equilibrium is then determined at the wage rate and level of employment at which market demand equals market supply, as illustrated in Figure 15.2.

Figure 15.2 *Equilibrium Price and Employment for a Factor*

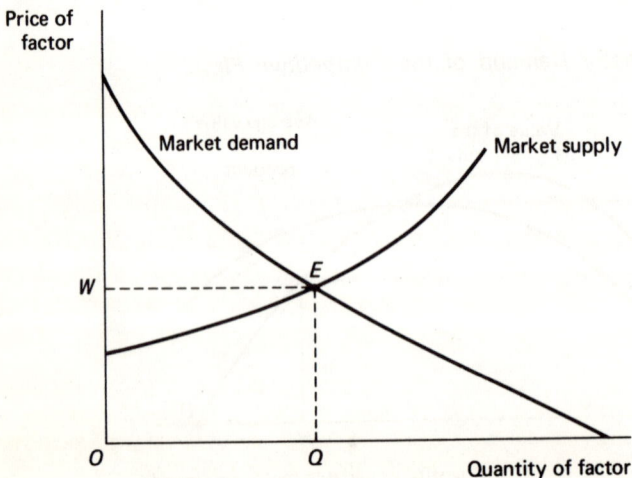

The equilibrium levels of factor price and employment are thus determined essentially by three factors: the willingness of individuals to supply factor services, the physical productivity of the factors, and the demands and hence prices of the goods produced with the use of this factor.

Note that in this competitive case the wage rate is equal to the value of the marginal product of this factor in each of its uses among all the firms employing the factor, for each firm is hiring the factor up to the point at which the factor's price (which is the same to all employing firms) equals the value of the marginal product of that factor in that firm.

THE EFFICIENCY OF THE COMPETITIVE FACTOR EQUILIBRIUM

Three aspects of the efficiency of this competitive factor equilibrium can be noted (continuing to use labor as the illustrative example). First, because the value of the marginal product of this factor is the same in all its uses, no reallocation of this factor among different firms can increase the total value of the product produced by these firms. A requirement for efficiency in the allocation of a resource is that the value of the marginal product of the resource be equal wherever that factor is used, a condition satisfied in the present competitive case.

Second, the value of the marginal product of each worker equals the wage rate and therefore equals the worker's marginal rate of substitution between effort and leisure. If, for example, the equilibrium wage rate is $5, each worker supplies effort up to the point at which the disutility of an extra hour of work is just worth $5, which is also the amount that hour adds to the value of the output produced by the worker. If less effort were supplied, inefficiency would result because the extra value of the product that would result from an added hour of labor would exceed the real cost of the extra effort to the worker. Conversely, if more effort than the equilibrium quantity were supplied, the real cost of the extra effort to the worker (measured in money terms) would exceed the value of the additional product produced.[2]

Third, because all workers of a given type in a particular market receive the same wage rate, the marginal rate of substitution between money and effort is the same for all. No reallocation of the existing amount of effort among workers would raise efficiency. That is, no worker would be willing or able to hire another worker at the

---

[2]In practice, standard work days limit the ability of the worker to vary his hours of work. There is probably a kink in the demand curve for an individual worker at, say, eight hours a day. In this situation it would be preferable to define the services of the factor in terms of days of effort, rather than hours.

existing wage rate to take over some of his work. This also is a requirement for efficiency.

TWO OR MORE VARIABLE INPUTS

In practice, firms can vary quantities of more than one input. How does this affect the theory of the competitive determination of factor prices?

Assume a firm with two variable factors (for example, labor and equipment), where the price of equipment remains constant. The firm's marginal physical product schedule for labor will shift depending on how much equipment is used with the labor. Given the price of the firm's output, a curve of the marginal revenue product of labor can be determined corresponding to each of the schedules of the marginal physical product of labor. The relevant portions of these marginal revenue product curves constitute the demand of the firm for labor, each of which assumes a particular quantity of equipment is being employed with the labor. A group of such firm demand curves for labor is shown in Figure 15.3. For each curve, the quantity of equipment (E) employed is also indicated.

Figure 15.3   _Factor Pricing with Two-variable Inputs_

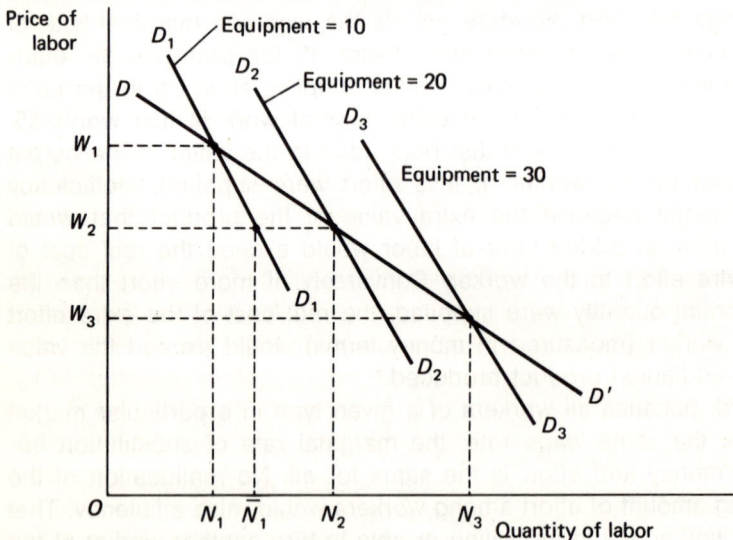

Figure 15.3 illustrates the case in which labor and equipment are assumed to be complementary factors in production. For complementary factors, an increase in the quantity of one employed raises

the productivity of the other. (For substitute factors, an increase in the quantity of the first lowers the productivity of the second.)

Assume that if the price of labor is OW_1, the optimum (that is, profit maximizing) quantity of equipment to utilize (given its price and its productivity) is 10. Labor demand curve D_1D_1 is therefore relevant, and the firm would hire ON_1 workers. If the wage rate dropped to OW_2 and the firm did not change the quantity of equipment, the firm's demand for labor would rise to $\overline{ON_1}$. But the firm finds it profitable to provide more equipment for the added labor and increases the quantity of equipment to 20. This increase in equipment raises the productivity of labor and shifts the firm's demand curve of labor to the right, to the curve labeled D_2D_2. The firm then hires ON_2 workers at the wage rate of OW_2.

The same process of changing the quantity of equipment, inducing shifts in the demand curve for labor, would result from other changes in the wage rate. The firm's demand curve for labor, in this case where the quantities of two factors are variable, is thus indicated by points on successive marginal product curves, curve DD' in Figure 15.3.

The effect here of varying the quantity of equipment optimally as the wage rate changes is to make the demand for labor more elastic. As a general but not universal principle, the longer the period for adjustment, and the more variable factors there are, the more elastic will be the demand curve for any single input. This is simply a further application of the general principle that demand and supply functions are more elastic in the long run than in the short run.

No matter how many factors are variable, in competitive equilibrium the price of each factor will be equal to the value of the marginal product of the factor, and all the earlier comments about the efficiency of the competitive determination of input prices would continue to hold.

The analysis can be extended to many factors, with complex relationships of substitution and complementarity. The net results do not differ significantly from those above: Under competitive conditions, the prices of variable factors are equal in equilibrium to the value of the marginal product of the factor.

MONOPOLY AND MONOPSONY IN FACTOR MARKETS

The competitive results of the previous sections must be modified if elements of monopoly or monopsony exist in the factor or product markets. The buyer of the factor services may be a monopolist in selling his output, the supplier of the factor services may be a monopolist, and the buyer of factor services may be a monopsonist.

Demand for Factors by a Monopolist

Consider the determination of the equilibrium price and quantity of employment for a factor sold in a competitive factor market to firms which sell their products in noncompetitive markets. A firm that has a monopoly in the sale of its output must lower its price to sell added production. It will naturally take this into account in purchasing inputs. The physical marginal productivity schedule of such a firm will have basically the same nature as that of a competitive firm. But unlike the competitive firm, the monopoly will not hire a factor up to the point at which the factor's price equals the value of its marginal product. If the selling firm is a monopoly, offering for sale the increased product resulting from added employment of a factor will require the firm to reduce the price of its product. The added return to the firm from hiring one additional unit of the factor is less than the value of the marginal product of the factor by the drop in revenues caused by reducing the price on the previous volume of output sold. The net addition to the revenues of the firm when an additional unit of factor is employed is the *marginal revenue product,* and equals *MPP* $\times$ *MR*. For the firm selling in competitive markets, the price of the product equals the firm's marginal revenue, and therefore the marginal revenue product equals the value of the marginal product. The two schedules are the same. For the monopoly firm, however, marginal revenue is less than product price; its marginal revenue product is therefore less than its value of the marginal product. The monopoly's demand curve for a factor is derived from its schedule of the marginal revenue product. The firm hires a factor up to the point at which the price of the factor equals the factor's *MRP.*

For any given schedule of the marginal physical product of a factor, the monopolist will hire fewer factors than a comparable competitive industry. The monopolist hires to the point at which $P_F = MPP \times MR;$ the competitive industry to the point at which $P_F = MPP \times P_p$. Since P_p (price of the product) will exceed the monopolist's *MR* (marginal revenue), the monopolist stops short of the competitive employment level.

The monopolist thus hires fewer factors than does a comparable competitive industry. This is simply a restatement of an earlier conclusion: A monopolist produces less (and hence hires fewer factors) than does the perfectly competitive firm and industry with comparable cost and demand functions.

As noted in Chapter 11, this results in economic inefficiency. For efficiency, a factor should be hired to the point at which its marginal supply price (which, for labor, is a money measure of the disutility of effort and in general measures the opportunity cost of the factor in alternative uses) is just equal to the added value of the product produced with the use of this factor. The monopoly firm stops short of this point because its marginal revenue is less than the value of the product to the buyer.

Factor Supplied by a Monopolist

If the supplier of a factor of production is a monopolist, the usual monopoly analysis of Chapter 11 applies. The case is illustrated in Figure 15.4 where DD' is the demand for the factor and CC' represents the marginal cost or marginal supply price of the factor.

Figure 15.4 *Monopolistic Supplier of a Factor*

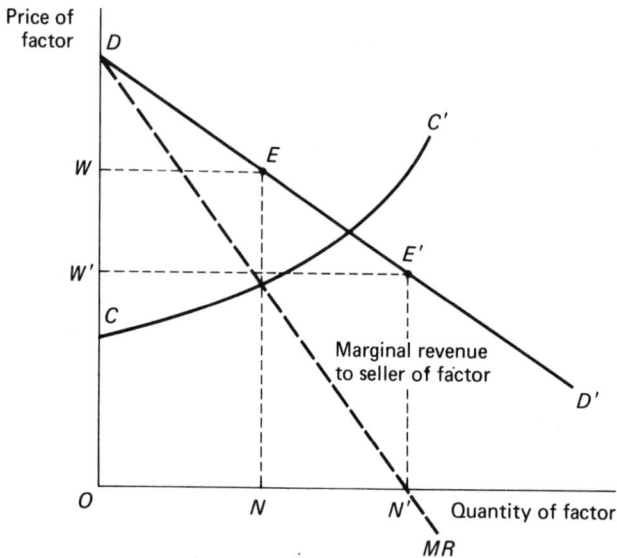

The curve D–MR is marginal to the demand curve, and measures the marginal return to the seller of the factor as additional supplies are offered. The seller maximizes the excess of his returns over the real cost of supply by restricting supply to ON, which results in a factor price of OW. The result is not efficient, for the standard monopoly reasons.

This case might be applied to a labor union. The difficulty lies in determining what a union attempts to maximize. A union which wished to maximize total wages received by its members, for example, would set a wage rate OW' with employment ON', at which point the marginal revenue to members of the union is zero and total wages are maximized. Or one could perhaps conceive of a union's preference map relating the wage rate to the level of employment. If such a map were overlaid on Figure 15.4, the opportunity line facing the union would be represented by the demand curve *DD'* for labor. The union would then choose the wage rate and level of employment indicated by the point of tangency between the demand curve and a union indifference curve.

Many other variations are possible.[3]

A Monopsonist Buying Competitively Supplied Factors

The monopsonist, a single buyer of a factor or other input, knows his purchases will affect the price of the input and acts accordingly. Given his *MRP* curve[4] of Figure 15.5 and the competitive supply

Figure 15.5   *Monopsonistic Buyer of a Factor*

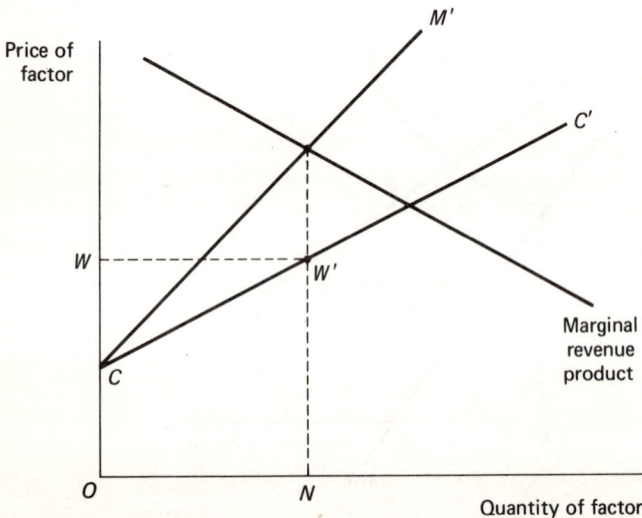

curve of the input, curve *CC'*, the marginal factor cost to the buyer of an additional unit of the factor is represented by curve *CM'*, which is marginal to curve *CC'*. When this buyer employs additional units of the input, not only must he pay a higher price for the added factors; he must also pay the new higher price to all other units of

[3]See, for example, Allan M. Cartter, *Theory of Wages and Employment* (Homewood, Ill.: Irwin, 1959), chaps. 7–8.

[4]If the monopsonist sells his product in a competitive market, his **MRP** curve will also constitute a curve of the value of the marginal product.

the factor employed. This raises the marginal factor cost to the buyer above the factor supply curve.[5]

The monopsonist hires factors up to the point at which marginal factor cost (curve *CM'*) equals the marginal value to him of the factors (as shown by his *MRP* curve). He employs *ON* units of the factor. For this quantity he must pay a price of only *OW* (= *NW'*), which is the price at which this quantity would be supplied.

Again, the existence of an imperfect market restricts the employment of a factor and hence the supply of the good produced by this factor below the efficient level.

Bilateral Monopoly

When a single buyer meets a single seller, bilateral monopoly results. As the theory of exchange of Chapter 5 suggested, several different results are possible, depending on the relative strengths and behavior patterns of buyer and seller. Some possibilities are sketched in Figure 15.6.

Figure 15.6 *Bilateral Monopoly*

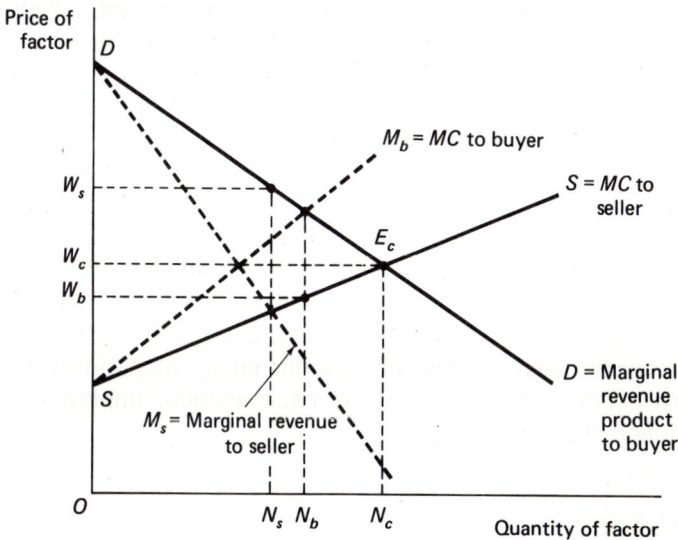

For reference, note that the competitive equilibrium would be at point E_c, with ON_c units of the factor employed, at a price of OW_c.

[5]The *CC'* and *CM'* curves should be carefully distinguished. The *CC'* curve measures the marginal cost to the *supplier* of supplying further units of the factor; the *CM'* curve is the marginal factor cost to the *buyer* of employing extra units of the factor.

If the buyer is the price-maker, he would set price OW_b, hiring ON_b units; if the seller is the price-maker, the price would be OW_s, and employment ON_s; these are the results discussed in the preceding sections. These two prices set limits to the range within which the factor prices will fall if neither buyer nor seller can discriminate. Employment will be at least as large as the smaller of these two figures (in the case illustrated, it will be at least ON_s) and will not exceed the competitive level, ON_c.

The employment level would be ON_c if either the buyer or the seller discriminated perfectly in setting prices. With a perfectly discriminating buyer, offering for each unit of the factor the minimum price at which that unit would be supplied, prices for the factor would range from a low of OS to a high of the competitive price OW_c. The perfectly discriminating seller would charge for each unit of the factor supplied the maximum price the buyer would pay for it; prices would range from a high of OD to a low equal to the competitive price OW_c. In both of these cases ON_c units of the factor would be sold (that is, the competitive level of employment). The joint surplus, area SDE_c, will be completely appropriated by the stronger party.

Joint surpluses (or profits) are maximized at employment level ON_c. If the buyer and seller combine in an effort to maximize their combined surplus, they will seek that employment level. Such joint efforts are rather likely to founder on disagreements over the division of the spoils. The area SDE_c represents the surplus available to the two transactors, but how is it to be divided? The two parties will not accept the competitive division of the surplus (that is, with a factor price of OW_c), for the stronger of the two could increase his gains by enforcing a monopoly (or monopsony) price level.

As seen in Chapter 5, the competitive solution and the perfectly discriminating solutions are all efficient points. They differ in the distribution of gains, and hence will be judged unequal in terms of equity. The equilibrium of the nondiscriminating monopolist or monopsonist is not an efficient solution; each restricts employment below the efficient level.

REVIEW QUESTIONS

1. Explain the following concepts:
   Marginal revenue product (MRP)
   Marginal factor cost (MFC)
   Value of the marginal product (VMP)
   Monopsony
   Marginal physical product (MPP)
   Bilateral monopoly

2. Is bilateral monopoly a zero-sum game? Explain.
3. Why is it that virtually all forms of market imperfection appear to lead to output *below* the efficient level?
4. Demonstrate that perfect price discrimination by either a monopsonist or a monopolist selling the services of a factor of production promotes economic efficiency.
5. Discuss the factors which determine or influence the marginal productivity of an individual. How many of these factors are subject to the control of the individual himself? To what extent can an individual influence his own marginal productivity?
6. Discuss the equity of distributing incomes according to the marginal productivity of factors of production.

FURTHER READING

American Economic Association, *Readings in the Theory of Income Distribution.* New York: McGraw-Hill–Blakiston (1949).

Cartter, Allan M., *Theory of Wages and Employment.* Homewood, Ill.: Irwin (1959).

Hicks, J. R., *The Theory of Wages.* 2nd ed., London: Macmillan (1963).

Phelps, E. S., *et al., Microeconomic Foundations of Employment and Inflation Theory.* New York: Norton (1970), esp. pt. I.

Stigler, George J., *Production and Distribution Theories.* New York: Macmillan (1941).

16

TOPICS IN FACTOR PRICE THEORY

The theory of factor prices of Chapter 15 is completely general and can be used to explain the determination of the prices of all factors—labor, capital, and land of all types. In this chapter a few selected aspects of factor pricing are discussed.

EULER'S THEOREM

If each and every factor of production is paid a price equal to the value of its marginal product, will the total value of the product produced be sufficient to pay all the factors? The basic principle here is Euler's Theorem, which states that if the production function is linear and homogeneous, that is, if there are constant returns to scale, the sum of the values of the marginal products will exactly add up to the total value of the product. Thus, for the production function $Q = f(L, C, N)$ with constant returns to scale

$$Q = L \cdot MP_L + C \cdot MP_C + N \cdot MP_N$$

If returns to scale are increasing, the total value of the product is less than the sum of the marginal products; with decreasing returns to scale, the reverse is true.

Applications of this principle have been seen in previous chapters. In long-run equilibrium the perfectly competitive firm will be operating at the minimum point of its average total cost curve. Up to this point, the firm has increasing returns; beyond it returns are decreasing. At this minimum point where the firm shifts from increasing to decreasing returns, the firm's returns to scale are constant, and Euler's theorem applies. The firm producing at this point in long-run competitive equilibrium will be paying all factors the value of their marginal products, including the payment of normal profits on the capital invested (which equals the value of the marginal product of capital). The firm's income (revenue) exactly equals its expenses.

The competitive firm operating under decreasing returns (that is, to the right of its minimum *ATC,* with a price of the product in excess of average total cost) receives profits in excess of normal. This indicates that total income is more than enough to pay all factors the value of their marginal products; the excess income goes to the residual claimants, the owners, as excess profits. Conversely, the competitive firm operating to the left of its minimum *ATC* with a product price below average cost (for example, in the short run, when demand has declined below the expected level) is earning less than normal profits. Total revenues are insufficient to pay all factors the value of their marginal products; the residual claimants—the owners—receive less than the value of the marginal product of their capital.

Under conditions of monopoly or monopolistic competition, firms quite commonly make normal profits or better, even while producing under conditions of increasing returns. This does not mean that Euler's Theorem has failed. As explained in Chapter 15, in this situation the factors of production used by the firm are receiving less than the value of their marginal products.

Prices of factors equal their marginal revenue products, which are less than the value of marginal products of factors employed by firms that sell their output in noncompetitive markets. In these cases, the residual claimants (suppliers of capital) may be getting more or less than their marginal revenue products, depending on whether profits are above or below the normal profit level.

Paying factors less than the value of their marginal products is sometimes termed "exploitation."[1] Whether it is or not depends on how one defines the word. The point to note here is simply that, where production is carried on under increasing returns, it is possible that *all* factors are being paid less than the value of their marginal products, for total revenue is not sufficient to make the full payment to all factors.

[1] See in particular Joan Robinson, *Economics of Imperfect Competition* (London: Macmillan, 1933), book ix.

RENTS—ON LAND AND OTHERWISE

Four concepts of rent can be distinguished:

(1) Rent is payment for the use of property, particularly housing, and commercial space. Here the rent includes not simply payment for land, but often for capital (the building and furnishings) and labor services (janitors, repairmen, and so on). This definition of rent is most common in practice but is least useful in economics, because it may include so many different types of factor payments.

(2) Rent may be the payment for the use of land. In this context it is analogous to the categories of wages and salaries paid labor, and the interest or profits paid for the use of capital.

(3) *Economic rent* is defined as any payment to a factor of production in the long run in excess of the amount needed to keep a factor in its current use. Rent is a factor surplus analogous to consumer surplus. It does not constitute a real cost of using a factor. Real cost is the value of a factor in its next best use. Payments of economic rent are the excess of the money cost of a factor over this real opportunity cost.

A factor will receive economic rent only if the supply of the factor is not perfectly elastic.

(4) Quasi-rent is similar to economic rent but with this difference: quasi-rent is a short-run payment in excess of its supply price to a factor the supply of which in the short run (but not in the long run) is less than perfectly elastic.

For example, all revenues to a firm in the short run in excess of total variable costs constitute quasi-rent on the firm's fixed factors of production, the short-run supply price of which is zero.

Both economic rent and quasi-rent are due to the inelasticity of the supply of factors; the former refers to long-run inelasticity, the latter to short-run inelasticity of supply.

Economic rent is most obvious in the payments to land, the quantity of which is (with a few trivial exceptions) absolutely fixed in the long run. Taking land as a whole, assume the supply is perfectly inelastic, as in Figure 16.1, indicating that no alternative use for land exists, and that the owners of the land would be willing to supply it at any price.[2] Given the demand for the services of land, as indicated by *DD*, under competitive conditions the price or rent per unit of land will be *OR*. Total receipts of land owners are *OREQ*, *all of which* in this case *constitutes economic rent.*

---

[2]This extreme case of a perfectly inelastic supply of land requires that the owners have no uses of their own to which they wish to put the land, and use of the land in the current period does not affect its future usefulness.

Figure 16.1   *Economic Rent on Land*

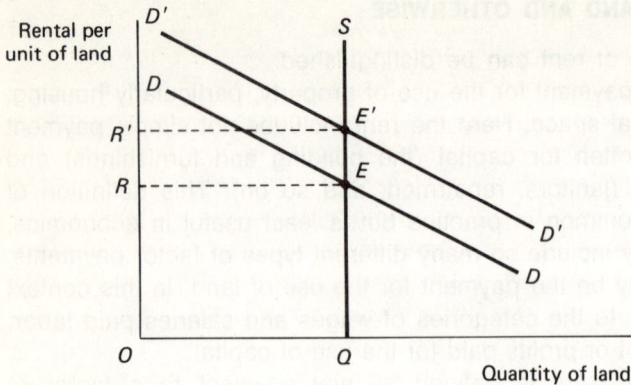

An increase in the demand for land, arising for example from an increase in population, raises the demand curve to *D'D'*. The quantity supplied remains the same, but when the price rises to *OR'* total receipts of land owners and their economic rent rise to *OR'E'Q*.

HENRY GEORGE AND THE SINGLE TAX

Given the competitive assumptions we are using, these results are efficient. The higher price serves to allocate the available supply of land to those uses in which its productivity is greatest. But is it fair? Henry George, an influential American writer of the late nineteenth century, thought not.[3] He argued that the increases in land values and rents were not due to the efforts of the landowners, but to social causes. The landowners therefore did not deserve the rents. These returns, he argued, should be appropriated by those responsible for them, namely the general public. George therefore proposed a *Single Tax* on land values, one which would not affect the rents paid for the use of land but would tax away the gains received by land owners. George believed that this single tax on land would be sufficient to finance all government services, and that all other taxes could be eliminated, thus freeing business activity from their restrictive influences.

George's notions were widely popular and remain so in some quarters today. The Single Tax movement lives on, for example, in the Henry George Institute in New York, where the basic textbook is George's *Progress and Poverty*.[4] The British Fabian Society and Labour Party were strongly influenced by George.

[3]Henry George, *Progress and Poverty* (London: Routledge & Kegan Paul, 1906).

[4]George believed that poverty continued in spite of obvious economic progress, because the gains were appropriated by landowners.

His arguments are in principle rather attractive. The property tax upon which local governments place such reliance, is in part a tax on land. But George would not approve of a tax on buildings or other property other than land, essentially because it would discourage building and lead to inefficiency in the allocation of resources. In operation, the property tax is more a tax of expediency than of principle.

Objections to George's specific proposals include the following:

(1) It is difficult in practice to determine the appropriate tax for individual pieces of land, and the process can easily lead to political maneuvering and abuse.

(2) A single tax on land would surely not be sufficient to finance the present level of government operations.

(3) Land is not the only factor of production to receive economic rents. Any type of factor may receive it, if the supply of that factor is less than perfectly elastic. (Note the salaries in the entertainment world.) On grounds of equity (which is the chief basis for his program), should not these other forms of economic rent also be taxed?

RENT AND DIFFERENTIAL RETURNS

Whenever the supplies of a factor are not homogeneous (for example, lands of different fertilities or at different distances from markets) rent may arise in stages. At first, so long as there are abundant supplies of homogeneous land of the best quality, no rents will exist. All land will be free, and only the first quality land will be used. But as demand for land grows, for example with population increase, lands of poorer quality will be brought into use. When this occurs, the owners of the better lands will be able to charge a rent equivalent to the excess in productivity of their land over the poorer land. The process may continue with ever poorer lands brought into cultivation and with rising rents on the inframarginal lands.

Accompanying this extension to the extensive margin is a second process, the more intensive utilization of the original higher quality lands. As the price of the better lands rises, it becomes profitable to economize on their use, which conversely means employing more labor and capital per unit of land. Hence skyscrapers.

QUASI-RENTS

A factor which is fixed in the short run is in effect in perfectly inelastic supply. As noted earlier, a firm will continue operating a plant in the short run as long as revenues cover variable costs. Any return on fixed factors constitutes a rent. But because in the long run these fixed factors of a firm would not continue to be supplied unless their costs are covered, these rents on the fixed factors are only temporary, and are called quasi-rents.

Virtually all factors can receive quasi-rents—workers as well as capital and land. In Figure 16.2, a general case is illustrated. With a demand for a factor of DD' and a long-run supply curve of the factor AA', equilibrium factor price is OP, and the quantity of factor employed is OQ. Total receipts of the factor are $OPEQ$, of which $OAEQ$ is a necessary payment to induce the factor to be supplied, and APE constitutes economic rent.

Figure 16.2 Rent and Quasi-Rent

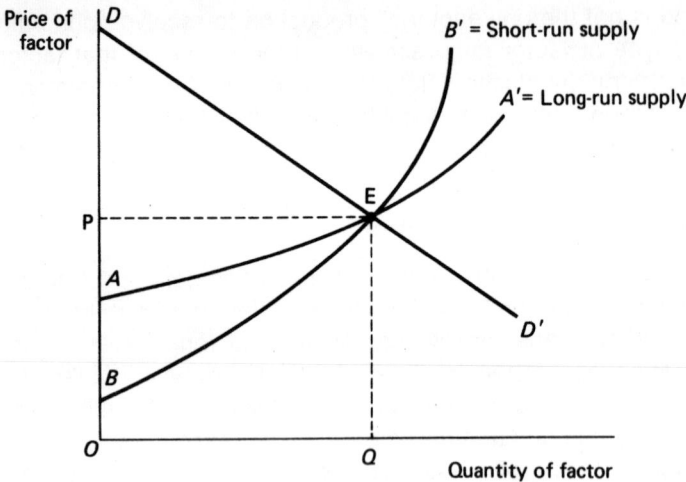

Once the factors are committed, however, their short-run supply function is less elastic, as indicated by BB'. While in the long run they would leave if they did not receive the higher prices indicated by curve AA', in the short run most of them would continue at much lower prices. Reading Figure 16.2 as a description of a short-run equilibrium, price and quantity are the same as in long-run equilibrium, as is the total income of the factor. But now quasi-rents of BPE are received, which is significantly larger than the pure economic rents of the long run equilibrium.

Rents to factors are surpluses, not necessary to induce the supply of their services. If they are not paid, or if they are taxed, the allocation of the factors will not be affected, nor will the efficiency (or inefficiency) of production. The rents may be appropriated by a buyer of the services of the factors of production who can practice price discrimination in the factor market. The perfectly discriminating monopsonist appropriates all the rent of factors, in fact.

The fact that rents can be appropriated without affecting factor supplies or utilization makes rents attractive candidates for taxation, as Henry George well knew. The difficulties are in identifying rents, and in ensuring that a tax does not also fall on marginal units of factor. The latter are not receiving rents, and an attempt to tax their earnings will cause a shift in the supply of these units of the factor away from the taxed area.

These difficulties are magnified with any attempt to tax quasi-rents. Only a temporary tax on quasi-rents would satisfy efficiency requirements, and temporary taxes are, to say the least. hardly common.

CAPITAL

As a factor of production, capital presents many complex and controversial problems of analysis. The essence of capital is time—a time lapse between the period or periods when a firm expends money on factors of production or intermediate products, and the time when the product of those expenditures adds to the revenues of the firm. Part of the cost of using capital goods, then, is the opportunity earnings on the money invested in them, either the amount the firm must pay in interest to borrow the financing, or the returns the firm could have made on investments elsewhere with its own funds.

The firm employs capital equipment because the productivity of indirect or roundabout methods of production exceeds the productivity of productive techniques not involving capital goods. The use of capital will be profitable to the firm only if the productivity of the capital-using method of production is great enough not only to pay the original costs of the capital equipment but also the interest cost on the amount of money invested.

The productivity of an act of investment is determined by the following formula, where MP_c is the marginal productivity of the investment, n is the number of periods the firm uses the good in production, C is the original cost of the capital good, SV is the salvage value of the good when the firm no longer uses it, and the $R's$ are the net returns of the capital good in each of the future periods (designated with subscripts):

$$C = \frac{R_1}{1 + MP_c} + \frac{R_2}{(1 + MP_c)^2} + \cdots + \frac{R_n}{(1 + MP_c)^n}$$
$$+ \frac{SV}{(1 + MP_c)^n} \tag{1}$$

The marginal product of capital (MP_c) is that rate of discounting that makes the sum of the discounted future returns of a capital good equal to its original cost.

The firm determines the marginal product of capital for various types and scales of investment in capital goods. It thus derives a schedule of the marginal product of capital, as in Figure 16.3. This schedule then constitutes the firm's demand curve for capital, analogous to its demand curve for any other input. We assume the marginal productivity of capital declines as the quantity of capital used by the firm rises.

Figure 16.3 *The Firm's Demand for Capital*

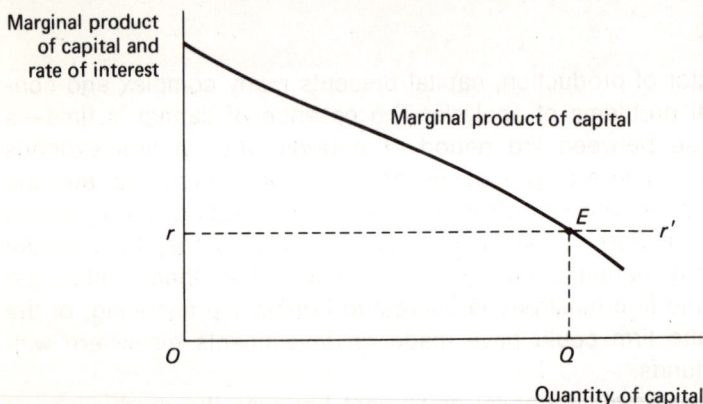

For profitability, the marginal product of capital must exceed the rate of interest, the cost of financing the capital goods. The market rate of interest is indicated by *rr'* in Figure 16.3. Equilibrium for the firm is point *E*, where the marginal product of capital equals the rate of interest; *OQ* quantity of capital is employed by the firm. Note that the quantity of capital used by the firm will vary inversely with the rate of interest.

The same results can be reached by an alternative route with which the firm compares the present discounted value of an investment with the cost of the investment. The present value of a future stream of earnings from the use of a capital good, net of the cost of the other variable factors employed with it, is found by summing these future earnings, each of which is discounted back to the present by the market rate of interest. The present value (*PV*) of a future earnings (*R*) to be received in *n* years, when the market rate of interest is *r* is

$$PV = \frac{R}{(1 + r)^n}$$

Thus the present value of $100 to be received in five years, if the prevailing rate of interest is 10 percent, is $100/(1 + .1)^5$, or $65.51, which is the amount one would have to invest with compound interest of 10 percent, to receive $100 after five years.

The present value of a stream of future earnings, then, is

$$PV = \frac{R}{1 + r} + \frac{R_2}{(1 + r)^2} + \cdots + \frac{R_n}{(1 + r)^n} \qquad (2)$$

Note the similarities and differences between equations (1) and (2): In equation (1), the value of all variables except MP_c is known, and the equation is solved for the value of MP_c. In equation (2), the unknown is PV; all other variables are assumed known to the firm.

The firm then compares the present value of a projected investment with the cost of the investment and invests in those projects for which the marginal product of capital exceeds the market rate of interest.

The demands of various firms for capital are then aggregated into market demand curves.[5] In the long run the supply of financing for investment is provided by individual savers (acting directly or through the saving of businesses in which the individuals have an interest), and an equilibrium rate of interest is determined by the interaction of demand and supply. On the margin the rate of interest will be equal both to the marginal productivity of capital for each firm and to the marginal rate of substitution beween present and future use of income on the part of each saver. In general, this represents an efficient scale and allocation of saving and investment.

These conclusions are subject to many reservations, particularly with respect to the short run capital market on which the behavior of lending institutions and governments have a significant influence. Consideration of these factors would thrust us into questions of macroeconomic behavior and policy, disequilibrium paths, and other dynamic considerations beyond the scope of this book.

The theory of capital is an unfinished chapter in economics, and the validity of the analysis of capital based on the marginal productivity of capital and the savings propensities of individuals is still highly controversial.

REVIEW QUESTIONS

1. Explain the following concepts:
    Euler's theorem
    "Exploitation"
    Economic rent

---

[5]Included in this market demand will be the demand of individuals for consumption loans, as discussed in Chapter 4.

Quasi-rent
The "Single Tax" of Henry George
Marginal productivity of capital
Capital
Present value of discounted future earnings

2. Discuss the advantages and disadvantages of taxes on economic rent and on quasi-rents.
3. Compare and contrast the nature of economic rent and consumer surplus.
4. Should capital gains, the rise in the value of capital assets, be taxed at the same rate as ordinary income? Discuss.

FURTHER READING

Dewey, Donald, *Modern Capital Theory*. New York: Columbia University Press (1965).

George, Henry, *Progress and Poverty*. London: Routledge & Kegan Paul (1906).

Scitovsky, Tibor, *Welfare and Competition*. Homewood, Ill.: Irwin (1951), chap. 9.

6

**THE
PUBLIC
SECTOR**

17

THE PUBLIC SECTOR AND THE EFFICIENT ALLOCATION OF RESOURCES

THE MICROECONOMIC ROLE OF GOVERNMENT

Microeconomic analysis is concerned with the allocation of resources in all contexts. Traditionally, economic theory courses and textbooks have virtually ignored the large and growing influence of governments on this allocation.[1] Part VI of this book constitutes an attempt to reduce the analytical imbalance between private and public sectors.

Criticisms of private markets are based on two factors, inefficiency in the allocation of resources and inequity in prices and the distribution of incomes. Without too much violence to reality, we can perhaps assume that the microeconomic function of government is to attempt to reduce these imperfections within the limits of feasible political processes.

Governments use three techniques in attempting to achieve the desired goals of efficiency and equity: (1)

[1]In recent years in the United States over one-sixth of all workers have been directly employed by governments. Government goods and services have accounted for over a quarter of the nation's output, and total government expenditures, including transfer payments, have amounted to over 35 percent of national income. In addition, governments influence private markets extensively through regulation of the terms on which individuals and firms may engage in private transactions.

goods and services provided directly by governments, (2) taxation and subsidies, and (3) government regulation of firms and individuals.

The present chapter deals primarily with the reasons private markets may not produce the economically efficient type and quantities of goods and considers some public policies that may improve the efficiency in the allocation of economic resources. The following Chapter 18 deals more specifically with the effects of various forms of taxation and subsidies, and Chapter 19 discusses the impact of government regulation of the activities of private firms and individuals.

THE BASIS OF INEFFICIENCY IN PRIVATE MARKETS

Inefficiency in the allocation of economic resources can arise in private markets only when the revenues and costs of the profit-maximizing firms do not correspond to the monetary benefits and costs to society of that firm's production. Efficiency calls for the production of any good if its benefits exceed its costs; profit maximization induces production whenever revenues exceed the firm's costs. Only divergences between benefits to society and revenues to firms, or between social and private costs, can cause inefficiency in private markets.

Four closely interrelated types of cases in which inefficiency arises in private markets will be discussed: (1) simple monopoly; (2) external costs and benefits resulting from the operation of firms, costs that firms do not pay, and benefits for which the firm is not compensated; (3) pure public goods, which are goods that can be supplied to additional consumers at no extra cost; and (4) natural monopoly (that is, the firm with decreasing costs).

In all four cases inefficiency arises either because of a lack of control by firms over the price or prices consumers must pay for a good or service, or because those on whom costs fall cannot control the prices that must be paid them to compensate for these costs.[2]

Accentuating the problem in many cases is the decreasing cost nature of production, the fact that the marginal cost of supplying an additional consumer is often less than the average cost of supply.

[2]The inability of a firm to withhold a benefit from an individual and hence its inability to require payment is sometimes referred to as the "principle of exclusion," but the phrase is awkward and imprecise. Inefficiency arises not only when a firm cannot exclude those benefiting from its production, but also when the firm is required to set the same price for all users. As standard monopoly analysis shows (see the following section on simple monopoly and monopsony and Chapters 11 and 12), nondiscriminatory pricing by a monopolist leads to inefficiency, but it is stretching language almost to the breaking point to say this standard monopoly case illustrates the "impossibility of exclusion."

SIMPLE MONOPOLY AND MONOPSONY

The general principle that inefficiency results in private markets when the firm's revenues do not correspond to the value or benefit of its product will first be illustrated with a repetition (Figure 17.1) of the familiar case of the simple (that is, nondiscriminating) monopolist operating in an otherwise efficient economy.

Figure 17.1 *Monopoly and Inefficiency*

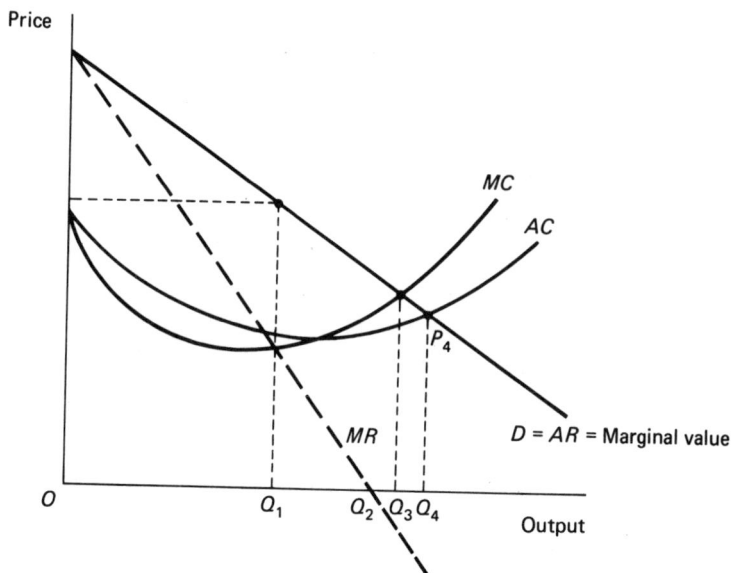

The demand curve measures the marginal benefit of the good to buyers (that is, the monetary value of additional units of output). For efficiency, the product should be supplied to any user whose benefit exceeds the marginal cost of supply; output should be produced to Q_3. The simple monopolist, however, produces only to point Q_1, even though the additional benefit from units Q_1 to Q_3 is greater than the extra costs of supplying them.

If benefits for the added output exceed the costs, why does not this private firm produce it? The answer is clear: The firm cannot appropriate all the gains from expanding its output. True, it will collect revenues from the new users. But the firm's total profits will not increase because in order to attract the added users the firm must lower its price to all of its customers. In fact, beyond output Q_2, the firm's revenues actually decline, as the negative marginal revenue curve indicates.

Inefficiency results because the firm cannot control the price to each buyer individually.

A perfectly discriminating monopolist does not have this difficulty in collecting revenues from the gainers and would expand output to the efficient point Q_3.

This hardly constitutes a policy solution, however, since perfect discrimination is rarely practicable and, where feasible, gives all the gains of trade to the producer leaving no consumer surplus for the buyers.

The inefficiency of the simple monopolist results whether the firm has constant, increasing, or decreasing costs. When remedies for this source of inefficiency are considered, the cost function of the firm becomes important. If the firm has constant or increasing costs, a price that induces the efficient level of demand also provides revenues sufficient to cover the total costs of production. Price regulation or antitrust enforcement policies may then be used to handle cases of simple monopoly. These techniques are not adequate, however, for dealing with the decreasing cost natural monopoly.

Like that of the simple monopolist, the output of the simple monopsonist is less than the efficient level for an analogous but converse reason: The simple monopolist cannot appropriate all the gains from his production; the simple monopsonist pays *more* than the real cost of the marginal factors employed. As the monopsonist hires additional factors, he not only pays the new factors the higher price needed to attract their services, but he must also increase the price he pays to existing suppliers. These latter extra payments are a rent, not payment for a real cost. Thus the money costs to the monopsonist exceed the real cost to the suppliers. As a consequence, the monopsonist fails to hire some factors whose real cost would be less than the benefit to buyers of the output the factors would produce.

As in the monopoly case, the perfectly discriminating monopsonist avoids the inefficiences of simple monopsony, but at a cost of giving all gains of trade to the employing firms and leaving no gains or rents to the factors.

EXTERNAL EFFECTS

The current concern with problems of air and water pollution i belated recognition of a deficiency of private production long recog nized by economists[3]—external costs and benefits.[4]

[3]See for example, A. C. Pigou, *The Economics of Welfare*, 4th ed. (Londo Macmillan, 1932), especially chap. 9, "Divergences Between Marginal Social N Product and Marginal Private Net Product"; K. W. Kapp, *The Social Costs Private Enterprise* (Cambridge: Harvard University Press, 1950); E. J. Mishan, *T Costs of Economic Growth* (New York: Praeger, 1967); E. J. Mishan, "Reflectio

External costs and benefits in production arise when the firm, in the process of producing goods it sells made with inputs it buys, also creates other benefits for which it is not remunerated, or causes cost to fall on individuals or other firms for which they are not compensated.

External benefits and costs are not bought and sold in the market; they do not have prices. The firm causing these effects does not take them into account in planning its production because the external benefits give the firm no revenues, and the external costs are free to the firm.

These are unpriced effects produced jointly with other priced goods and services. A firm produces goods for which it receives no revenues only because the goods are created jointly with another product that can be sold. The two outputs can be produced together at lower cost than if only the marketable good alone were produced. The advertiser on television is not particularly pleased to provide entertainment for individuals who will never buy his product, but it is cheaper to do so than to attempt to exclude them. Similarly, the firm produces undesired outputs or external costs (for example, noise, odors, smoke) because it would cost the firm more to exclude these outputs than to continue them.

External benefits are unpriced because the producer cannot feasibly exclude beneficiaries from enjoying them. It may be impossible for him to identify the beneficiaries or legally to levy a charge upon them. Even when pricing is possible, the costs of implementing a price system may exceed any revenues that would be gained. It is not feasible for the firm creating external benefits to exclude the beneficiaries from the benefits.

External costs are unpriced because those on whom they fall can neither exclude nor avoid them except at still greater cost, and the economic institutions provide no way by which they can enforce a claim for compensation on the firm responsible for them. One may say that the appropriate price of such unwanted effects would be negative, and negative prices cannot be enforced in private markets unless those bearing the cost have the power to exclude the effect.

The inability of firms to exclude persons receiving external benefits, and the inability of individuals and firms that incur external costs to enforce these costs on the firm responsible for them de-

---

Recent Developments in the Concept of External Effects," *Canadian Journal Economics and Political Science* 31 (1965), 3–34, reprinted in E. J. Mishan, *elfare Economics* (New York: Random House, 1964), pp. 98–154, is a comprehensive and rigorous theoretical analysis of externalities.

[4]They are also sometimes called "third party" costs and benefits, or neighborhood effects.

pend on the legal environment (that is, whether the firms have a legal right to charge for benefits or are legally liable for payment of cost). Many proposals have been made recently for changes in the laws—in particular, to require firms to pay what have previously been external costs.[5]

External effects can also result from consumption by individuals. The pleasure that neighbors receive when an individual paints his house or keeps his yard neat are examples of external consumption benefits, while the unpleasant noise from a neighbor's stereo or dog and the smoke from his burning leaves are external consumption costs.

How prevalent are external effects? Because such effects are unpriced and their impact is often widely diffused, they are often difficult to identify and measure. It seems clear, however, that external effects (costs in particular) increase with growing population density, urbanization, and industrialization. Nationally and locally we seem to be becoming more conscious of such externalities as air and water pollution, and traffic congestion on streets, highways, and in the air, and more insistent that these unpleasant aspects of "civilization" be abated. Growing doubts of the desirability of "progress" are evidence of the concern with externalities.

The objections to externalities (costs in particular) are based in part on equity considerations. It is believed unfair that householders who moved in before an airport was located nearby have to bear the noise of jets without compensation, or that neighboring residents of a paper mill have the unpleasant odors inflicted upon them.

The efficiency argument is that so long as firms ignore external costs and benefits, economic resources will be allocated inefficiently. Goods will be produced which, if all costs were included would be found wasteful; other products remain unproduced or with too little produced because firms ignore the external benefits of these goods. Perhaps even more important, so long as firms are not required to pay external costs, they have no incentive to reduce those costs.[6] The presence of external costs in the production of a good need not mean the product should not be produced. I counting all costs, the benefits of production exceed the costs efficient allocation of resources calls for production. But as long a some of the costs are ignored, it is impossible for profit-maximizin firms to achieve economically efficient methods and scales of pro

[5]See, for example, E. J. Mishan, *The Costs of Economic Growth*, especia chaps. 4–6; and J. H. Dales, *Pollution, Property and Prices* (Toronto: Univers of Toronto Press, 1968), especially chap. 6.

[6]The writer knows of one case of a lumber products mill which, forsee legislation on pollution, revised its methods of waste disposal and discovered new methods were less costly than the old!

duction. Should the SST be used if all costs are considered? Only a careful study will answer this question, and the results of the study would no doubt be debatable. But ignoring important costs is certainly less likely to provide a correct answer.

PUBLIC POLICIES TOWARD EXTERNALITIES

How can public policies help reduce the inefficiencies caused by external costs and benefits? Two general approaches may be distinguished. First, the externalities may in some way be priced so that consideration of these external costs and benefits becomes a normal part of the operation of private markets. It would then pay the firm to create external benefits and avoid external costs. Second, direct regulation or prohibition of the activities of firms giving rise to external costs may be established, and goods with strong external benefits may be provided by public agencies.

Pricing Externalities

An externality may be priced in several ways. First, the external effects may be internalized by a merger of the two parties. If the activities of one firm create an external cost or benefit that falls on a second firm, a merger of the two firms leads to an internalization of the effect, which would then be taken into account when the merged firm makes its production plan. Some proponents of socialism argue that the ability to take all benefits and costs into consideration in planning production is a major advantage of public economic activity, inducing efficiency in the use of resources.[7]

Second, externalities become priced if those on whom costs fall are provided with a legal claim for damages against those responsible for the cost, and when firms responsible for external benefits can legally claim compensation from those enjoying the benefits. The nature of the laws of legal liability is crucial in determining whether external costs and benefits are internalized in this fashion.

Third, in some cases compensation in the *reverse* direction will induce efficiency in the presence of externalities. If those on whom costs fall offer to pay the person or firm responsible to discontinue the activity creating the cost, or if a legal obligation is enforced on the firm creating external benefits to compensate the beneficiaries if the firm should withdraw the benefits, the external effects become priced.

The feasibility of such reverse compensation is limited. Paying

[7]Oscar Lange and Frederick Taylor, *On the Economic Theory of Socialism* (Minneapolis: The University of Minnesota Press, 1938), pp. 103 ff.

people or firms *not* to do something raises difficult problems of identifying those to whom payments should be made. To pay a firm *not* to create smoke when the firm had no intention of doing so anyway conflicts with equity (or should one say common sense?), and does not increase efficiency. Presumably, such reverse compensation would be limited to those already creating the undesired effects. Even in this case there is the problem of handling possible increases in the external costs. The basic difficulty is determining who would in the absence of compensation create external costs, and in what degree.

Where feasible, either the direct or the reverse forms of compensation will promote efficiency in resource allocation. In both cases the firm will be worse off when causing external costs and better off when creating external benefits than it would be without these effects. The firm will therefore take these costs and benefits into consideration in its planning.

A choice between the two forms of compensation would ordinarily be based on considerations of feasibility and equity. At first sight it might appear that equity would be furthered if firms were required to pay for external costs and be compensated for external benefits. But in some situations the reverse can be argued. For example, if the external cost is smoke from A's factory, which existed before B moved into the area, one could argue that it would be unfair to require A to compensate B for this cost. The smoker on the bus may give rise to external consumption costs to nonsmokers. Should the smoker compensate those offended? Or should those bothered by the smoke have the responsibility of offering to buy off the offending smoker? Needless to say, on questions of fairness differences of opinion are inevitable.

The practical difficulties of developing and enforcing a compensation scheme for payments between private parties suggest a fourth way of incorporating externalities into the pricing system: levying a tax on those creating external costs and providing public subsidies to those responsible for external benefits.[8] By these methods the cost and revenue functions of private firms are shifted to incorporate the external effects, they are taken into consideration in its planning, and efficient allocation of resources is encouraged.

Apart from the difficulties of administering such a plan, the chief criticism of this approach is basically one of equity: The taxpayer, rather than those harmed by external costs, receives the payment; conversely, the taxpayer, rather than the beneficiaries, finances the production of goods with external benefits.

---

[8]Taxation of consumption of alcoholic beverages and subsidies to private transportation companies may perhaps be justified on these grounds.

Regulation of Externalities

The practical difficulties of devising a method of incorporating externalities into the pricing mechanism often make such plans administratively impossible. The practical alternative to inaction then is direct regulation. The direct approach to activities with broad external benefits is for the government to undertake the production of the goods involved, an activity to be considered in the following section under the heading "Public Goods." When external costs arise from the activities of private firms or individuals, the government may (and often does) establish regulations prohibiting or restricting the activity. Examples are innumerable: zoning ordinances; smoke control legislation; requirements that vehicles be equipped with antipollution devices; even simple provisions against disturbing the peace.

Direct regulation of activities creating external costs tends to reduce the inefficiency inherent in the unregulated private markets, but not to eliminate it. It is virtually impossible to frame regulations that have the same effect on the behavior of firms as does incorporating external costs into the firm's cost function. External costs are not bad *per se*. The question is whether they provide benefits greater than the costs, a question that direct regulation answers rather clumsily.

No general rule can be established to determine whether externalities should be ignored, priced, or regulated. A price system established with complete accuracy and costless administration would be more effective than direct regulation in encouraging the efficient utilization of resources. But it is also true that an ideal framework of regulation would be more effective than a price system that was imperfectly developed and administered. The choice is therefore more likely to be determined on grounds of feasibility than of ideology.[9]

PUBLIC GOODS

External benefits arise as byproducts from the production or consumption of other goods. Since the beneficiaries do not pay for these gains, firms have no incentive to provide them. Goods and services with external benefits are therefore underproduced in private markets.

[9]The costs of a price system are further discussed in the section on income redistribution.

To encourage the production of such goods and services, governments may grants subsidies to private firms. Transportation subsidies—commuter train and bus services, and airports—are often defended on the grounds that the benefits accrue not only to the users of the facilities but also to the wider community. Where strong external benefits exist, however, and particularly with goods for which most of the benefits are so diffused that private firms may not produce the goods at all, a case can be made for public provision of the good.

The extreme case of a good which, once produced, provides benefits to a wide and diffused group is the *pure public good*.[10] The characteristics of a pure public good are that the good or service provides benefits to additional consumers without added cost; consumption by one person does not reduce the amount of the good available to others. National defense and various community health measures (for example, malaria control) are often cited as examples. Lighthouses, streets and highways, bridges, and many other public services may also have characteristics close to those of a pure public good.[11]

With the normal private good, the total quantity of the good produced equals the sum of the consumptions of that good by all individuals. When one individual increases his consumption of the product, less is available for others. The dominant characteristic of a pure public good, on the other hand, is that consumption of the good by one individual does not decrease the amount available to others. The consumption of *each* individual is equal to the total amount of the good produced. Individual consumptions are not added to get the total.

Using C's for the consumption of individuals 1, 2, and 3, we define

$$\text{Output of private good} = C_1 + C_2 + C_3$$
$$\text{Output of public good} = C_1 = C_2 = C_3$$

Three important questions arise with respect to pure public goods. First, how much of the good should be supplied? This is the question of the efficient allocation of resources between private

---

[10]See Paul A. Samuelson, "Diagrammatic Exposition of a Theory of Public Expenditure," *Review of Economics and Statistics 36* (1955), 350–356, and "Pure Theory of Public Expenditure and Taxation," in J. Margolis and H. Guitton, eds., *Public Economics* (New York: St. Martin's, 1969), pp. 98–123.

[11]The similarity of a pure public good to a "natural monopoly" is obvious; the cost of supplying the latter to additional users is not zero (as with a pure public good), but is less than the average cost of production. The natural monopoly is discussed in the following section.

and public production—a question of much current interest.[12] Second, how should the supply of public goods be financed? This question is discussed in greater detail in Chapter 18. Third, can profit-maximizing firms in private markets be expected to produce the efficient kinds and quantities of products that have the characteristics of pure public goods?

For private goods, the demands of the individuals are summed horizontally to determine a market demand curve which, combined with the cost curves, determines the efficient output. For the pure public good, however, each unit of the good is (or at least can be) consumed by all individuals. The demand curves of the individuals are therefore summed vertically in order to find the total value placed on each unit of the good by all consumers combined.[13] Figures 17.2 and 17.3 compare the two types of goods.

Figure 17.2 Private Good

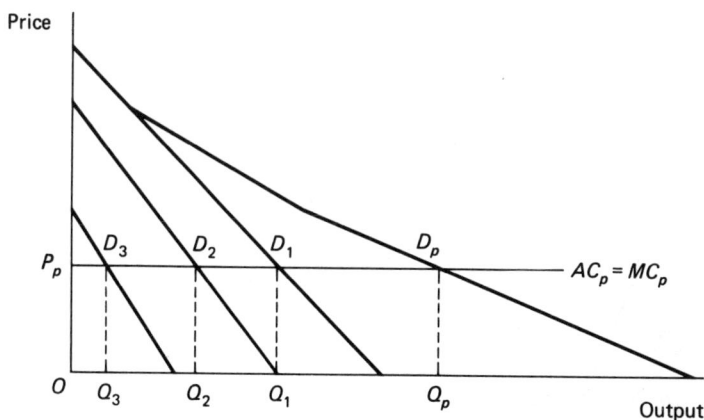

Assume three individuals with demand curves D_1, D_2, and D_3. To facilitate comparison between the two cases, assume that they have the same demands for the private and the public goods. Here D_p of Figure 17.2 is the kinked market demand curve for the private good derived by summing the three individual demand curves horizontally. With the assumed costs of production of the private

[12]See, for example, J. K. Galbraith, *The Affluent Society* (Boston: Houghton Mifflin, 1958), chap. 18, and Francis M. Bator, *The Question of Government Spending* (New York: Harper & Row, 1960).

[13]The same procedure would be followed by a family deciding on the value to it of one or more units of a good (for example, a car, a magazine subscription), which all members of the family would consume. The value of each additional unit and hence the price the family would be willing to pay for it would be the *sum* of the values placed on that unit by all members of the family.

good (for simplicity, average cost is assumed constant and there-fore equal to marginal cost), the efficient output of the private good for the market as a whole is OQ_p. This output is then allocated efficiently among the three individuals by setting the "rationing" price OP_p, and each individual consumes the good up to the point at which this price (which equals marginal cost) is just equal to the marginal value the individual places on the good. This gives consumption of OQ_1, OQ_2, and OQ_3, respectively, for the three individuals, which sum to OQ_p.

Figure 17.3 Pure Public Good

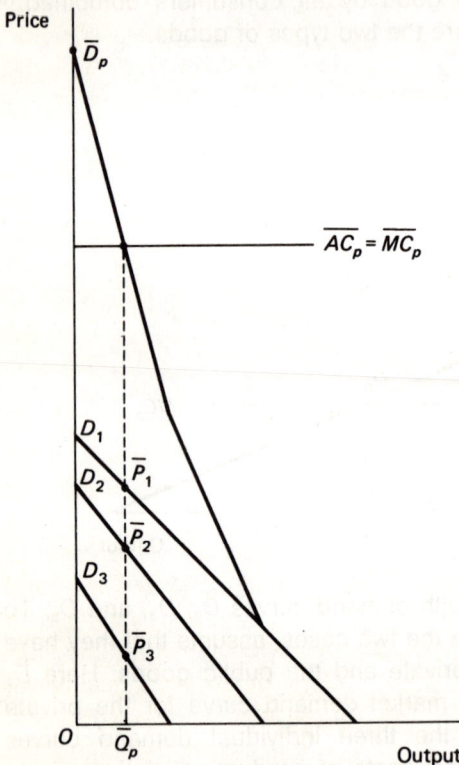

Compare the case of the public good of Figure 17.3. Each unit of that good is consumed by all three individuals. The aggregate "demand" curve of Figure 17.3 for the public good is therefore $\overline{D}_p$. The term "demand curve" is a misnomer; it would be better called an "aggregate value curve," for it shows the value, summed over all three individuals, placed on successive units of the public good.

Given the indicated costs of production for the public good

$(\overline{MC}_p = \overline{AC}_p)$, the efficient output is $\overline{OQ}_p$. Since the good is consumed equally by all, $\overline{OQ}_p$ is also the amount of the public good consumed by each of the three individuals.

Note that no single price can efficiently allocate this public good. In fact, in the case illustrated, each consumer has a different price at which he would choose to consume this efficient quantity $\overline{OQ}_p$ of the public good ($\overline{P}_1$, $\overline{P}_2$, and $\overline{P}_3$). Note also that the marginal cost of production exceeds all three of these prices. Marginal cost is, in fact, equal to the *sum* of these three prices.

The marginal cost of supplying the fixed quantity to an additional consumer, however, is zero. For efficiency, the good should be supplied to any individual who wants it at any price.

It is in fact this difference between the marginal cost of a unit of the good and the marginal cost of supplying the good to an additional consumer that creates the difficulties in supplying this good efficiently. The average cost of production *per consumer* necessarily exceeds the marginal cost of supplying an additional consumer. The zero price to consumers, which induces efficient use of the good, fails to provide the revenues to cover the costs of production. The pure public good is thus a special limiting example of the decreasing cost case.

It is obvious why it is difficult in practice for governments to provide exactly the right amount of a public good to satisfy the efficiency test. To do so the government must determine (estimate, guess) the values that all individuals would place on various quantities of the good.

Note also the difficulty of allocating the costs of the public good among individuals. If, for example, the government wished to finance the production of the public good illustrated in Figure 17.3 with taxes levied on individuals, which are equal or proportional to the marginal benefit or value each person receives from the good (as do prices in private markets), the government would have to estimate, as a minimum, the three prices (marginal values) the individuals would pay on the margin for the predetermined quantity of the good (that is, $\overline{P}_1$, $\overline{P}_2$, and $\overline{P}_3$). Alternately, if the government wished to impose taxes on individuals in proportion to the *total* value each receives, it would somehow have to determine the area under each individual demand curve up to the point of common consumption.

Furthermore, if individuals believe that they will be assessed taxes in some manner related to the government's estimate of the benefit each receives from the good, each has an incentive to conceal or understate the benefits he would receive from the good. It is then even more difficult for the government to determine the benefits likely to result from provision of some public good; the result may be to discourage the production of goods for which the test of efficiency is satisfied.

NATURAL MONOPOLIES

Cases of pure public goods with zero marginal costs of supplying added consumers are perhaps rare. But their basic characteristics are found in lesser degrees with virtually every "natural monopoly" (that is, a good subject to decreasing costs) for which the marginal cost of supplying additional consumers is positive but significantly below average cost. As we have seen,[14] an efficiency test requires that persons be provided the good if they are willing to pay marginal cost. If marginal cost is less than average cost, production of the good by private firms is likely to be restricted below the efficient level, and public provision of the good is suggested. A price equal to marginal cost will not provide sufficient revenues to cover total costs.

When the marginal cost of supplying an additional consumer or user is extremely low, a product may be supplied by the government free of charge. Parks, bridges, and streets are examples. If the marginal cost of supply is less than average cost but still not negligible, the good may be produced by private firms operating under price, output, and quality constraints established by regulatory commissions. Such regulation is discussed in Chapter 19.

A basis for public production closely related to the natural monopoly argument is the suggestion that certain types of production require such large capital commitments or involve such high risks that they are beyond the capabilities of private industry. In view of the finances of AT&T or General Motors, compared with the average state or local government, the argument is not too persuasive. However, governments may insure private firms against risks (for example, government insured mortgages).

INCOME REDISTRIBUTION AS A BASIS FOR PUBLIC GOODS

Public production or distribution of goods free or below cost is sometimes used as a method of redistributing income. It would usually be more efficient to distribute money income directly rather than through the distribution of goods and services, but it is often more feasible politically to distribute goods. Their distribution (for example, free education, parks, medical care) no doubt often reflects a political judgment that fairness requires some minimum standard of consumption of such goods for all individuals. Public

[14]See Chapter 11.

distribution also often reflects the belief that the good is subject to decreasing costs, or gives rise to external benefits which are diffused throughout society. Public education and health measures are examples of the latter.

PRICING AND THE PUBLIC SECTOR

When considering public policy to reduce inefficiencies in private markets, an important question is whether improvements can be accomplished through a pricing system, or whether direct action (for example, regulation or free distribution of goods) is preferable. The compensation, tax, and subsidy plans mentioned in our discussion of externalities represent efforts to incorporate those effects into the pricing mechanism. Even if goods are to be supplied by governments (for example, highways and parks), one must ask whether the product should be priced or not.

The advantages of a price system are its automaticity, its possibilities for decentralization of decision making, its separation from arbitrary personal judgments about the "proper" production and distribution decisions. A price system can be a remarkably effective tool to encourage the efficient allocation of resources. No private individual or firm has to decide anything more than whether he wants to participate and, if so, to what extent. Prices provide information about the alternatives available to an individual and permit the individual to make his own choice among them. The price system is no doubt coercive, but to many people its coercion is less objectionable than that of a personal authority.

Pricing systems are, however, not costless. In the first place, the expenses of determining benefits and costs (as a basis for pricing) can be substantial. Without such information, however, no intelligent decisions can be made. Even if a public pricing system is not expected to be established for a good or service (as, for example, with national defense), a knowledge of benefits and costs is necessary for rational decision-making.

A second question is whether prices should be charged and, if so, how complex a price structure should be established for public goods and the output of private firms (for example, natural monopolies) whose prices are regulated. There is a fundamental conflict here: the more closely a pricing system reflects the costs of production, the greater contribution prices can make to the efficient allocation of resources; but the more complex the pricing system, the higher its costs of implementation. A price system decreases efficiency unless its costs are less than the inefficiencies arising from its absence.

Should a toll be levied on users of a bridge, for example? Apart from questions of equity and financing, would a toll encourage efficient use of the bridge? If the marginal cost of an additional vehicle is small, the costs of collecting the sum would often exceed the efficiency savings. But if the bridge is congested the marginal cost of an additional vehicle is high, including as it does, an external cost, the congestion cost inflicted by this vehicle on other drivers. Here, the expenses of toll collection may well be justified by the reduction in traffic induced by the toll, and the consequent improvement in the efficient flow of traffic.

Clearly, whether any particular good should be priced or not and, if so, how complex a pricing system should be established, can only be determined with careful analysis of the facts of the particular case.[15] Further, equity is in practice as important as efficiency in evaluating a price structure.

BENEFIT-COST ANALYSIS

The general principles for efficiency in the supply of public goods are difficult to apply in practice, but a rising level of economic sophistication has marked developments in this area of applied economic analysis. Benefit-cost analysis—the explicit attempt to compute the direct and indirect costs and benefits of a proposed public project—has become increasingly popular and useful since its beginnings with the evaluation of water resource development plans. The literature mirrors two basic concerns: (1) the analytical issues of how the costs and benefits of government programs should be measured and compared, and (2) the empirical question of determining the actual costs and benefits of various specific proposed projects. The concern here is with the analytical questions, but it may be noted that empirical studies have been made in a wide range of fields, including transportation, urban renewal, crime prevention and punishment, recreation, and health.[16]

The typical project to be evaluated has uneven streams of costs and benefits extending over time. For comparison between the

[15]While this problem of the optimum price system is particularly acute with public goods (for example, parks, parking space in congested areas), it also plagues private business firms, which know that customers do not like complicated pricing structures, even though they might lead to lower prices. For example, a firm may wish to increase the utilization of its capacity by setting low prices during off-peak business periods, but customers often object to this apparent discrimination.

[16]A. R. Prest and R. Turvey, "Cost-Benefit Analysis: A Survey," *Economic Journal 76* (1965), 683–735, reprinted in *Surveys of Economic Theory*, vol. 3 (New York: St. Martin's, 1966); Robert Dorfman, ed., *Measuring Benefits of Government Investments* (Washington, D.C.: Brookings, 1965).

streams of costs and benefits, they must be reduced to a common denominator. The standard approach is to compute the present values of the stream of benefits and the stream of costs. The benefit-cost ratio is thus the ratio of these two present values.

The present value of a stream of future benefits or costs is found by discounting future values or costs back to the present.[17] The choice of a rate of interest to use in discounting is crucial, particularly because benefits are likely to occur in the future, whereas costs are often incurred at the outset. A change in the interest rate employed thus will change the present value of the stream of benefits more than the present value of the stream of costs, and may raise or lower the ratio of benefits to costs quite significantly. A project that appears desirable at one rate of interest with a high benefit-cost ratio, may be indefensible at another rate.[18] It is not surprising, therefore, that the question of the proper rate of interest to use is widely discussed, and remains controversial.

Projects are often ranked in the order of their benefit-cost ratios. Efficiency would call for the initiation of all projects for which the benefit-cost ratio exceeds one. However, policymakers are often faced with a budgetary constraint that does not provide sufficient funds to finance all projects with a favorable benefit-cost ratio. This is a problem of a "second best" or a constrained optimum.[19] Given such a constraint, the efficient ranking of projects is not necessarily in the order of their benefit-cost ratios.

Efficient ranking of projects within an agency operating with a

[17]Using r for the rate of interest and n for the number of years in the future a benefit or cost will occur, the formula for determining the present value is

$$\text{Present value} = \frac{\text{Future cost or benefit}}{(1 - r)^n}$$

See Chapter 16 (p. 240).

[18]To illustrate with a simplified example, consider a project costing $100,000 with all costs incurred at the beginning of the project. All benefits accrue in a lump-sum of $150,000 five years after the project is constructed. The present values of costs and benefits and the corresponding benefit-cost ratios, for interest rates of 5 percent and 10 percent are as follows:

	Present value of costs	Present value of benefits	Benefit-cost ratio
Interest rate = 5%	$100,000	117,555	1.18
Interest rate = 10%	$100,000	93,168	.93

Thus a rise in the interest rate from 5 percent to 10 percent drops the benefit-cost ratio below 1; at 10 percent costs exceed benefits and the project is not defensible.

[19]See Chapter 20 (p. 310).

budget constraint (assuming all projects have standard benefit-cost ratios in excess of one) requires ranking of projects by the rate of return they promise on the agency's scarce factor, capital funds. For the agency, the opportunity cost of developing one project is the next best use of the limited capital within the agency itself. In terms of the formulas developed in Chapter 16 the agency would compute the marginal productivity of capital investment in each of its possible projects (using equation (1), page 239) and rank projects in the order of these marginal productivities.

A second major problem in developing benefit-cost analysis for proposed projects lies in attempting to include external benefits and costs in the calculations. Because these external effects are unpriced in markets, estimating their values is often difficult. What is the value, for example, of a human life saved because of higher safety standards in highway construction? What monetary valuation should be placed on the costs of river pollution caused by logging operations on the slopes of a stream?

Benefit-cost analysis cannot capture all the advantages and disadvantages of projects. The benefit-cost ratio is, after all, a ratio of money benefits and costs. It is a tool to investigate and evaluate the efficiency implications of a project. A high benefit-cost ratio does not guarantee that establishment of a program will raise economic welfare. Benefit-cost analysis tends, in particular, to slight questions of income distribution (not to mention political back-scratching considerations). There is always the danger that the use of this type of analysis will lead to the overemphasis of efficiency considerations at the expense of other factors relevant to the social welfare.[20] This, however, is a criticism of the misuse, not the use, of benefit-cost analysis.

REVIEW QUESTIONS

1. Explain the following concepts:
   External costs
   External benefits
   Pure public good
   Benefit-cost analysis
   Benefit-cost ratio
2. Give specific examples of goods with external costs or external benefits. What public policy is appropriate for dealing with each?
3. How would you determine the proper rate of interest to use in discounting future benefits of public projects? Discuss.
4. Should government provide tax incentives to firms which reduce air

[20]See Arthur Maass, "Benefit–Cost Analysis: Its Relevance to Public Investment Decisions," *Quarterly Journal of Economics 80* (1966), 208–226.

and water pollution? Or should polluting firms be taxed? Apply your analysis and conclusions to a specific case.

5. What is the relationship among pure public goods, externalities, and natural monopoly?

6. Discuss the economics of blacking out TV coverage of an athletic event in the city where it takes place.

7. Apply the concept of a pure public good to a family's decision to purchase a color TV set. If the public good concept is relevant here, how can TV sets be private goods?

FURTHER READING

Mishan, E. J., *The Costs of Economic Growth.* New York: Praeger (1967).

Mishan, E. J., "Reflections on Recent Developments in the Concept of External Effects." *Canadian Journal of Economics and Political Science* 31 (1965), 3–34.

Musgrave, Richard A., and Alan T. Peacock, eds., *Classics in the Theory of Public Finance.* New York: St. Martin's (1967).

Musgrave, Richard A., *The Theory of Public Finance.* New York: McGraw-Hill (1959).

Prest, A. R., and R. Turvey, "Cost-Benefit Analysis: A Survey." *Economic Journal 76* (1965), 683–735.

Samuelson, Paul A., "The Pure Theory of Public Expenditure." *Review of Economics and Statistics 36* (1954), 387–389.

Samuelson, Paul A., "Pure Theory of Public Expenditure and Taxation," in J. Margolis and H. Guitton, eds., *Public Economics.* New York: St. Martin's (1969), pp. 98–123.

18

TAXES AND TRANSFER PAYMENTS

BASIC ISSUES

Taxes provide revenue to finance government goods and services and transfer payments. The tax structure has an important influence on the distribution of income and the allocation of resources in an economy. The characteristics of alternative tax systems are considered in this chapter in both positive and normative terms. What effects do various taxes and transfer payments have, and to what extent do these effects conform to concepts of a desirable system of finance?

While the definition of a "good tax" is a matter of individual judgment, there is perhaps broad agreement that a tax and payments system should have the following characteristics:

(1) It should be simple enough to be comprehensible to the taxpayer, and inexpensive to administer.

(2) It should promote the pattern of income distribution desired by the public.

(3) It should be nondiscriminatory.

(4) It should encourage the efficient allocation of resources.

Needless to say, no tax would satisfy all these objectives. There would be disagreement on the definitions of the terms, and also on the proper trade-off between objectives (for example, how much inefficiency the nation would be willing to accept in order to achieve a more equitable tax structure).

This chapter considers some criteria of equity in taxation, the relationship between efficiency and taxes, and the impact of specific forms of taxes on the allocation of economic resources and the distribution of incomes.

EQUITY AND ABILITY-TO-PAY

Before the economics profession became sensitive to charges that it was "unscientific," it was more common for economists to consider explicitly the fairness of alternative tax structures. Two general principles of equity arose: the benefit theory and the ability-to-pay principle. By the former, equity was believed to require that taxes be assessed according to the benefit an individual was presumed to receive from the functions of government. By the latter, the individual's ability-to-pay, usually represented by his income or wealth, was the proper criterion for the size of his tax liability. Note that if one determines both benefit and ability-to-pay by the size of an individual's income (as did Adam Smith), the two principles reduce to one.

In analyzing the ability-to-pay principle of equity in taxation, early writers on public finance investigated the properties of tax structures that would minimize or equalize the burden or sacrifice of taxes on individuals, or make that burden proportional to the total utility individuals enjoyed from their incomes. Proportional, progressive, and regressive taxes on incomes (that is, those for which the tax rate is constant, increasing, or decreasing as income increases) were considered in combination with various assumptions about the schedule of the marginal utility of income of individuals.

For the purpose of analyzing the fairness of income taxes, it is necessary to make assumptions about the utility of income to individuals. Consider the implications of two assumptions commonly employed:

(1) The schedules of the utility of income are the same for different individuals (that is, the total utility of income is the same for any two individuals with equal incomes). This implies also that all individuals have the same schedule of the marginal utility of income.

(2) The marginal utility of income decreases as income increases.

Using these two assumptions, the taxation principle of equal sacrifice—that the total disutility of a tax be the same for all individuals—would require that the *amount* of taxes assessed rise with an individual's income.[1] Proportional taxes have this effect. Whether

---

[1] The "equal sacrifice" concept in the text is sometimes called the principle of equal absolute sacrifice, in contrast with equal marginal sacrifice (on the

a progressive tax is needed to impose equal sacrifice or a regressive tax is sufficient depends not on whether the marginal utility of income declines but on how fast it declines (that is, on the elasticity of the marginal utility function). If the elasticity of the marginal utility of income schedule is unitary, a straight proportional tax gives equal sacrifice. With a tax rate of 10 percent, the disutility of the $500 tax paid by the man with a $5000 income is the same as the disutility of the $1000 paid by the man with twice the income, for the marginal utility of a dollar under unitary elasticity is exactly half as much at the $10,000 income level as at $5000. The equal sacrifice principle requires a progressive tax if the elasticity of the marginal utility of income is less than one, but a regressive tax for elasticities greater than one.

If, alternately, one wishes the total burden or disutility of a tax to be minimized, the entire tax should be imposed on those with the lowest marginal utility of income (that is, those with the highest incomes). If all individuals have the same schedule of the marginal utility of income, no individual would pay any tax so long as any other individual had a higher after-tax income.

A logical extension of the minimum sacrifice principle would apply the same reasoning to income grants and supplements to low income individuals through transfer payments. Transfers from high to low income individuals could be enforced by the state until the marginal utility of income (after taxes and income supplements) is the same for all individuals. If, further, all individuals are assumed to have uniform schedules of the utility of income, the result would be equal incomes for all.

The conclusion that equal incomes maximize the utility of income for a group is often attacked. First, the conclusion holds only if (1) all individuals have the same utility function, and (2) if the marginal utility of income does in fact decline. Neither of these assumptions is provable or disprovable. Second, equal incomes conflict with the popular equity concept that incomes should bear some relationship to the effort or abilities of different individuals. Third, in a private enterprise economy that relies so heavily on monetary incentives, equalization of incomes would presumably have substantial deleterious effects on the productivity of the economy. The size of the pie depends in part on how it is divided. As Frank Knight once said, "Equality conflicts with efficiency, and both conflict with justice."

---

margin of taxation the marginal disutility of a tax is the same for all individuals) and equal proportional sacrifice (the total disutility of a tax is the same proportion of the total utility of income for each individual). See Richard A. Musgrave, *The Theory of Public Finance* (New York: McGraw-Hill, 1959), pp. 95–98.

THE BENEFIT PRINCIPLE

The principle that individuals should pay taxes in accordance with the benefits they receive from government goods and services is of long standing. It not only accords with many persons' concepts of fairness, but also may be conducive to efficiency in resource allocation.

It would clearly be self-defeating if the government followed the benefit principle with respect to welfare and other forms of transfer payments. The purpose of these payments is to change the distribution of income, which would be negated if the recipients were taxed to finance the payments.

Questions do arise, however, when the benefit principle is applied to financing public goods. There is perhaps wide agreement that, when the beneficiary of a public good is easily identifiable, that person should pay the costs of the good. Postal fees are the obvious example. With most public goods, however, further complexities arise:

(1) To raise low incomes the public may wish to provide goods below cost as a method of income redistribution. As with transfer payments, the benefit principle of taxation is here explicitly repudiated.

(2) The good may be supplied under conditions of decreasing costs. In such cases, a tax or price to beneficiaries, which covers average costs, will lead to a restriction of output below the efficient level. A conflict thus arises between the benefit principle and the efficient allocation of resources.

(3) While the primary benefits of a public good may accrue largely to a readily indentifiable group, it is often argued that external benefits exist, often diffused through a larger group. Public education and mass transportation are often cited as examples. Here, the benefit principle would call for a broadly based tax, perhaps combined with user fees that do not cover the full cost of the service.

(4) The difficulties of determining the amount of benefit received are often insuperable, particularly when individuals expect to be taxed on the basis of benefits, in which case they have an incentive to understate their benefits.

(5) Finally, as noted in the discussion of public goods, the benefits of a particular public good, when measured in money terms, may vary widely among individuals. A price system equating taxes to benefits would have to be enormously complex, with different people paying different amounts. Even if such a system were practicable,

the costs of enforcement would be high, and a charge of discrimination could be levied against the tax.

For financing general government expenditures such as national defense, police, the judicial system, and so on, it is sometimes argued that benefits can be adequately approximated by the individual's income. A relatively broad but simple sales, income, or expenditures tax might then satisfy the benefit criterion.

ECONOMIC EFFICIENCY AND TAXATION

The imposition of a tax will affect the amount of the taxed good or service that will be supplied or demanded, thus influencing the allocation of resources and the efficiency of the economy. Several questions arise:

(1) How can the revenues necessary to finance public expenditures be acquired with the least efficiency loss on the taxed goods and services?

(2) How can taxation be employed to reduce the inefficiency of private markets (for example, to offset sources of inefficiency in those markets resulting from noncompetitive conditions, or the presence of external costs or benefits arising from the production or consumption of those goods)?

(3) How can objectives of income redistribution be achieved with the minimum distortion of the efficiency of the economy?

Any tax collected from one group to finance payments to another will have an effect on the allocation of resources, for it is hardly likely that those gaining income would demand the same types and quantities of goods that would have been chosen by those paying the taxes. But the imposition of a tax does not necessarily mean that the efficiency of the system has been affected. An efficient economy is not unique. As seen in the discussion of the Edgeworth box diagram (Chapter 5), all points on the contract curve represent efficiency in exchange, although they involve vastly different distributions of income. Efficiency (that is, a Pareto optimum) simply means that there is no change that can benefit one person without hurting another. A tax affects efficiency only if the gains resulting from a tax are not equal to the losses when both are measured in money terms. A pure, lump-sum redistribution of money from one person to another does not affect efficiency, for example, even when the two individuals have quite different tastes or income levels and the redistribution changes perceptibly the allocation of resources.

The phrase *excess burden* is used to describe the effect of a tax on efficiency. A neutral tax is one that has no excess burden and therefore does not affect the efficiency of the economy. The size of the excess burden of any tax is measured by the excess of money losses over gains resulting from the tax.

To facilitate the measurement of excess burden, we shall here arbitrarily assume that the benefits of a tax equal the amount collected. Presumably, legislatures believe that gains from government expenditures usually exceed the tax cost. Our assumption will therefore tend to cause an overestimate of the excess burden of a tax. Somewhat compensating for this, the costs of administering the tax will be ignored. With these assumptions, then, the burden of a tax will be measured by how much worse off, in money terms, are the individuals who are affected by the tax. The excess burden is then these losses minus the amount of tax collected.

It might appear that under these assumptions any tax would have a neutral effect, that both losses and gains would simply be measured by the amount of tax revenue. However, this is not true. Losses can exceed the amount paid in taxes. It is this possibility that leads to the excess burden of taxation.

In analyzing the effects of a tax, it is important to consider the incidence of the tax (that is, who actually bears the burden of the tax). The incidence of a tax imposed on the operations of a business firm, for example, may fall on the firm and its owners, but it may be shifted, wholly or in part, to customers or suppliers.

The concepts of incidence and excess burden are illustrated in Figure 18.1, which shows the long-run effects of a unit excise tax imposed on the product of a perfectly competitive increasing cost industry. The price before the tax is OP, the output OQ. The im-

Figure 18.1   *Incidence and Excess Burden of an Excise Tax*

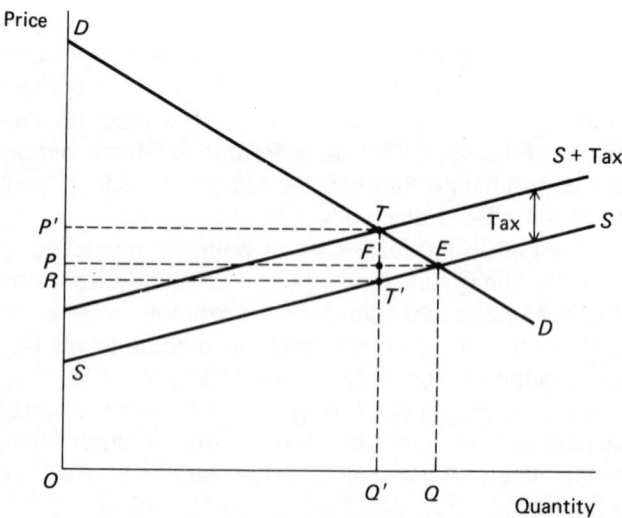

position of a tax of TT' per unit raises the price to the consumer to OP' and reduces the net revenue per unit to the seller to OR; output declines to OQ' and total tax yield is $TT'RP'$.

Of the total tax yield, amount $TFPP'$ is paid by customers. The burden on them, however, also includes area TFE, which is a measure of the loss to those demanders who have stopped buying this good because of the rise in price. Total burden on demanders is therefore area $P'TEP$. Note that this is also the decline in the area of consumer surplus (that is, the area below the demand curve and above the price line) from the pretax surplus of PED to the posttax surplus of $P'TD$.

On the supply side, in the short run some of the burden of the tax would fall on the individual firms in this perfectly competitive industry, forcing their profits temporarily below the normal level. In the long run illustrated in Figure 18.1, however, all the firms remaining in this competitive industry after the imposition of the tax would again be making normal profits, and the burden of the tax not absorbed by consumers would fall on the suppliers of the scarce factor of production responsible for the rise in this long-run competitive supply curve. Remember that for the increasing cost competitive industry costs rise because as the industry expands the price of some scarce factor of production increases. The imposition of the tax in Figure 18.1 will reduce the rents of this scarce factor from area PES before the tax to $RT'S$ after the tax. The burden of the tax on the factor thus equals area $PET'R$, which includes the tax that falls on the factors (area $PFT'R$), plus area FET' (the drop in rents caused by the imposition of the tax on factors no longer employed in producing the good). The total burden on the factor suppliers is thus the decline in their rents from PES before the tax to $RT'S$ afterwards.

The total burden of the tax then equals area $P'TET'R$, the sum of the burdens on demanders and suppliers.

Against this total burden must be set the gain from the tax revenues to whoever benefits from them. By our current assumption, this is equal to the tax yield—area $P'TT'R$.

The excess burden, therefore, is the triangle TET', which represents the efficiency loss resulting from the imposition of the tax.

Note that the excess burden of this efficiency loss results solely because demanders and suppliers change the quantities of the good or service they demand and supply. If either demand or supply were perfectly inelastic, the quantity of the good produced would not change, and no efficiency loss would be incurred.

Some possible extensions and qualifications to this analysis should be noted. In the case discussed, the changes in the prices of the product and the scarce factor would have further ramifications throughout the economy. The effects of these price changes would be felt in industries producing products that are close substitutes or complements of the item taxed, and also in other industries using the scarce factor whose price has decreased.

Further, it has been implicitly assumed here that the taxed industry is operating in an otherwise efficient economy. The existence of monopoly or of externalities in the economy would require a modification of the analysis and conclusions. If, for example, the taxed industry causes significant external costs, the reduction in the output of this industry induced by the tax would reduce those external costs and raise the level of the efficiency of the economy.

The tax theory here is intended to provide some general tools of analysis; applying them to specific situations requires broad knowledge of actual conditions.

NEUTRAL TAXES

A neutral tax is one that does not affect the efficiency of the economy; the burden of a neutral tax equals the amount of the tax. Except for a random tax or a head tax bearing equally on all persons, the only tax that does not affect efficiency[2] is one that falls exclusively on economic surpluses. A tax on economic rent, an appropriation by government of consumer surplus, or a tax on excess profits, will not affect efficiency. (This, of course, was the basis for Henry George's espousal of the single tax on land.)

The practical difficulties of identifying, measuring, and appropriating such surpluses are great; it is unlikely that any modern government could rely on such sources for financing its expenditures.

Suppose a government wished to tax consumer surplus on some good. Unless the supply or demand function is perfectly inelastic, an excise tax would inevitably affect the quantity of the good purchased. To tax only consumer surplus, the tax must not apply to the marginal unit of consumption. Clearly, it would be virtually impossible for such a tax to be devised.

Analogously, a tax on economic rents can be neutral with respect to efficiency only because it does not apply to marginal units of the supply of the factor of production being taxed.

A tax on the excess profits of a profit-maximizing firm is neutral because the tax will not cause the firm to change its price or output policy. Excess profits are a surplus over the amount the capital could

[2]A government may of course *want* to use taxes to affect the efficiency of the economy, particularly if it considers that private markets are for some reason operating inefficiently. In such cases the neutral taxes mentioned would *not* be effective.

earn in alternative uses. Until a profits tax cuts into normal profits, it will cause no reallocation of capital. It is, of course, difficult in practice to devise a tax that falls only on excess profits as defined by the economist.

INCIDENCE AND BURDEN OF EXCISE TAXES

The incidence of an excise tax can fall on three groups: buyers, firms supplying the good, and the factors employed in producing it. The share of a tax that would be paid by each group depends on the slopes of the demand and supply functions (including the supply functions of the factors), and on the competitiveness of the industry taxed.

Consider first the long-run effects of a tax. In a perfectly competitive industry, none of the tax will fall on the firms, which by definition will be making normal profits both before and after the tax. For a constant cost competitive industry, the entire tax falls on buyers, the price rising by the amount of the tax. In the increasing cost industry, only part of the tax falls on buyers; the rest is shifted to that factor of production responsible for the increasing costs of the industry. The price of this factor falls as the tax induces a decline in the industry's output and a reduction in the employment of this factor. The steeper the demand curve and the less steep the supply curve of the industry, the larger will be the share of the tax falling on the buyers, and the less on the factor.

In a decreasing cost competitive industry, an excise tax will lead to a rise in the price of the product that is even greater than the amount of the tax. This excess price rise in effect goes to pay the higher average costs of production for this industry as output declines.

In the short run, part of the tax will fall on the profits of the firm. The steeper the slope of the industry's supply curve, the greater is the proportion of the tax that will come out of the profits of the firms.

In general, a given excise tax will raise the price of a monopolist's product less than the increase in the price of a product produced competitively under comparable demand and cost conditions. In contrast to the competitive case, even in the long run, part of an excise tax may fall on a monopolist's profits.[3]

---

[3]For example, a monopolist with constant costs facing a linear demand curve will raise his price by only half the amount of the tax, the other half coming from the firm's profits. In general, the increasing cost monopolist will raise price by less than half the tax (but more than half the comparable competitive price rise), and a decreasing cost monopolist will raise price by more than half the tax (but by less than half the increase of a competitive industry with comparable demand and costs). (These cases are based on linear demand and cost functions.)

Returning to the competitive case, the incidence of an excise tax depends on the slopes of supply and demand functions, but the excess burden of an excise tax is a function of the elasticities of supply and demand. The excess burden is equal to that reduction in surpluses—of consumers, firms, and factors—not offset by the yield of a tax. An excise tax causes output to be reduced. The burden is then measured by the surpluses that buyers, sellers, and factors lose as a result of the reduction in output.

As the size of an excise tax on a product increases, the excess burden increases more than proportionally. With linear demand and supply functions, for example, the excess burden is proportional to the square of the unit tax. The total tax *yield* from raising the size of a unit excise tax on any one product, on the other hand, first increases and then decreases. In the limit the yield of a tax becomes zero when the tax rate is prohibitive and no one is willing to buy the taxed product.

Figure 18.2 *Excess Burden and Yield*

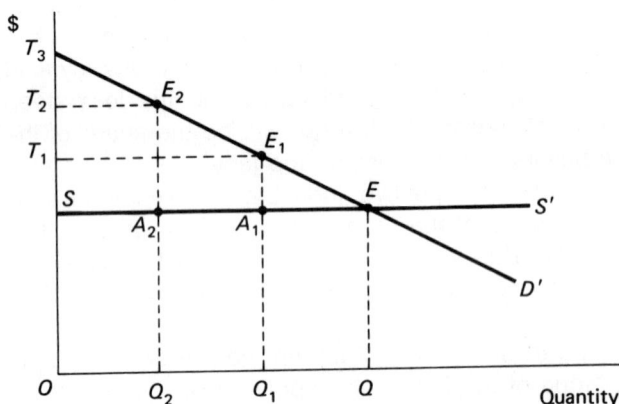

These points are illustrated in Figure 18.2 where the excess burdens and yields of different rates of excise taxation are shown for a constant cost competitive industry in the long run. With a tax per unit of ST_1, the yield is $ST_1E_1A_1$; the excess burden is E_1EA_1. A doubling of the unit tax to ST_2 does not here increase the yield ($ST_2E_2A_2 = ST_1E_1A_1$), but the excess burden with the second tax is E_2EA_2, which is four times the excess burden created by the first tax. In the limit, a tax of ST_3 (which is three times the size of the first tax) has a zero yield—the amount demanded drops to zero—but has an excess burden (ST_3E) nine times as great as the excess burden of the first tax.

As the size of the tax increases, the yield first rises and then falls to zero, but the excess burden increases geometrically.[4]

MINIMIZING EXCESS BURDEN

An objective of policy might well be to maximize the ratio of yield to excess burden, that is, to minimize the excess burden per dollar of yield. A useful construct here is a curve that plots the output of the good against the measure of the vertical distance between the supply and demand curves. This might be called a net benefit curve because it measures the sum of the marginal surpluses or benefits to buyers and sellers. The area under this curve represents the

Figure 18.3   *Derivation of Net Surplus Curve*

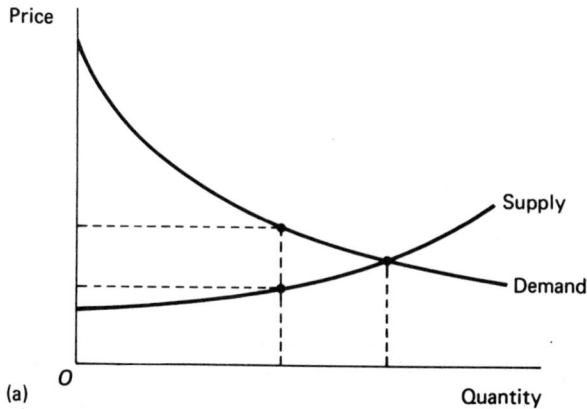

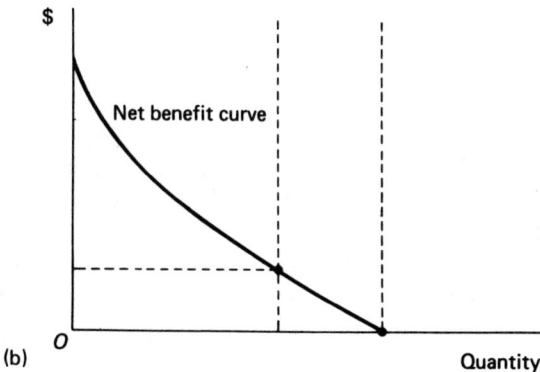

[4]With nonlinear demand and supply curves, the yield may rise and fall more than once; nevertheless, the total yield will be zero at two points: with a zero tax and with a prohibitive tax.

surpluses out of which tax revenues can come. The net benefit curve of Figure 18.3b is derived from the demand and supply curves of Figure 18.3a. The net benefit curve reaches zero at that output at which demand and supply curves intersect.

It can be shown that the ratio of yield to excess burden is an inverse function of the elasticity of this net benefit curve.[5] The elasticity of the net benefit curve approaches zero as the net benefit curve approaches zero. Generally, the smaller the tax, the greater the ratio of yield to excess burden. The optimum excise tax structure, from the point of view of minimizing excess burden per dollar of yield, is therefore that which imposes a small tax on many goods, rather than a large tax on a few goods. A general sales tax is thus less distorting than excise taxes of equal yield placed on a few goods. The optimum excise tax structure for a smaller number of goods would tax each good to the point at which the elasticities of the net benefit curves of all goods would be equal, thus equalizing the marginal ratio of yield to excess burden for all goods.

Although excise taxes on individual goods are popular and convenient sources of revenue for governments, they are, from an efficiency viewpoint, difficult to defend except in one important situation: when the production or consumption of the good gives rise to external costs. This is presumably one argument for taxes on liquor. In such cases, the objectives of revenue and regulation happily and untypically encourage the same policies.

Conversely, a negative excise tax (that is, a subsidy) may be appropriate when external economies exist and the government wishes to encourage the production and distribution of a good. The extreme case is free distribution of a good (for example, primary and secondary education).

TAXES ON INCOME

Income taxes are popular methods of raising revenues, and progressive income taxes are commonly defended as a way of redistributing incomes from high to low income groups. Because of the ubiquity of taxes on income it is important to analyze their economic consequences.

An income tax may cause an individual to increase, decrease, or leave unchanged the quantity he offers of the services of the factors from which he derives income. This inconclusive statement

---

[5]Specifically, the ratio of marginal yield to marginal excess burden (dY/dB) equals $(1 - e)/e$ (where e, the elasticity of the net benefit curve, has the conventional positive sign). If the elasticity of the net benefit curve is greater than one, an increase in the tax rate results in a greater excess burden but a *reduced* total tax yield.

has the advantage of being true, which cannot be said for such assertions as that taxes discourage people from working or saving. A tax, say on labor income, has two types of effects—income and substitution—on the amount of labor an individual will offer to supply, which may well work in opposite directions. The net result of a tax on income then depends on which effect is dominant.

A tax on labor income means that the individual gets less (after-tax) income for each hour of work. This by itself would induce him, through the substitution effect, to shift from work to leisure, and to work fewer hours. But there is also an income effect. His income is lower than before, which *ceteris paribus* lowers his marginal rate of substitution between money and effort. He has less money, and hence is willing to supply more effort to get money.[6] When a factor of production is supplied perfectly inelastically, we know the income and substitution effects exactly balance each other, so that the same quantity of the factor is supplied regardless of its price, or of a tax.

Figure 18.4 illustrates the effects of an income tax. The hori-

Figure 18.4   *Income and Lump-sum Tax*

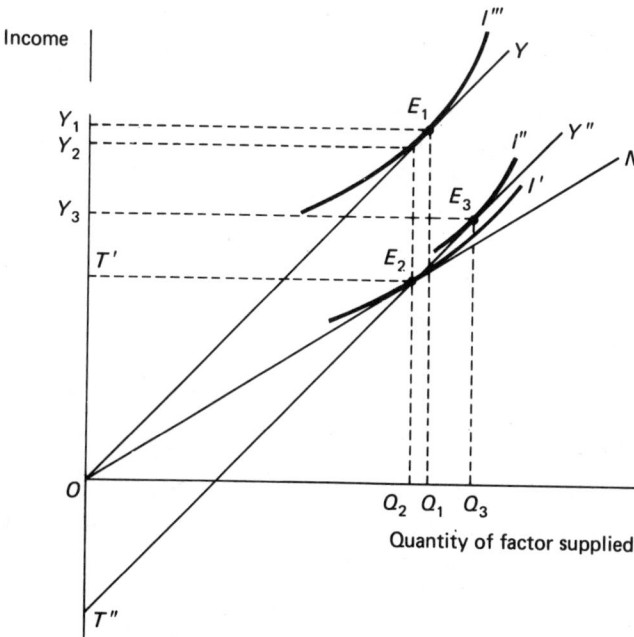

[6]In utility terms, the tax lowers his income and hence raises the marginal utility of money to him. He extends his hours of work to the point where the marginal disutility of effort equals the marginal utility of money.

zontal axis measures units of the productive service supplied (for example, hours of labor or quantity of capital-savings); income is measured on the vertical axis. The indifference curves show the individual's preference pattern for various combinations of effort and income.

If the individual has no income other than that received from the supply of his services, his opportunity line OY begins at the origin and rises with a slope equal to the price at which he can sell his factor services. His equilibrium is at point E_1, supplying OQ_1 units of the factor for a total income of OY_1. Assuming (as we shall here) that the market price of the factor is equal to the value of the factor's marginal productivity, the equilibrium is efficient.

A proportional income tax of 40 percent has the effect of lowering the individual's opportunity line. Each point on it is 40 percent below the corresponding point on his original opportunity line. Line ON is the new opportunity line showing his after-tax income for each quantity of service supplied. The vertical distance between OY and ON is the amount of the tax collected. Responding to the after-tax income line ON, the individual's new equilibrium is at E_2. He offers OQ_2 units of the factor, for which he receives total before tax income of OY_2, pays a tax of $T'Y_2$, and has a net income of OT'.

In the case illustrated the substitution effect dominates and the individual supplies fewer services as a result of the tax; but another individual might offer more hours of effort in response to this tax, depending on the shapes of his indifference curves and, hence, on the relative impacts of the income and substitution effects.

The result is not efficient. The individual's marginal rate of substitution (MRS) between income and leisure is not equal to the marginal productivity of his services. The marginal productivity is equal to the slope of line OY (that is, what the services are worth to the employer), but the individual's MRS is equal to the lesser slope of line ON.

LUMP SUM TAXES

The inefficiency is caused by the form of the tax, not by the existence of the tax. To illustrate this, let us assume another tax of the same amount—a lump-sum tax rather than one varying with the individual's income. The individual's opportunity line would then begin at a point T'' below the origin, where OT'' is the lump-sum tax, equal to $T'Y_2$, the amount that would have been collected with the proportional income tax. The opportunity line with the lump-sum is then $T''Y''$. Note that this opportunity line necessarily goes through point E_2.

The equilibrium of the individual under these new conditions would be at point E_3. His after-tax income, is OY_3, and he offers OQ_3 units of the factor in supply.

Compared with the original untaxed situation, there is no substitution effect here because the price the individual receives per unit of his services is unchanged. The income effect does operate and is likely to cause him to offer to supply more units of the factor than he would have supplied if he had not been taxed at all.

The result of the lump-sum tax is efficient. Clearly, the individual is better off (that is, on a higher indifference curve) with the lump-sum tax than he would have been with the proportional income tax. The individual's equilibrium with the lump-sum tax at E_3 must lie on a higher indifference curve than the equilibrium with the income tax E_2 because the opportunity line $T''Y''$ with the lump-sum tax intersects the indifference curve at point E_2 and must therefore be tangent to a higher indifference curve. Thus the consumer is better off with the lump-sum tax, while the government is indifferent between the two forms of taxes, giving the same yield.

Furthermore, at the equilibrium (E_3) with the lump-sum tax, the individual's marginal rate of substitution between income and effort is equal to the value of the marginal productivity of his factor services, a necessary condition for efficiency. The slope of the opportunity line with the lump-sum tax, and hence the slope of the indifference curve at the point of tangency, equals the price of the factor, which by assumption measures the value of the factor's marginal productivity.

INCOME SUBSIDIES

The principles discussed here create problems in practice. Lump-sum taxes are not particularly feasible. And even if they were, they would run contrary to the basic intent of many income taxes. If we wish to use a tax to redistribute income, quite obviously the tax must be based on income and cannot be a lump-sum tax.

This problem, and indeed many of the principles developed in this discussion of taxes, also appear when income subsidies are considered. One way of distributing income is to finance payments to low income individuals from taxes on high income persons. As with taxes, lump-sum grants have less impact on efficiency than do grants that vary with earned income. The problem here is how to raise the incomes of low income persons without affecting their incentive to work. As a minimum, one might suggest that welfare payments should not be tailored so the individual receives no net monetary gain when he seeks employment; he should be permitted to retain at least part of his earned income.

Figure 18.5   *Effects of Income Guarantee*

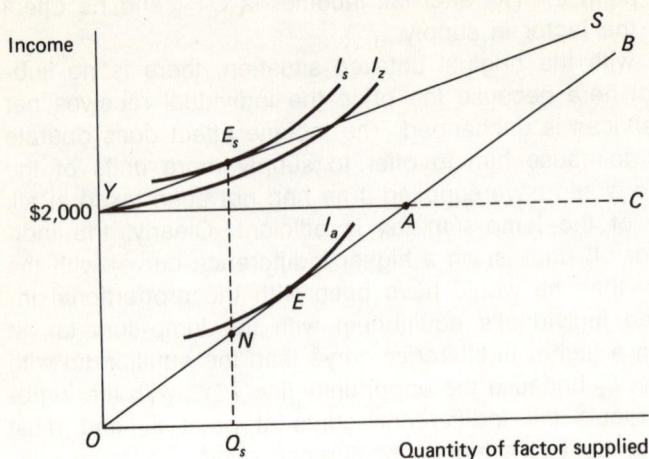

The idea that every individual should be guaranteed a certain minimum income is discussed with increasing frequency. The effect of a minimum income guarantee is illustrated in Figure 18.5. Without an income guarantee, the individual's opportunity line is *OB*, the slope of which equals the wage rate. Opportunity line *OB* is tangent to an indifference curve at the equilibrium point *E*. If the government then commits itself to pay an individual any difference between $2000 and his other income, his opportunity line becomes the kinked line *YAB*. Up to point *A* his income is $2000, regardless of whether he works or not. The highest indifference curve the individual can reach along opportunity line *YAB* is I_z at point *Y* itself. He does not work.

A rise in the wage rate the individual could earn would swing line *OB* up and move the location of the kink to the left along line *YC*. Only if *OB* rose enough to cut indifference curve I_z would the individual ignore the income guarantee and rely on wage earnings.

If the individual were instead allowed to retain some portion of his wage income, say half, his opportunity line would be *YS*, the slope of which would equal half the wage. Equilibrium is at point E_s. His total income is $E_s Q_s$, of which $Q_s N$ comes from wages and the rest from the income supplement. Note that the supplement is less than $2000—reduced by an amount equal to half the wages earned by the individual.

TAXATION AND EQUITY

The discussion of taxes here is necessarily incomplete. Taxation issues go far beyond considerations amenable to objective economic analysis. Taxation touches each of us deeply and sensitively. Equity considerations cannot be ignored.

The existing tax structure of a nation, a state, a village, is rooted in history. Any change will almost inevitably affect some individuals with force. An argument can be made that the fairest tax structure is that which exists and has existed because individuals have adjusted to it and have made lasting commitments in response to it. It has been said that anything is fair if it was correctly anticipated at the time decisions were made. The homeowner regards an unexpected rise in property taxes as unfair. The traveler is convinced that transportation taxes are inequitable. Such considerations of equity dominate our personal views of taxation—and perhaps rightly so.

In this area, above all, one is aware that economics is not just a matter of efficiency, that economic policies must be responsive to the prevailing views of equity, for they too—when sustained or violated—affect the welfare of society.

REVIEW QUESTIONS

1. Explain the following concepts:
   Ability-to-pay
   The benefit principle
   Incidence of a tax
   Burden of a tax
   Excess burden of a tax
   Neutral taxes
   Principle of equal sacrifice
   Proportional, progressive, and regressive taxes
2. Under what conditions does the principle of equal sacrifice require a proportional tax?
3. Compare income, property, and sales taxes, from the standpoint of efficiency and equity. (Define carefully your concept of equity.)

FURTHER READING

Musgrave, Richard A., and Alan T. Peacock, eds., *Classics in the Theory of Public Finance*. New York: St. Martin's (1967).

Musgrave, Richard A., *The Theory of Public Finance*. New York: McGraw-Hill (1959).

19

GOVERNMENT REGULATION

PRICE AND NONPRICE REGULATION

Governments influence economic activity through the direct regulation of the behavior of private individuals and firms, as well as with the budgetary methods discussed in the last two chapters. The regulation has a significant impact on the allocation of resources—the types and amounts of goods produced, and the methods and locations of production—as well as on the level and stability of prices and the incomes of various groups and individuals.

Price regulation is perhaps the most obvious type of such regulation. In the private economy, individual consumers, suppliers of factor services, and business firms respond to the prices of goods and services in making their economic decisions. It is therefore natural for governments to attempt to influence prices directly, as with minimum and maximum price controls or laws against discriminatory pricing.

In addition, governments establish a wide range of regulations over nonprice variables: entry, quality and performance standards, production methods, information requirements, even location.

PRICE REGULATIONS: PURPOSES AND EFFECTS

Price regulation has two types of consequences: it affects the incomes of sellers and buyers, and it influences the allocation of resources by encouraging or discouraging production and sale of products. The usual defense of price regulation is that it protects buyers against unjustifiably high prices or supports the incomes of sellers at a level deemed equitable by legislatures. The allocational effects of price control are often considered secondary and are, unfortunately, often undesirable.

Price regulation is a means, not an end. Its objectives may often be achieved with other techniques—regulation of output, taxes, and subsidies. A combination of techniques is frequently more effective than a single technique. In fact, to be effective, price control almost always must be supplemented with regulation of output (for example, rationing). Effective price control implies the existence of excess demands for maximum prices or excess supplies for minimum prices. Price regulation by itself does not eliminate these excess market pressures which, if left uncontained, may in practice destroy the effectiveness of the price controls.

Consider the effects on a competitive industry of price regulation unaccompanied by any supplementary controls. Both minimum and maximum price control by themselves tend to reduce the amount of the good being produced. When supply and demand are not in equilibrium at a market-clearing price, the "short side" of the market will dominate.[1] In general, buyers cannot be forced to purchase more nor sellers required to supply more at any given price than the amounts they are willing to buy or sell, as shown by their demand and supply curves. At a regulated minimum price above the equilibrium level, for example, OP′ in Figure 19.1, only OQ′ will be sold; at a regulated maximum price below the equilibrium level, for example, OP″, only OQ″ will be supplied. Both quantities OQ′ and OQ″ are less than the equilibrium output OQ. Maximum price regulation leaves some buyers unsatisfied, while minimum price control creates unsatisfied sellers.[2]

These results are often inconsistent with the basic purposes of price regulation. Maximum price control is usually designed to protect buyers, while the usual function of minimum price regulation is to help sellers.

To achieve these objectives, price regulation is often combined with further controls. Maximum price control, especially for public utilities, is often accompanied by a requirement that sellers supply all customers who wish to buy, thus protecting buyers from unavailability of supplies.

[1]Robert Clower, "Keynes and the Classics: A Dynamical Perspective," *Quarterly Journal of Economics* 74 (1960), 318–323.

[2]Exceptions to these generalizations, to be noted below, may arise if the unregulated price is set monopolistically or monopsonistically.

Figure 19.1 *Effects of Price Regulation on Output*

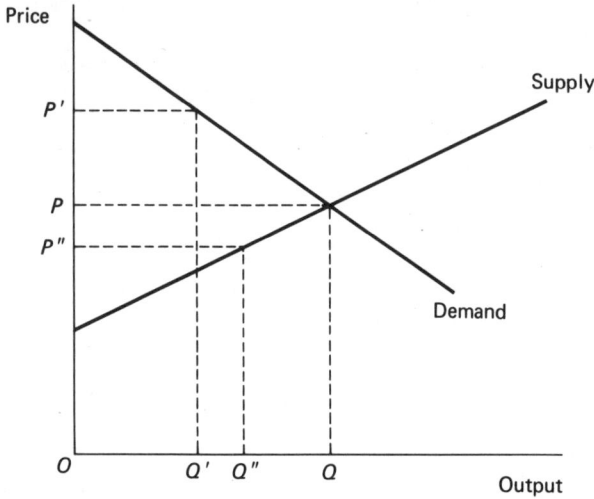

Unfortunately, these secondary regulations create further problems. Unless they are protected against competition, sellers may be
unwilling to produce at all in a market if their price is regulated and
they are required to serve all customers. Maximum price control,
originally conceived as a protection for buyers, therefore often leads
to restrictions on entry into the field to protect the market position
of sellers. The original objectives of the regulation can thus be
completely reversed.

Minimum price control by itself may create unsatisfied sellers
who are unable to find buyers at the price support level. A secondary provision of minimum price laws is therefore often an offer by
the government to buy any output not purchased by other buyers
at the regulated price. This, in turn, often leads to further regulation
in the form of restrictions on production of the regulated product
in order to limit the amount of excess supply the government would
be required to purchase.

Price regulation is indeed complicated, and often has broad and
unanticipated consequences. By weakening the role of prices in
determining the allocation of resources, price regulation makes
necessary the establishment of alternative allocative devices that,
unfortuntately, are usually cumbersome and rarely as effective as
prices.

MINIMUM PRICE REGULATION

Minimum price regulation is effective only if the minimum price
level is higher than the unregulated price would be, which implies
an excess of supply over demand at the regulated price.

Figure 19.2 *Minimum Price Regulation*

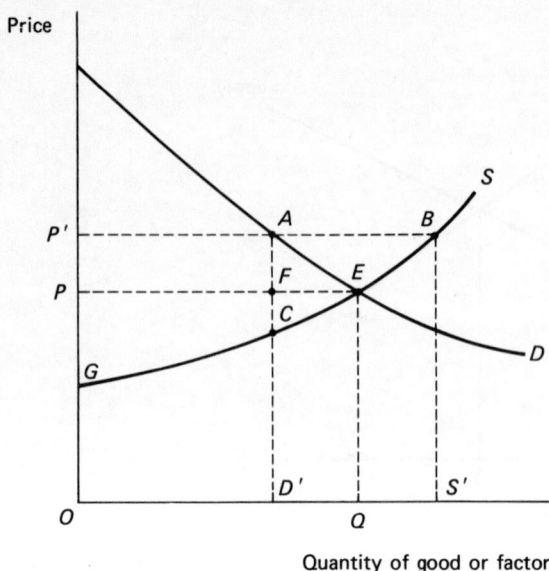

Quantity of good or factor

Consider the competitive situation illustrated in Figure 19.2. Without price regulation, output would be *OQ,* price *OP,* and the total income of suppliers area *OPEQ.* Assume that the government establishes a minimum price of *OP'.* If the government does not offer to purchase the excess supply, but only makes sales at prices lower than *OP'* illegal, the income of the suppliers will be *OP'AD'.* This may be more or less than the suppliers would have received under unregulated market conditions, depending on the elasticity of demand for the product. If demand is elastic over the range between output *OD'* and *OQ,* minimum price regulation will cause the incomes of suppliers to drop; if, however, this section of the demand curve is inelastic, price regulation will raise the suppliers' revenues.

Even if the gross incomes of suppliers are no larger under price regulation, they may be better off. At the lower level of output their total costs of production are reduced. In the case illustrated, the suppliers are slightly better off with price regulation. Without regulation the suppliers' surplus of revenues over costs is area *PEG;* with regulation their surplus is area *P'ACG.* The less elastic the demand and the more elastic the supply, the more likely price regulation will increase the surplus of suppliers.

Consumers of this product, on the other hand, are worse off under price regulation by an amount equal to area *P'AEP.*

The net efficiency change induced by the price regulation is the sum of the changes in supplier and consumer surpluses. In the case illustrated there is a net efficiency loss equal to the area of the triangle *AEC.* Whenever the unregulated price is a competitive market-clearing price, the establishment of a minimum price will reduce efficiency.

Whether the efficiency loss is worth the presumed improvement in income distribution is, of course, a political question. One might note, however, that as an alternative to price control the same improvement in the suppliers' surpluses could have been accomplished with a government grant to them of an amount equal to area *P'AFP* less *CEF,* with no loss to consumers and no efficiency loss *in this market.*[3] One could argue, also, that the latter policy is more fair in that it puts the burden of raising the income of the suppliers on the general taxpayer rather than on the customer who purchases the good supplied.

Maintenance of prices above the private market level may alternately be accomplished if the government offers to buy any amount offered at the minimum price. In Figure 19.2, the government would then purchase quantity *AB,* the amount of the excess supply. Incomes of producers in this case would definitely be higher than incomes in a private unregulated market would have been, the amount of the increase depending on the elasticity of supply. Incomes would increase at a minimum by the percentage by which the regulated price lies above the private market price, as would be true for a perfectly inelastic supply. The more elastic the supply, the more the incomes of suppliers would increase for any given fixed price, and, of course, the higher the cost to government.

Elasticity of demand does not in this case affect the degree of rise in suppliers' income, but it does have a strong influence on the degree of inefficiency induced by this fixed price policy, as well as the cost to the government and the amount of excess supply it must buy. The efficiency loss cannot be computed without a measure of the value of the supplies purchased by the government, although the limits can be indicated. In one extreme case the government simply discards the supplies it purchases. The efficiency loss in this market, compared with the market equilibrium, is represented by the oddly shaped area *D'AEBS'.*[4]

At the other extreme, if the government's offer price is assumed to be a true measure of the value of the good in the uses to which

[3]The efficiency loss, if any, would be associated with the method of taxation used to finance the subsidy.

[4]Consider it as area *D'CBS',* the marginal cost of the quantity purchased by the government, plus area *AEC,* the loss in surplus on the quantity diverted from private consumption to government purchase.

it is put by the government, there is no efficiency loss from the price fixing; in fact, the private market equilibrium would represent an inefficient situation.[5] In such a case, of course, the government purchases would be justified on efficiency grounds, independent of their effect on the incomes of suppliers.

The dollar costs of a price-fixing program depend on the elasticity of supply for the good whose price is fixed. Long-run supply functions are typically more elastic than short-run supply functions. The costs of a given program will therefore be likely to increase with time, as more producers enter to produce the fixed-price product. Without control of entry, the process of entry will continue until costs of producing the good (including normal profits) rise to meet the fixed price.

In the long run, however, at least in competitive industries, the costs of production rise as the industry output expands, primarily because of the inelasticity of supply of some factor employed by the industry.[6] The income gains from such a fixed price policy will in the long run accrue only to owners of such factors with inelastic supplies and not to the producers themselves. A policy designed to raise wages or profit rates in an industry may, in the long run, simply raise the prices of some other factor used in the industry, the supply of which is not perfectly elastic.[7]

The long-run effects of a policy may thus be quite different from the short-run consequences. A policy that makes sense in the short run may have undesired long-run consequences. Yet it is difficult to phase out a policy or to retain the short-run advantages without incurring the undesired long-run consequences.[8]

Efforts of governments to maintain prices or incomes inconsistent with those arising from private competitive markets conflict with the pressures toward efficient allocation of resources inherent in the variable prices of competitive private markets. Low prices or incomes induce the owners of the factors to move to uses of higher

[5]The exact efficiency gain from the fixed price can be shown only if we have a government demand curve showing the marginal value of various quantities when consumed or purchased by the government. If, for example, the government gives food acquired under a price support law to the schools or as foreign aid, the net efficiency loss of the price support is reduced by the value of the good in those uses.

[6]Recall the discussion of the increasing cost industry, Chapter 9. If the industry has constant or decreasing costs, there will be no limit on the entry of new firms attracted by the excess profits available.

[7]An example is support of tobacco prices, the long-run tendency of which is simply to raise the rents of lands suitable for tobacco growing.

[8]Many efforts of states and municipalities to attract new industry appear to illustrate the principles discussed here.

productivity. Any artificial elevation of these prices in the interests of fairness is likely to encourage inefficiency in the allocation of the resources. Whether the benefits are worth the costs is a question of public policy.

MINIMUM PRICE CONTROL IN A MONOPSONISTIC MARKET

The proposition that minimum price regulation induces inefficiency in the allocation of resources must be qualified when applied to a market dominated by a monopsonist. Here, price regulation may constitute an offsetting imperfection that increases efficiency.

Figure 19.3 *Minimum Price Regulation and Monopsony*

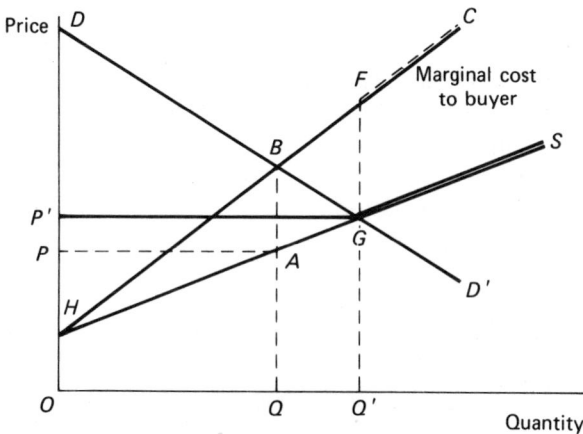

The case is illustrated in Figure 19.3 for the monopsonistic buyer of the services of a factor of production. Curve *DD'* shows the value to the buyer of each additional unit of the factor, and curve *HS* is the factor supply curve. The marginal factor cost to the buyer shown by curve *HC* lies above the factor supply curve because when the monopsonist hires an additional unit of the factor he must raise the price paid to the factors he currently employs. In profit-maximizing equilibrium the employer hires *OQ* units of the factor at a price of *OP*. As noted earlier,[9] this will be below the efficient, competitive quantity of *OQ'*.

If the government introduces minimum price control for this factor at *OP'*, the level that would result from a competitive market, the supply curve of the factor to this buyer becomes the kinked curve *P'GS,* and the marginal factor cost coincides with the supply

[9]See the analysis of monopsony in Chapter 15.

curve to point *G*, at which point it jumps to segment *FC* of the original marginal factor cost curve. For quantities of the factor up to *OQ'*, the regulated price must be paid; for larger quantities, the minimum price regulation is ineffective and the unregulated supply and marginal factor cost curves are applicable.

Under these conditions, the monopsonist finds it profitable to employ *OQ'* units of the factor (that is, the competitive quantity). Minimum price regulation here offsets the inefficiency of monopsony, and competitive efficiency is achieved.

The case illustrated assumes an omniscient government that chooses exactly the right price to set. Although only price *OP'* would move the monopsonist exactly to the efficient level of employment, any price above *OP* and below *QB* would cause the employment of the monopsonist to move closer to the efficient level.

Minimum price regulation for a factor will improve the utilization of the factor only when applied to imperfect markets. A government that uses minimum price control to raise factor prices may discover the reason for the low prices is low productivity rather than monopsony. In that event, the minimum price control will simply cause unemployment of the factor; then, alternative methods of raising incomes should be considered.

MAXIMUM PRICE REGULATION

Maximum price regulation is often employed to hold prices down to what is considered a fair level and is used in two types of situations: (1) with monopolies—especially natural monopolies such as public utilities, and (2) in periods of general inflation, particularly wartime.

While many definitions of what constitutes a fair price level could be advanced, the discussion here is limited to what is probably the most commonly employed criterion of fairness—nondiscriminatory prices equal to average cost.

Maximum Price Regulation for the Monopoly

As minimum price regulation can lead to increased efficiency in the presence of monopsony, regulation of maximum prices can induce monopolists to produce at a more efficient level. At the same time, the public's desire for greater fairness in the prices of a monopolist may be achieved.

The effects of maximum price regulation on a monopolist depend on the nature of the monopolist's cost function. If a nondiscriminating decreasing cost monopolist is required to set a price equal to average cost, thus eliminating its excess profits, the firm's output will move closer to an efficient point. In Figure 19.4,

Figure 19.4   *Maximum Price Regulation: Decreasing Cost Monopolist*

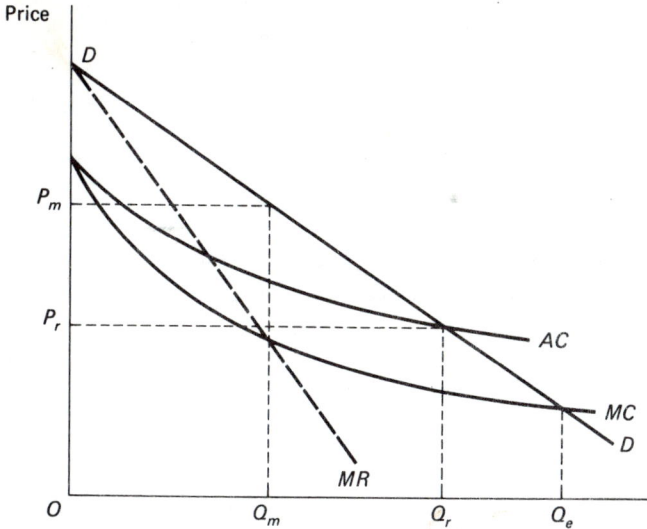

the profit-maximizing price of the unregulated monopoly is OP_m, and the output of OQ_m falls short of the efficient output OQ_e. If the monopolist is required by law to charge a price no higher than OP_r, he expands output to OQ_r. His profits here are normal. Output under regulation is greater than the unregulated output, but for the decreasing cost monopolist it still falls short of the point of maximum economic efficiency. Some inefficiency will still exist because customers willing to pay marginal cost but not average cost will not be served. This is the perennial paradox of pricing for a decreasing cost firm: the efficient price will not produce revenues sufficient to cover total costs.[10]

The reaction of an increasing cost monopolist to maximum price regulation depends on whether he is also required to serve all customers who wish to buy. In Figure 19.5 for example, OP_r is the legal maximum price the firm may charge. The effective demand curve for the firm under regulation is P_rCD'; the marginal revenue curve follows the demand curve from P_r to C and then jumps down to MS.

Under these conditions, the profit-maximizing monopolist will wish to produce only OQ' units of the good; beyond that point his marginal cost exceeds marginal revenue. Demand for his product at the regulated price exceeds this output, and the firm would have to institute some form of rationing. Further, at this output the firm would still be making some excess profits.

[10]As discussed in Chapter 12, discriminatory pricing is one method of achieving the efficient output while generating revenues sufficient to cover total costs.

Figure 19.5 *Maximum Price Regulation: Increasing Cost Monopolist*

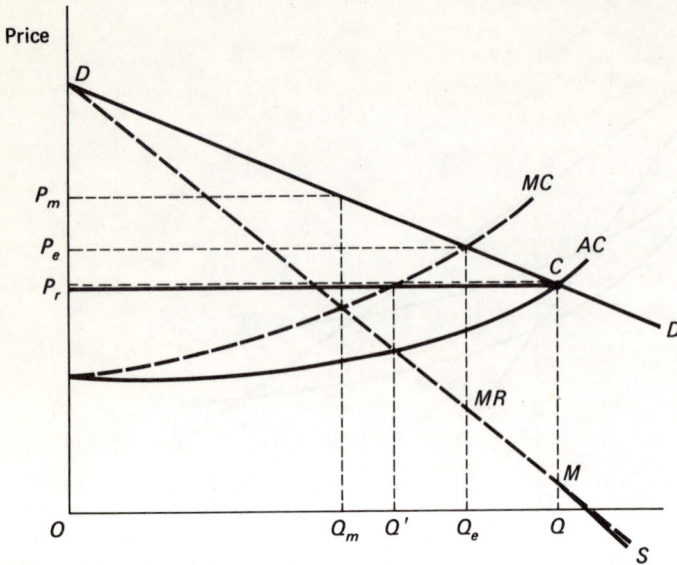

By requiring the firm to serve all customers, regulation would induce an expansion in output to OQ at which point all customers would be supplied, price would equal average cost, and the firm would be making normal profits.

The effect of regulation here is to cause output to be expanded *beyond* the point of efficiency. The efficient output is OQ_e, with price OP_e. This price does not, however, satisfy the requirement of equity (interpreted as the absence of excess profits).

Increasing cost monopolists are probably uncommon, but the same type of conflict between efficiency and equity can arise with a regulated firm whose costs have been increasing over time as part of a general price inflation. Efficiency price should be equal to *current* marginal cost. Because many of the firm's costs were incurred at periods of a lower general price level this may exceed the firm's *accounting* average cost (which forms the basis for determining the regulated price), even when technologically the firm has decreasing cost.

A combination of techniques that can help reconcile efficiency and equity objectives in cases where the efficient price provides profits that are regarded as excessive would be to combine an efficiency price for the product with an excess profits tax. The analogous mixture of techniques for the decreasing cost firm for which the efficient price fails to provide sufficient revenues to cover costs is an efficiency price plus a subsidy to cover the deficiency in revenues.

Maximum Price Regulation for Competitive Industries

In the short run, competitive prices may rise well above an average cost level, particularly when demand has increased suddenly and sharply (as in wartime) and the supply of the good is quite inelastic (for example, housing). Maximum price control in such a situation has essentially the same effects as for the increasing cost monopolist, and producers will not voluntarily supply the existing demand at the regulated maximum price. In contrast to the monopoly situation, however, when many firms exist it is not feasible for the government to require the suppliers to satisfy the demand. The excess demand is therefore likely to continue, and the good will be rationed not by price but by some alternate technique. Rationing may be by an informal method (for example, priority to friends, first-come first-served), or the government may itself institute a rationing system, as with a point system in wartime.

The pressure of excess demand creates incentives for illegal black market sales at prices above the regulated level. Prices are more likely to be held down if illegal *buyers* are penalized than if the *sellers* are liable for violations. Maximum price control creates excess demand. Excess demand is reduced by a decline in demand but is accentuated by a drop in supply. A penalty on buyers has the effect of reducing demand at prices above the regulated level (for example, from DD_1 to $DFGD_1$ in Figure 19.6), thus reducing the excess demand at prices above the regulated level. A penalty on

Figure 19.6   *Black Market: Penalties on Buyers and Sellers*

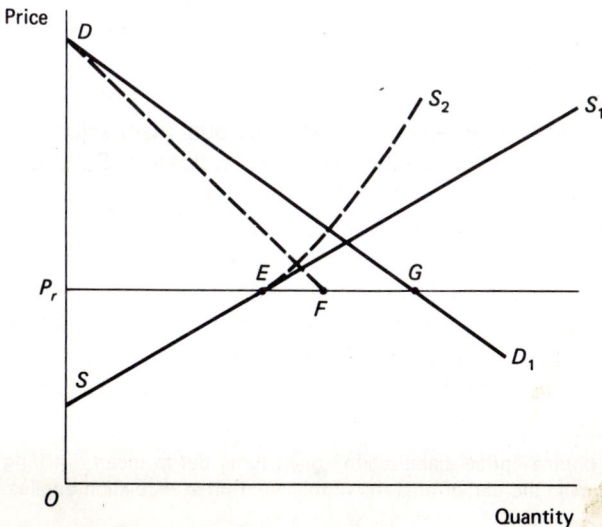

sellers for black market activities has the effect of reducing the amount offered for supply at prices above the regulated level. The penalty on sellers shifts the supply curve from SS_1 to SES_2, which increases the excess demand at prices above the legal limit.

Inefficiency results from maximum price legislation for two reasons. First, it reduces the amount supplied below the efficient level. Second, the supplies that *are* made available are not likely to be distributed efficiently. The seller has no incentive to allocate the available supplies to those demanders who place the highest monetary value on the good.

When excess demand persists, methods of bypassing the legal price limits often develop. They may take many forms: deterioration in the quality of the product; the disappearance of those goods with low profit margins so the customer must shift to less preferred models with higher profit margins; under-the-counter bonuses (as with housing leases); tie-in sales, where the buyer is required to purchase some good he does not wish as a condition for buying a desired product. The speed and ease with which such subterfuges develop suggest that to be effective maximum price controls must either be strongly enforced or must be accepted by the overwhelming majority of the population, who voluntarily reduce their demands for the goods.

PRICE STABILIZATION

Most people appear to prefer stable prices rather than unstable prices. Therefore, governments sometimes attempt to stabilize prices.[11] Prices in private markets are expected to respond to changes in market condition (that is, to fluctuate). Insofar as price variations are considered undesirable (for example, on grounds of unfairness) it may be appropriate public policy to attempt to stabilize them.

In a competitive world of perfect knowledge, price stabilization would be damaging to efficiency, as the previous discussions of maximum and minimum price regulation have indicated. Stabilization of prices is also likely to lead to greater fluctuations in the quantity produced and in the employment of factors than would otherwise occur, and may even cause incomes to vary more than they would in the absence of price stabilization.

An efficiency case for price stabilization can be constructed, however, if one recognizes the prevalence of imperfect knowledge in the economy. Economic efficiency requires that individuals and

---

[11]In practice, the phrase "price-stabilization" often turns out to mean "holding prices up," in which case the earlier analysis of minimum price regulation applies.

firms respond to correct knowledge about the alternatives open to them. Prices play the role of summarizing alternatives. Unless individuals and firms are aware of the prices of all goods and services that are or might be incorporated in their economic activities, they cannot make efficient production and consumption decisions.

The prices that are relevant to the behavior of individuals and firms include not only existing prices but also the future prices of the relevant goods. Most decisions of firms, and many decisions of individuals, commit the firm or individual to a course of behavior over time. Correct knowledge of future opportunities, including future prices in particular, is essential.

Unfortunately, future prices are rarely known with any certainty. Individuals therefore often assume that current prices will continue, and hence base their planning on them.

Price stabilization at levels consistent with longer run economic conditions can facilitate planning and improve long-run efficiency. At a cost of some short-run inefficiency in the allocation of economic resources (short-run excess supplies or demands), stable prices can promote efficiency by improving longer run planning. In addition, the costs of uncertainty and of change associated with fluctuating prices may be reduced.

In an individual case it is a neat judgment whether the short-run costs of stability are less than the advantages gained from stable prices. Only a careful consideration of the characteristics of individual markets (including, in particular, the degree of knowledge of the future on the part of buyers and sellers) can lead to a solution.[12]

REGULATION OF NONPRICE VARIABLES

Nonprice regulation of private economic activity is often used to induce behavior consistent with legislators' concepts of social objectives. Perhaps the most common techniques are control of entry and establishment of performance standards. The two are often used together. A firm or individual is required to obtain government permission before engaging in a specific activity, with performance standards required as a condition for receiving the entry permit. Public utilities, the professions, even taxicabs, require licenses and

[12]A case for stable incomes (especially of factors) can also be developed in utility terms, if one is willing to assume (as many are) that the marginal utility of income declines with increasing income. This implies that the utility lost when income declines is greater than the utility gained when income rises by an equal amount from the same base level. A stable income of $100 a week gives more utility than one which fluctuates but averages $100 weekly.

If a perfectly operating capital market exists, an individual can stabilize his cash receipts in the face of a variable (but predictable) income by borrowing and lending—a fact of slight consolation to most individuals.

have performance standards. Analogous are zoning laws, where permission to build is conditioned on the type of business to be conducted or residence to be constructed.

Several basic reasons for the regulation of entry and performance may be advanced.

(1) Economies of scale may suggest that only a limited number of firms be permitted to operate in a given industry. The results of such limitation could easily be monopoly exploitation of the public. Performance standards—including safety standards, product quality, and the obligation to serve all buyers without discrimination—are added to the standard price or rate regulation.

(2) Much antitrust legislation is based on the opposite grounds, restricting mergers and on occasion requiring the dissolution of companies in order to increase the level of competition.

(3) Entry may be regulated with the purpose of raising the incomes of the producing group. The result is likely to be inefficiency. Entry control may complement minimum price control or public subsidies to ensure that the higher incomes induced by these latter policies are not dissipated in higher costs, as more firms or individuals move in to take advantage of the higher prices or subsidies. Effective control of entry and of the production of existing suppliers can, in fact, make price controls and subsidies unnecessary because prices will rise by themselves in response to the lessened supply. Such entry or production control is often more feasible politically than the alternative price control or subsidies as techniques to raise the income of a group, because the cost of the program is often effectively hidden in the higher prices paid by buyers. Tariffs are an obvious case in point.

(4) Private activity may involve external costs that nonprice regulation may eliminate or reduce (for example, control of air and water pollution, and zoning). External benefits may be encouraged by allowing entry only to those agreeing to operate in such a way that the benefits result.

(5) Information requirements may be placed on firms in order to improve the public's knowledge of the characteristics of the firm's product, thus presumably increasing the effectiveness of the private markets. The efficient operation of a private enterprise economy depends heavily on the availability of information—of prices, the characteristics of goods and services, the availability (present and future) of jobs and productive capacity, or productive techniques, and so on. In a highly productive economy with many products available, the need for information is accentuated, but so are the costs of acquiring and comprehending information.

Closely related to information requirements are laws establishing minimum quality standards for products or services where the characteristics of the good may be important to the buyer but are not readily apparent at the time of purchase. Drugs and foods are obvious examples.

It is clear then that economic theory can provide no broadly applicable rules for the optimum degree and types of regulation of private business. Individuals will necessarily differ in their judgments.

Judgments will no doubt improve and conflicts are likely to be reduced as information concerning the costs and benefits of alternative policies grows. The increasing scope of empirical research in economics and the growing availability of data offer promise.

REVIEW QUESTIONS

1. Explain the following concepts:
   Excess demand
   Excess supply
2. Under what conditions will maximum price control lead to an increase in production? a decrease?
3. Under what conditions will minimum price control cause a decrease in production? an increase?
4. What effect do minimum and maximum price controls have on the gross and net incomes of suppliers?
5. Under what conditions will maximum or minimum price control increase the efficiency of the allocation of economic resources?
6. Discuss the advantages and disadvantages of price stabilization.
7. Discuss the interrelationships between maximum price control and rationing.
8. Compare penalties on sellers and on buyers as methods of discouraging black market transactions.

FURTHER READING

Phillips, Charles F., Jr., *The Economics of Regulation.* rev. ed., Homewood, Ill.: Irwin (1969).

Wilcox, Clair, *Public Policies Toward Business.* 3rd ed., Homewood, Ill.: Irwin (1966).

7

WELFARE ECONOMICS

20

THE
SOCIAL
OPTIMUM

THE NATURE OF WELFARE ECONOMICS

Positive economics describes what is or might be. Welfare or normative economics deals with the evaluation of alternative economic situations.

Through the years most economists have been willing to use economic analysis as a tool for evaluating public policies. More recently, they have been challenged to make their work "value-free," to eliminate the subjective elements of judgment, and to restrict economics to objective, "scientific" statements. Partly in response to this challenge, a branch of economic theory called welfare economics has developed. The aim of welfare economics is not so much to make economic judgments, as to analyze and state formally the conditions or assumptions under which such judgments can be made.

One can distinguish between making judgments and discussing the judgment-making process. The latter can be conducted objectively; the former necessarily involves subjectivity. The statement "The nation should grow faster" is normative and judgmental; but "If we want national income to grow faster, more saving would be useful" is not. To say "All income should be distributed equally" is judgmental; but to say "To maximize the utility of a given amount of income, it should be distributed so that the marginal utility of money is equal for all individuals" is not.

While some economists believe that they should concern themselves only with testable propositions and avoid the use of any nonoperational concept,[1] most economists follow the approach taken in this book. Welfare propositions can and should be discussed but welfare judgments should not be imposed.

The discussion of welfare economics here is divided into two parts. The present chapter deals with the concept of a social optimum (that is, the best possible economy), its characteristics, and the conditions under which it might exist. The following chapter considers changes in a suboptimal world in which the basic question is under what assumptions we can say that a given *change* in economic institutions or behavior will increase or decrease the welfare of society.

A fundamental difficulty is that welfare cannot be measured. One must recognize from the start that it is never possible to assert objectively that any particular economic situation represents higher or lower welfare for society than another. Welfare statements must be based on unprovable assumptions. Welfare economics analyzes the implications of various assumptions. The search is for simple, plausible assumptions on which the broadest and most general statements can be based. Unfortunately, but predictably, the more plausible an assumption, the less useful it is likely to be. Conflicts thus develop. The purpose here is to survey this field of conflict, not to urge the acceptance of any particular assumptions or their welfare implications.

THE SOCIAL WELFARE FUNCTION

The search for a description of a social welfare optimum can begin with a simple concept, the social welfare function, the purpose of which is chiefly to help organize our thinking. It is simply a statement, often written in equational form, that social welfare is a function of a number of variables. We ask what variables affect welfare, what assumptions we wish to make about the functional relation, and what implications follow from alternative assumptions about the function.

The question, "Under what conditions will welfare be maximized?" is converted to the query, "Social welfare is related to what variables, and what is the nature of the relationship between welfare and each variable?"

---

[1]If science is restricted to operational propositions, the truth of which can, at least in principle, be tested, many of the statements of welfare economics are not scientific, although they may involve no valuational statement. By the same test, any mathematical statement about infinity is also nonscientific.

If, for example, we believe that social welfare (W) depends on the amount of goods produced (Q), how those goods are distributed (D), the amount of various factors used in production (F), the political structure (P) and even the rainfall (R), we have

$$W = f(Q, D, F, P, R) \tag{1}$$

The economist is first likely to exclude "noneconomic" variables from consideration (political structure, rainfall, and so on), assuming that their influence on welfare is constant. This means not that they are irrelevant to welfare, but only that we choose not to include them in our investigation.

Using bars over variables to indicate their assumed constancy, the social welfare function now becomes

$$W = f(Q, D, F, \bar{P}, \bar{R}) \tag{2}$$

If the welfare of a group is assumed to depend only on the welfare or utilities of the members of the group the function becomes

$$W = f(U_1, U_2, \cdots, U_n) \tag{3}$$

where U_i is the utility of an individual.

This form of the social welfare function raises the possibility of assuming that group welfare is simply the summation of the utilities of the individual members

$$W = U_1 + U_2 + \cdots + U_n \tag{4}$$

This assumption denies the possibility that the social welfare might be considered to increase when the utility of some individual (no doubt an unpopular one) is reduced. Nevertheless, this assumption is widely used and is often taken for granted.

An individualistic society assumes a social welfare function of the form of equation (3) or (4): The welfare of a group is taken to be a function only of the welfare or utilities of the individuals in the group.

Because utilities of individuals are not measurable, nor can the utilities of different individuals be compared objectively, assumptions are necessary to establish a social ranking of alternative situations.

Specifically, some method is needed for deciding whether the group welfare is higher in one economic situation than in another. Following are some possible decision-making criteria for ranking situations:

(1) The *authoritarian approach* suggests that the determination of the specific nature of the social welfare function should be left to some authority or dictator, perhaps to a political or religious leader. While this position seems inconsistent with democratic con-

cepts, it is commonly employed within subgroups or organizations such as a church or a family.

(2) The *voting approach* suggests that decisions about the social welfare function (for example, whether a proposed economic change would raise or lower total welfare) should be made through the democratic process of majority voting. This proposal is analyzed in the final section of this chapter.

(3) The *Pareto approach* provides only a partial ranking of alternatives: A new situation is preferable to the old (that is, gives greater social welfare) if no individual is worse off, and at least one individual is better off in the new situation than he was in the old.[2] Conversely, social welfare has declined if no one is better off and at least one person is worse off.

The Pareto ranking is incomplete. It does not rank changes that make some individuals worse off and others better off.

The Pareto criterion establishes a necessary but not sufficient condition for the maximization of social welfare. There must be no change possible that can make any person better off without at the same time making someone worse off. The criterion is not sufficient to define the social optimum because more than one situation can satisfy this condition.

(4) *Distributional approaches* incorporate some type of assumption about the effects of various distributions of income on the level of social welfare. Typically, this is done with an assumption about the utility of money to different individuals. For example, it may be postulated that the marginal utility of money is the same for all individuals or, alternately, that all individuals have the same schedules of diminishing marginal utility of money. The latter would mean that the marginal utility of money is an inverse function of individuals' income levels and is the same for all individuals with equal incomes.

Distributional assumptions such as these make it possible to use money measurements as a measure, complete or partial, of welfare.

(5) A *compromise approach,* perhaps the attitude toward social ranking most commonly used by economists and exemplified by this book, first accepts the Pareto criterion. For cases not ranked by the Pareto criterion (changes that benefit some persons but harm others) the compromise approach makes no judgments but suggests a technique of approaching a judgment. Welfare depends on efficiency and equity; the efficiency effects of a change are relatively objective and should be computed in money terms; then the efficiency gain or cost of a change is compared subjectively with the effect of the change on equity. Proponents of this decision-

---

[2]Recall that "better off" means that given a choice between the two situations he would choose the new.

making technique do not specify how or by whom the final judgment is made.

REQUIREMENTS FOR PARETO OPTIMALITY

As noted, most economists would accept the Pareto condition for maximization of social welfare. This criterion is incomplete and could be satisfied by many economic situations.[3] It does not identify *the* social optimum, but it does establish some necessary conditions for that optimum.

The conditions under which a Pareto optimum will exist, therefore, play an important role in welfare economics. Perhaps frustrated with their inability to describe more fully the nature of the social optimum, economists have tended to concentrate attention on what they feel they can say with some assurance, that is, that if a Pareto optimum does not exist, social welfare is not being maximized. The conditions for Paretian optimality should therefore be noted carefully.

The necessary and sufficient condition for a Pareto optimum is simply that there be no possible change that can make one person better off (that is, give him a preferred collection of goods) without making another person worse off.

It is traditional and somewhat useful to ask for further rules that will ensure the achievement of a Pareto optimum. The nature of such rules will depend on the particular context. Unfortunately, it is not uncommon for rules that are valid only for particular contexts to be misunderstood as sufficient rules in a more general sense (that is, for rules that are valid only in a restricted context to be taken as general rules and for a Pareto optimum to be defined in terms of such limited rules).[4] Much misunderstanding can be avoided if that danger is understood.

To illustrate, when considering pure exchange (as in Chapter 5), we saw that a Pareto optimum exists at every point on a contract curve. However, a contract curve may run along the border of an Edgeworth box diagram. If indifference curves are postulated and *if* we assume that the contract curve lies within the box and not on

[3]Recall, for example, that every point on a contract curve in an Edgeworth box diagram for pure exchange (see Chapter 5) is a Pareto optimum.

[4]Only under rather strict and extensive assumptions, for example, is each of the following common statements correct: (1) A necessary and sufficient condition for a Pareto optimum is that all prices be equal to marginal costs; (2) every competitive equilibrium is a Pareto optimum, and every Pareto optimum is a competitive equilibrium; (3) perfect competition is necessary and sufficient for maximization of social welfare. It would be instructive for the student to state the further assumptions necessary to validate each of these statements.

the border, *then* a necessary condition for a Pareto optimum is that the marginal rate of substitution between any two goods must be the same for all individuals. But this is a derivative rule, only applicable under the conditions specified.

Assuming then the simple case with smooth and convex utility and production functions, fixed factor supplies, and the absence of "border" solutions and externalities, the sufficient conditions for a Pareto optimum can be stated rather quickly. While they can be phrased in many different but equivalent ways, they can be reduced to three conditions.

First, Pareto optimality requires that the marginal rate of substitution between any two goods be the same for any two individuals consuming those goods. By defining *goods* broadly to include services, leisure, products at different points of time, and so on, this condition covers many cases. Basically, however, it is an exchange condition which, if violated, indicates that some reallocation of goods can increase efficiency.

To revert to a simplistic example, if one individual values apples and oranges equally (that is, has a marginal rate of substitution of one), and the marginal rate of substitution of a second individual is two oranges for one apple, it is obvious that each person can gain through exchange and that further exchange will be advantageous until their marginal rates of substitution between these two goods are equal. Note that this first condition is concerned with subjective valuations by the individuals concerned.

A second broad requirement for Pareto optimality is technological: It must not be possible to produce any more of one good without at the same time reducing the output of another good. In essence, this means that the economy must be on its production

Figure 20.1 *Production Possibility Frontier*

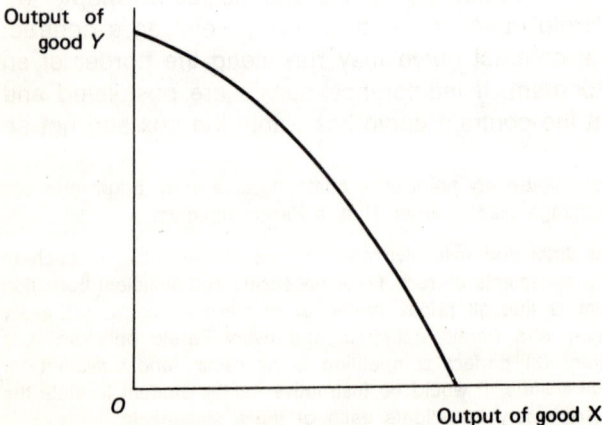

Output of
  good Y

O   Output of good X

possibility frontier, illustrated in Figure 20.1 for the two-good case. Each point on the frontier shows the maximum quantity of one good that can be produced with the fixed supply of factors available, for a given production level of the other good.

The slope of the production possibility frontier equals the marginal technical rate of transformation between the two products. The slope is the amount by which the production of one product must be reduced in order for the output of the second to be increased by one unit.

The conditions necessary for an economy to be on the production frontier are two: First, the marginal physical product of any one factor must be the same wherever that factor is used to produce a given product. If the marginal physical product of labor is not the same wherever labor is used to produce a given product, output of that good can be increased with no increase in the amount of labor employed by shifting labor from its low to its high productivity location.

A second technological requirement to put an economy on its production frontier is that the marginal technical rate of substitution between any two factors is the same in any use employing those two factors. This means that the ratio of the marginal productivities of any two factors in any two uses must be equal. Thus, using subscripts n and c for labor and capital and superscripts a and b for any two products,

$$\frac{MPP_n^a}{MPP_c^a} = \frac{MPP_n^b}{MPP_c^b} \tag{5}$$

Equation (5) necessarily means that the marginal technical rate of transformation between any two goods will be the same for any firm producing both goods. It is this marginal rate of transformation between two goods that is shown by the slope of the production possibility frontier.

These technical requirements for ensuring that the economy is on the production possibility frontier can be summed up in one statement: Pareto optimality in production requires that the technological rates of transformation or substitution between any two factors or any two products, or between a factor and a product, must be the same wherever the two are related in a production function. Otherwise some change exists (for example, shifting of factors, or of the amounts of products produced in different firms, or of the quantities of factors employed by different firms to produce any product) by which the total output can be increased without using more factors.

For Pareto optimality (that is, efficiency) in exchange, the marginal subjective rate of substitution between any two goods must be the same for all individuals consuming both; for technological efficiency, the marginal technical rate of transformation between any two goods must be the same throughout the economy. The third broad condition for a Pareto optimum, then, is that the marginal rate of subjective substitution be equal to the marginal technical rate of transformation between any two goods.

If, for example, two goods can be produced with the same amounts of factors, yet individuals value one good twice as highly as the other, efficiency does not exist. By shifting factors to the more highly valued good, some individuals can be made better off without harming any others. Only if the ratio of values of the two goods equals the ratio at which they can be substituted in production can Pareto optimality exist.

THE PRICE SYSTEM AND PARETO OPTIMALITY

Economists have been impressed (perhaps too much so) with the relationship between Pareto optimality and the price system. If one asks how the necessary conditions for a Pareto optimum can be achieved, and if one is willing to make all the assumptions necessary for the marginal conditions of the previous section to have validity, the answer is clear: A competitive price system is sufficient but not necessary to achieve a Pareto optimum.

In terms of the marginal conditions, Pareto optimality requires that the marginal rate of substitution (*MRS*) between any two goods must be the same for all consumers. But, as shown in Chapter 3, consumer equilibrium is achieved when the consumer's *MRS* between two goods is equal to the ratio of their prices. If all consumers are faced with the same two prices for two goods, as occurs under perfect competition, the buyers will adjust their consumption patterns of the two goods so that the marginal rate of substitution beween the two goods is the same for every individual.

Using subscripts a and b for two goods and superscripts 1 and 2 for the two individuals,

$$\frac{P_a}{P_b} = MRS^1_{ab} = MRS^2_{ab} \tag{6}$$

Competitive prices thus induce efficiency in exchange, the first requirement for Pareto optimality.

A Pareto optimum also requires that the *MRT* (marginal rate of transformation in production) of any two goods be the same wherever the two goods are produced. Under competitive conditions[5] the *MRT* between any two goods is the ratio of their marginal costs.

[5]Making the other necessary assumptions, for example, no externalities.

Firms produce each good up to the point at which its price equals marginal cost or

$$\frac{P_a}{P_b} = \frac{MC_a}{MC_b} = MRT_{ab} \tag{7}$$

Therefore, the ratio of the competitive prices of any two goods will equal the ratio of the marginal costs (that is, the MRT). Thus the second condition for Pareto optimality is achieved.

Third, the prices faced by consumers are, of course, the same prices faced by producers. Therefore, since the MRS equals the same price ratio as does the MRT,

$$MRS_{ab} = MRT_{ab} \tag{8}$$

thus satisfying the third marginal condition for Pareto optimality.

The proposition that competitive pricing leads to a Pareto optimum or perfect efficiency is important and is one of the major appeals of a competitive system. It is equally important, however, to remember the following extensions and qualifications.

(1) The proposition depends on the absence of externalities. Only if all costs and benefits are considered by the competitive firms and consumers will competitive pricing lead to a Pareto optimum. This often does not occur in private markets.

(2) The proposition does not apply to cases of increasing returns (decreasing costs), which are inconsistent with competitive production behavior. However, the principle is consistent with decreasing returns.

(3) On the other hand, corner and boundary equilibria are quite consistent with the proposition that competitive behavior leads to a Pareto optimum. It is not necessary that all production or demand functions be continuous and smooth.

(4) Finally, note that given our assumptions competitive pricing is only sufficient, but not necessary, to achieve a Pareto optimum. Perfect efficiency can also be achieved through various other schemes (for example, discriminatory pricing, direct allocation of goods, and so on). These alternative methods of achieving a Pareto optimum may not be feasible or may be considered unfair. On the other hand, these methods are able to induce a Pareto optimum even in the presence of externalities and increasing returns, which is not possible under competitive pricing.

(5) As often noted, many Pareto optima can exist. Yet the proposition that competitive behavior leads to a Pareto optimum seems to suggest a unique Pareto optimum (that is, that one induced by competitive behavior). The inconsistency is only apparent. The nature of any competitive equilibrium depends on the initial owner-

ship of assets.[6] The competitive equilibrium is the one Pareto optimum that would be reached through competitive pricing starting from any given initial distribution of the ownership of assets.[7]

(6) The last comment suggests that any of the available Paretian optima can be achieved in the absence of externalities and increasing returns through competitive pricing by a redistribution of the initial stocks of assets through lump-sum transfers. Simple money transfers can achieve this result.[8]

This point can be related to the earlier discussion of the social welfare function. Pareto optimality is a necessary but insufficient condition far maximizing social welfare. Efficiency is not enough; distributive equity is also required. We now see that efficiency and distributive justice may, in principle, both be achieved by a combination of lump-sum transfers of money among individuals plus competitive behavior in markets. Social welfare is thus maximized. The lump-sum transfers are adjusted so that the resulting efficient competitive behavior leads to the desired maximization of social welfare.

This is not intended as a practical proposal. Externalities and decreasing costs make competitive behavior unattainable. One could hardly expect political agreement on the optimum pattern of lump-sum transfers. Like a drawing of a six-legged elephant, perhaps the chief use of this description of a social welfare optimum is to see what one would look like if there were such a thing.

THE THEORY OF THE "SECOND BEST"

A Pareto optimum cannot exist in the presence of a man-made imperfection such as a monopoly or a legislative constraint on the price of some product or factor. If such an imperfection cannot be eliminated, how can the rest of the economy be ordered to achieve the maximum feasible level of efficiency? The answer is often called the theory of the second best; if the best is not attainable, what

---

[6]It is often incorrectly stated that the competitive equilibrium that will be reached depends on the initial distribution of income. While this is correct for a pure exchange economy in which no further incomes are received from the productive process, it is not correct when applied to production because income distribution is itself a function of the productive pattern, the equilibrium prices of factors, and the ownership of factors.

[7]Including ownership of a supply of labor services.

[8]The point is most easily seen in the pure theory of exchange, where a redistribution of initial holdings of assets on the standard Edgeworth box diagram means shifting the initial point from one location in (or on the edges of) the box to another point. Such a shift will tend to change the location of the resultant competitive equilibrium, but all such equilibria will lie on the contract curve.

principles should be followed to attain the next best position?[9] In particular, if one sector of an economy does not set prices that are in accord with the marginal equalities required for Pareto optimality, should those principles be followed in the rest of the economy?

The general principal of the second best—or, as it might better be termed, of a constrained optimum—is that there is no general principle. In particular, a constrained optimum cannot always be achieved by following the usual marginal rules in the unconstrained sections of an economy. Whenever a particular imperfection exists, particular counteracting measures must be devised to offset the imperfection as much as possible.

Consider an economy of fixed factor supplies with many goods, the price of one being arbitrarily fixed above its competitive market-clearing level. What prices should be set for each of the other goods?

The answer is complex and requires a knowledge of the inter-relationships among goods and the elasticities of supply and demand for various goods. The price of the constrained good is too high and its output would be too low for efficient allocation of resources if the price = marginal cost principle were followed in the rest of the economy. To encourage the expansion in the demand, and hence output of the constrained product, the general principle is that the prices of goods that are substituted for the constrained good should be higher than their marginal cost, and the prices of goods for which the demand is complementary with the constrained good should be priced below marginal cost. These pricing policies will expand the demand for the constrained good and cause its output to increase, thus offsetting the built-in imperfection of a price for the constrained good above the competitive level. The optimum price for each good will depend, however, not only on the relationship of this good to the constrained product, but also to other goods in the economy.

The problem of identifying the conditions necessary for the constrained Pareto optimum has considerable practical importance in several fields. In international trade policy, for example, how can a foreign tariff on U.S. goods best be offset? Can a public power organization such as the Tennessee Valley Authority use its price and production policy to improve the performance of privately owned utilities operating in the same area? Can public production of goods or services be used to offset the behavior of private monopolists?

The theory of the second best asks how a feasible, constrained

[9]Richard Lipsey and Kelvin Lancaster, "The General Theory of Second Best," Review of Economic Studies 24 (1956–1957), 11–32.

optimum can be achieved. Because even this optimum is far beyond practical attainment, a more common and important application of second best principles is the determination of how, in an imperfect and imperfectible economy, some piecemeal change in one sector will affect the efficiency of the economy. This question is considered in Chapter 21.

THE THEORY OF VOTING

At best, Pareto optimal conditions are a necessary but not sufficient condition for the maximization of social welfare. Our discussion so far leaves two questions unanswered.

(1) How can any two Pareto optima be compared or ranked in terms of social welfare?

(2) How can a choice be made between two situations, only one of which is Pareto optimal?[10]

To answer such questions a social welfare function is needed. No such function can be determined objectively, but we may agree on a decision rule. In a democratic society the rule is to accept the decision of the majority of the voters. In recent years extensive literature on the theory of voting has developed, fed by economists and political scientists.[11]

A crucial question is whether majority voting will lead to a consistent transitive ranking of social alternatives. A ranking is consistent or transitive if, when alternative A is ranked superior to B, and B to C, A will be ranked over C. If majority voting fails to rank policy alternatives transitively, voting would appear to be helpless in determining the nature of a social welfare function. If voting does give a transitive ordering of alternatives and if the public is willing to accept the rule of majority voting, a social welfare function can be determined through voting.

Further, if voting sometimes gives transitive rankings, and other times intransitive ordering, we may ask what conditions or assumptions are necessary or sufficient to provide consistency.

It has long been known that majority voting by individuals who are themselves consistent in their ranking of alternatives can lead to an inconsistent, intransitive social ordering or ranking of alternatives. For example, assume in the simplest possible case that

[10]Social welfare may of course be higher—although not at a maximum—in an inefficient economy than at a particular Pareto optimum, if, for example, the distribution of income in the inefficient situation is believed preferable to that of the Pareto optimum.

[11]See, for example, Kenneth Arrow, *Social Choice and Individual Values*, 2nd ed. (New York: Wiley, 1963); James M. Buchanan and Gordon Tullock, *The Calculus of Consent* (Ann Arbor: University of Michigan Press, 1962).

three voters are faced with a choice among three alternatives (for example, three candidates for an office or three possible policies with respect to the draft). Each individual has a consistent preference ranking among the alternatives, as indicated by the following table.

Table 20.1   Individuals' Ranking of Alternatives

	Alternative A	Alternative B	Alternative C
Individual X	1	2	3
Individual Y	2	3	1
Individual Z	3	1	2

In pairwise elections, A would be chosen over B, and B would be chosen over C. Consistency would then require that A be chosen over C. Yet C would win an election between A and C. Here, through majority voting, consistent individual rankings lead to an inconsistent social ordering. Majority voting fails this simple but elemental test.

A rigorous and formal analysis of this problem of arriving at social choices through voting has been made by economist Kenneth Arrow, who arrives essentially at the same conclusion as the simple example: In general it is impossible to achieve consistency in social choice through majority voting.[12]

The point is obvious in political processes where legislators know well that the eventual fate of a proposal depends not only on individual preferences but also on the form and order in which alternative solutions are voted on. Parliamentary maneuvering constitutes recognition of this.

The problem of developing a social welfare function through voting can be reduced, if not solved, if a method of measuring the intensity of preferences by individuals were available (that is, if some degree of cardinality were added to the ordinal expression of choices). To a limited degree, this is effected in elections where those with only mild preferences are less likely to go to the trouble of voting. In effect, the decision is made by those who feel strongly. Where everyone votes, those who are almost indifferent have as much power to influence the results as those who feel strongly about the issue.

Further analysis of the "paradox of voting" has shown that consistent social rankings can be achieved in elections if the alternatives are "single-peaked." This means that the choices can be arranged in such an order that the preferences of each voter decline monotonically as he moves away in either direction from his most preferred choice. In Figure 20.2 five alternatives (A through E)

[12]Arrow, *op. cit.*

Figure 20.2 *Single-peaked Preferences*

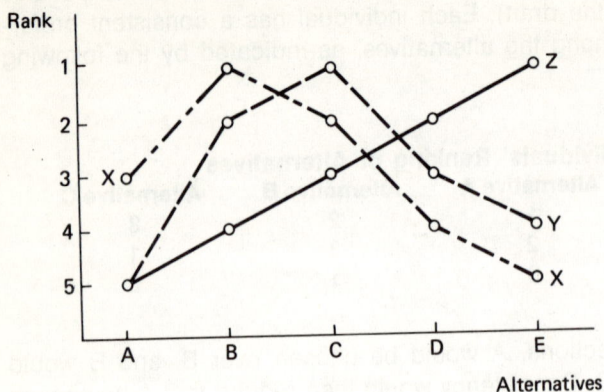

are arranged along the horizontal axis, with the rankings of three individuals, X, Y, and Z, plotted.

The preferences of X, Y, and Z are single-peaked, and elections among these three voters would lead to a consistent social ranking.

The earlier example of three voters facing three alternatives illustrates the absence of single-peakedness. There is no way to order the alternatives to achieve it. In that case, elections lead to inconsistent social rankings.

Whether consistent social rankings are achieved in elections therefore depends in part on a rather technical question: Can the alternatives be ordered in such a way that individuals are likely to have single-peaked preferences? Such a result is more likely if the alternatives differ from each other in only one dominant character-istic (for example, the size of a budget or the location of each alternative on a "liberal–conservative" continuum). But even in such cases, some voters may prefer extreme alternatives to those in the center (for example, "let's not do it at all if we can't do it properly"). Where alternatives differ from each other in several important characteristics, it is still less likely that single-peakedness will occur.

Finally, even if voting can be shown to lead to a consistent social ranking, this ranking is only as valid as the basic assumption that social ordering is properly represented by majority voting. The proposition is of course dubious, for it gives equal weight to each individual regardless of his intensity of feeling, his knowledge, and other factors that might be considered relevant to social ordering. At most, voting might be considered the best ranking method available in a world in which utilities cannot be measured and in-terpersonal comparisons of utility cannot be made.

REVIEW QUESTIONS

1. Explain the following concepts:
   Positive economics
   Welfare economics
   Social welfare function
   The Paretian test of a change in welfare
   Pareto optimality
   Production possibility frontier
   The marginal conditions for Pareto optimality
   The "Second Best"
   Transitivity in voting
   The "paradox of voting"
   Single-peaked preferences
2. Discuss the relationship of the price system to Pareto optimality.
3. Discuss the relationship of the price system to the maximization of a social welfare function.
4. Devise and defend a method of ranking social priorities, i.e., a social welfare function. Make your value judgments explicit.

FURTHER READING

Arrow, Kenneth J., and Tibor Scitovsky, *Readings in Welfare Economics.* Homewood, Ill.: Irwin (1969).

Arrow, Kenneth, *Social Choice and Individual Values.* 2nd ed., New York: Wiley (1963).

Bator, Francis, "The Simple Analytics of Welfare Maximization." *American Economic Review 47* (1957), 22–59.

Baumol, William J., *Welfare Economics and the Theory of the State.* 2nd ed., Cambridge: Harvard University Press (1965).

Boulding, Kenneth, "Welfare Economics," in B. F. Haley, ed., *A Survey of Contemporary Economics.* vol. 2, Homewood, Ill.: Irwin (1952), 1–34.

Henderson, James M., and Richard E. Quandt, *Microeconomic Theory: A Mathematical Approach.* New York: McGraw-Hill (1958), chap. 7.

Lipsey, R. G., and Kelvin Lancaster, "The General Theory of Second Best." *Review of Economic Studies 24* (1956–1957), 11–32.

Little, I. M. D., *A Critique of Welfare Economics.* 2nd ed., London: Oxford University Press (1957).

Mishan, E. J., "A Survey of Welfare Economics, 1939–1959." *Economic Journal 70* (1960), 197–256.

Samuelson, Paul A., "Social Indifference Curves." *Quarterly Journal of Economics 70* (1956), 1–22.

21

CHANGES IN SOCIAL WELFARE

- ▣ welfare criteria for changes
- ☐ the compensation principle
- ☐ money as a measure of utility
- ☐ the measurement of benefits and costs

WELFARE CRITERIA FOR CHANGES

The practical welfare question is not what the perfect world would look like, but whether a specific change in the economy would increase or decrease social welfare in an imperfect and imperfectible world. Making such judgments requires assessing and somehow comparing the gains and losses that would result from a change.[1]

Economists may simply assert the irrelevance of such inquiries to the "science" of economics because they would inevitably require value judgments. This attitude is quite defensible. Choosing it means making a value judgment about what economics should be. If, as Jacob Viner has suggested,[2] "Economics is what economists do," it seems clear that the majority of economists reject this interpretation of their discipline.

Scarcely more useful for the assessment of proposed changes is the Paretian test: A change increases welfare if, as a consequence, someone is made

[1]As Kenneth Arrow and Tibor Scitovsky say in the *AEA Readings in Welfare Economics* (Homewood, Ill.: Irwin, 1969), p. 3: "if the economist is to be something more than a preacher of optimality and market perfection, his policy recommendations in an imperfect, suboptimal world must mostly be based on the measurement of its costs and hoped-for gains."

[2]As reported by Kenneth Boulding. *Economic Analysis*, 4th ed., vol. 1 (New York: Harper & Row, 1966), p. 3.

better off and no one is worse off, and decreases welfare when no one gains and at least one person loses. The test is rarely applicable, except to legitimize transactions between freely participating parties.

Many economists are reluctant to restrict themselves to· either the agnostic or the Paretian approach to evaluating changes in welfare.

The basis for most contemporary welfare criteria lies in the recognition that utilities cannot be measured, but that monetary gains and losses of proposed changes can be determined. The critical question then is to what extent monetary measures of gains and losses can serve as proxies for changes in utilities or welfare. Among economists employing money as an incomplete indicator of utilities, two groups may be distinguished: (1) those who believe that economists should study money gains and losses, but leave to others the normative judgments of whether, given the other aspects of a change (particularly its effect on the distribution of income), the change is desirable, and (2) those who go farther to analyze the welfare implications of various assumptions about the relation between money and utilities. These two groups are considered in the sections that follow.

THE COMPENSATION PRINCIPLE

A major tool of the welfare analysis of changes is the compensation principle, which asks whether, as a result of a change, those who gain from it *could* compensate the losers and have net gains remaining.[3] The compensation principle is thus satisfied if the gains of a change exceed the losses when both are measured in money terms. The principle does not require that the gainers actually compensate the losers, only that they be capable of doing so.

Obviously, a change that satisfies the compensation principle could result in a decrease in social welfare if the accompanying change in the distribution of income is considered socially undesirable. When a change satisfies the compensation principle, it is sometimes said that *potential* welfare has increased or, alternately, that in some sense the national output or production has increased. In the terminology of this book, a change that satisfies the compensation test increases economic efficiency.

[3]See J. R. Hicks, "The Foundations of Welfare Economics," *Economic Journal 49* (1939), 696–712, and Nicholas Kaldor, "Welfare Propositions of Economics and Interpersonal Comparisons of Utility," *Economic Journal 49* (1939), 549–552, reprinted in Arrow and Scitovsky, eds., *Readings in Welfare Economics* (Homewood, Ill.: Irwin, 1969). For a critique of the compensation principle see I. M. D. Little, *A Critique of Welfare Economics,* 2nd ed. (London: Oxford University Press, 1957), chap. 6.

A deficiency in the compensation test was noted by Tibor Scitovsky, who pointed out that it would be possible for a change from situation A to situation B to satisfy the compensation test and, at the same time, for a reverse change from B back to A also to satisfy the test.[4] This possibility of intransitivity in ranking situations according to their degree of efficiency casts serious doubt on the legitimacy of the test. Scitovsky therefore proposed a dual test: Situation B is more efficient than situation A if a change from A to B satisfies the compensation test, while a movement from B to A does not satisfy it. In principle, this dual test has been accepted; in practice, the reversal test is usually ignored on the grounds that the perverse results are unlikely because they can occur only when the change from A to B changes the distribution of income very substantially. They cannot occur if either A or B is a Pareto optimum.

Note that if the original situation is a Pareto optimum no change from this situation could satisfy the compensation test. Conversely, if the compensation test is satisfied by a change, the original situation could not have been a Pareto optimum.

A change that satisfies the compensation test does not satisfy the Paretian test for an increase in welfare (that is, that no one be made worse off and at least one person be made better off) unless the compensation actually is paid. To insist on payment of the compensation reduces the compensation test to the Paretian test for an increase in welfare with its limited applicability. What is needed is a criterion for evaluating changes that help some persons but harm others.

The compensation test tells whether a change increases economic efficiency. A logical extension of the test is to use the net monetary gain resulting from a change (that is, the excess of monetary gains over losses) as an objective measure of the efficiency gain.

Few individuals explicitly argue that the extended compensation test should be used as the sole test of the desirability of a proposed change. A change may significantly increase the efficiency of the economy and yet be judged undesirable for other reasons, distributional or political. The suggestion is that judgments about the desirability of proposed changes can be made more easily with less likelihood of disagreement if a careful accounting is made of the money benefits and costs that would result from a change. The efficiency gain or loss can then be considered explicitly, along with the more subjective evaluation of the nonefficiency consequences of a change.

For example, should a tariff be placed on a certain product? Domestic producers will gain, and consumers will lose. Assume

---

[4]Tibor Scitovsky, "A Note on Welfare Propositions in Economics," *Review of Economic Studies 9* (1941), 77–88, reprinted in Arrow and Scitovsky, eds., *op. cit.*

that the resulting change in the distribution of income would be judged desirable. The extended compensation test would provide a measure of the net money loss, which would follow the imposition of the tariff. The test, in effect, measures the cost of the improved distribution of income, and thus helps the public to decide whether the change is worthwhile.

Conversely, consider a transportation service—perhaps an urban bus route or rail commuter service—that is losing money. An estimate can be made of the net money gains or losses that would result from discontinuing the service. If the gains from dropping the service would be positive, a political decision may still be made to continue the service. The economist argues not that the service should be discontinued, but that specific knowledge of the costs of maintaining the service is useful and perhaps essential in making the decision.

Not uncommonly, differences of opinion on a proposed change are narrowed substantially simply by a careful description of the size and distribution of the income effects of a change. For example, farm price supports lose much of their appeal when the facts on the recipients of such aid and the size of their receipts are publicized. Similarly, careful and detailed description of the impact of a proposed tax will often reduce the disagreements on its appropriateness. In this area the economist can make a significant contribution without attempting to impose the ultimate value judgment.

The extended compensation principle or some variation of it is the most widely used tool in the welfare analysis of economic policy issues. It is found in cost–benefit analysis of government projects, which began with studies of river development, and is now extended to the analysis of all forms of public expenditure, including health, defense, transportation, education, recreation, urban renewal, and even law enforcement.[5] The use of the principle is so broad that there is an unfortunate tendency in the professional economics literature to use the word "welfare" when only economic efficiency is meant—a practice that regrettably reinforces a natural tendency on the part of students and the public to believe that economists are only concerned with money.

Two arguments have been made to support the general use of the compensation principle as a complete guide to all policy

[5]See, for example, Robert Dorfman, ed., *Measuring Benefits of Government Investments* (Washington, D.C.: Brookings, 1965); A. R. Prest and R. Turvey, "Cost–Benefit Analysis: A Survey," *Economic Journal 75* (1965), 683–735, reprinted in *Surveys of Economic Theory* (New York: St. Martin's, 1966), vol. 3; Gary Becker, "Crime and Punishment: An Economic Approach," *Journal. of Political Economy 76* (1968), 169–217; and Chapter 17 of this text.

changes (that is, to urge as a practical matter that all policy changes be effected that satisfy the compensation test of money gains exceeding money losses). First, one may simply *assume* that the distribution of income generated in an efficient economy is good. A single-minded pursuit of efficiency would therefore also bring about the optimum pattern of income distribution: Both objectives would be achieved concurrently. The argument is particularly popular with high income individuals. As with all such arguments, it cannot be refuted, but it can be disbelieved. One obvious weakness to this attitude is that it fails to recognize that there can be many efficient situations, each with a different distribution of income. This criterion fails to rank such distributions.

More widely accepted is the argument that if the efficient allocation of resources were generally pursued it is *likely* that most individuals would incur a net gain. While any one specific change would harm some persons, it is argued that these individuals are likely to be more than compensated by gains from other changes. This result would be particularly likely if changes over a longer period of time are considered because over time the added productivity from efficiency changes would make possible significantly higher levels of income for all persons.[6]

If, in fact, a *series* of changes is being evaluated, the results of which will make everyone better off, there is no need for the compensation principle; the changes *as a group* satisfy the Paretian test of an increase in welfare. But the argument is generally advanced in a looser sense only as a probability.

Further, the argument that greater efficiency now will lead to higher future incomes for everyone must deal with the fact that different populations are involved in the present and future. The argument reduces, therefore, to the well-known question of how much the present generation should sacrifice to improve the incomes of future generations, a question that clearly involves value judgments of a most fundamental type.

It becomes clear that the compensation principle *by itself* is not a generally acceptable complete test for evaluating the welfare results of proposed changes. Further assumptions, particularly about the utility of money to different individuals and groups, are necessary.

MONEY AS A MEASURE OF UTILITY

Several answers have been offered to the question of how the money measures of costs and benefits shown by the compensation

[6]See Henry Wallich, *The Cost of Freedom* (New York: Harper & Row, 1960).

principle are related to measures of utility and disutility. There is, of course, no objective answer to this question. But in policy discussions, particularly in a world of imperfect knowledge, we are interested in the plausibility of various possible relationships between money and utility. Most policy, after all, is based on faith.

The essential question is how the utility of money, particularly the marginal utility of money, varies with various individuals and groups. To bridge the gap between money measures of gains and losses and a social welfare or utility function, some relationship between money and utility to different individuals must be established or assumed.[7] Two of the most commonly employed assumptions are to be considered: (1) the marginal utility of money is the same for all individuals, and (2) the marginal utility of money declines as an individual's income rises with all individuals having approximately the same *schedule* of the marginal utility of money.

If, as Alfred Marshall sometimes assumed, the marginal utility of money is a constant over any relevant range, and is the same for all individuals, any change that satisfies the compensation test (that is, results in net money gains) also increases the total utility of the group of individuals affected. Money is then an accurate measure of utility, and any proposed change can be evaluated simply by determining whether money gains would exceed money losses.

Few individuals would be willing to accept this assumption in all contexts. But it is used and perhaps useful in evaluating certain types of situations. If the group of individuals harmed by a change is believed to have economic characteristics (in particular, approximately the same distribution of income) as the group benefiting from a change, the marginal utility of money to those who as a group are gaining from the change may be roughly comparable to the marginal utility of money to the group of losers. This follows particularly if the marginal utility of money is largely a function of the income level of an individual. Under these conditions, it would then be likely, although not inevitable, that the money measures of the benefits and costs of a change would be a close approximation to the utility gains and losses, and therefore the compensation test would be a valid criterion of welfare changes.

Perhaps the most plausible common assumptions with regard to the utility of income are that the marginal utility of money diminishes as income rises and that most individuals have roughly comparable schedules of the marginal utility of money. Carried to its limit, as

---

[7]Assuming a social welfare function of the type of equation (3), Chapter 20, which asserts that group welfare is a function of the welfares of the individuals in the group.

few individuals do, this assumption would imply that maximization of social welfare would require equal distribution of income.

While the assumption that the schedules of diminishing marginal utility of money are uniform for different individuals is rarely heard in the extreme form, the popularity of a version of the assumption, modified by a recognition of the possibilities of some individual variations, is perhaps suggested by the various types of legislation aimed at reducing the inequality in the distribution of income.

THE MEASUREMENT OF BENEFITS AND COSTS

Assuming that we wish to utilize an efficiency test as at least one of the criteria of the desirability of a change, how are efficiency changes measured? In this section a few relatively simple examples are discussed in order to illustrate the questions that must be asked and the difficulties that arise. The measurement of costs and benefits, of gains and losses, is not easy. One could almost say that the chief skill of an economist lies in his expertise in handling this type of problem.

In the simplest case, assume that the economy is generally efficient, that all market costs accurately measure the opportunity costs of using resources, and that a proposed change will not cause any prices in the economy to change, except for the price of the good directly affected by the change. That is, the change to be evaluated will have only marginal effects elsewhere in the economy.

In this case, the efficiency consequences of a proposed change —a change in the output of the good in question, for example, or the introduction of a new good—can be determined simply by the standard efficiency tests: (1) a good should be produced if the total cost at any output is less than the total benefit derived from it measured by the willingness of consumers to pay, and (2) the good should be produced to the point at which marginal cost equals marginal value.[8]

In a single price system (without discrimination) the price of the good should be set equal to marginal cost.

For a second case, use the same assumptions as in the first case, but assume that external costs are associated with the production of the good concerned. Efficiency then requires a calculation of the amount of these external costs, which is added to the regular production costs in determining whether the good should be produced and, if so, at what output. If the good is to be produced,

---

[8]A more general rule: For each separable unit or group of units of the good produced, the avoidable costs of that unit or group should be not more than the benefits of that group.

its price should equal marginal social cost, which includes marginal private cost plus the marginal external cost of the good.

Conversely, a good with external benefits should be produced if total costs exceed total benefits, including the externalities, and up to a point at which marginal private plus external benefits equals marginal cost. The efficient price for such a good equals not marginal cost, but that cost less the amount of external benefits induced by the production of the good. Thus, if a product costs a uniform $1 per unit to produce, and each unit gives rise to 20 cents worth of external benefits, the good should be produced to the point at which the marginal private benefit to the buyer of the good equals 80 cents. A price of 80 cents per unit will give this result.[9]

Consider next the evaluation of the desirability of introducing a new good which, when priced at marginal cost, will substantially reduce the demand for some competing good B. Two important questions determining how the impact of the demand for product B affects the desirability of introducing product A are: (1) Is product B being produced competitively? (2) Is good B produced under conditions of constant, decreasing, or increasing cost?

The basic question in determining the efficiency consequences of a change is whether those who benefit incur greater monetary gains than the losses of those who are harmed. The gains and losses of consumers, firms, and factors of production must be considered.

If product B is produced competitively with constant costs (which implies that long-run analysis is being applied), it is surprising but correct to note that no one will be made better or worse off by the change in B's output, and attention can be concentrated on A. This is true even though the demand for B declines, and hence the area of consumer surplus to buyers of B declines. No past or present buyer of B is worse off. Those who still prefer B to A retain their previous advantage.[10] Those who have shifted to A are better off, and their willingness to pay for A (while the price of B remains constant) is a measure of the benefit they receive from A.

The producers of product B are not harmed under these assumptions because they are producing competitively and hence continue to make normal profits. (Obviously, there will be some short-run losses in industry B; a complete analysis of this case would require

---

[9]A price of 80 cents will not cover the cost of $1 per unit, and some supplementary source of finance would have to be devised.

[10]It is true that their willingness to pay for B may be decreased by the availability of A. But their utility level will not be changed. This shows the danger of attempting to add surpluses for two or more goods, and, by implication, the error in asserting that social welfare is maximized when some measure of a sum of surpluses is maximized.

computation of all short-run effects.) The factors used to produce product B are not harmed since by assumption they are supplied competitively and, when industry B declines, move to another industry at the same rate of pay.

When the impact of the introduction of product A falls on a competitive industry (call it D) that is subject to increasing cost, the introduction of product A will affect the surpluses being received by the customers and suppliers of D. If A and D are substitutes, the demand for D will fall with the introduction of A; D's price will also fall. Faithful buyers of D will receive increased surpluses, roughly equal to the fall in the price of D; on the other hand, the suppliers and factors in industry D will face a decline in their rents or quasi-rents. All changes in surpluses or rents must be taken into consideration when determining whether the introduction of A would raise the efficiency of the economy. If industries A and D are the only two affected, the introduction of A will be efficient if after all changes in D's price and output have occurred the total benefit to consumers of A exceeds the total cost of producing A. But the net gain will be less in this case than would have been indicated by an estimation of the benefits and costs of producing A prior to the changes in industry D.

Short-run supply curves are likely to be less elastic that long-run supply curves. The losses in surpluses in impact industries such as D are likely to be greater in the short run than they will be over a period of time when the suppliers of inputs (including capital) have time to redirect the allocation of their factor services. The measurement of the change in surpluses resulting from a proposed change therefore depends significantly on the time period of the analysis. A change intended to be permanent is much more likely to satisfy the efficiency test than will a temporary change. This conclusion is significant; it shows that two of the commonly listed goals of an economy, efficiency and short-run stability, are not necessarily antithetical.

If the impact of the introduction of product A falls on firms or industries that do not behave competitively, further complexities develop.

Special note should be taken of the impacts of proposed changes on unemployed or underemployed resources, the market prices of which exceed the real marginal costs of supply. Their price overstates the opportunity cost of using them. A decrease in their employment reduces the surpluses received by the suppliers of the factor, and an increase in employment significantly increases surpluses. These can be very important considerations in evaluating not only the fairness but also the efficiency of a proposed change that would affect employment levels substantially.

It is not easy in practice to assess the desirability of a proposed change. Even the efficiency implications of a change, involving as they do only monetary considerations, are difficult to estimate, because so many of the relevant monetary dimensions and prices do not appear explicitly in markets. This applies not only to external costs and benefits, but also to estimates of demand and supply functions at prices and quantities other than those currently existing. In addition, it is difficult to anticipate correctly on which products, industries, areas, and individuals secondary effects are likely to fall, and with what severity.

The prize, however, is increased efficiency in the allocation of resources which, combined with an appropriate distribution of the efficiency gains, means greater welfare for society.

1. Explain the following concepts:
   The compensation principle
   Marginal utility of money
   The Scitovsky test of a change in efficiency
2. Discuss the relation of the compensation principle to the following: Pareto optimality; the Paretian test of a change in welfare; the maximization of a social welfare function; the marginal utility of money.
3. Consider some specific proposed change in economic policy, for the nation or your own locality. What information would you need, and how would you use it, to determine whether the change would
   (a) increase the efficiency of the economy?
   (b) increase the social welfare?

FURTHER READING

Arrow, Kenneth J., and Tibor Scitovsky, *Readings in Welfare Economics.* Homewood, Ill.: Irwin (1969).

Hicks, J. R., "The Foundations of Welfare Economics." *Economic Journal 49* (1939), 696–712.

Kaldor, Nicholas, "Welfare Propositions of Economics and Interpersonal Comparisons of Utility." *Economic Journal 49* (1939), 549–552.

Little, I. M. D., *A Critique of Welfare Economics.* 2nd ed., London: Oxford University Press (1957).

Mishan, E. J., "A Survey of Welfare Economics, 1939–1959." *Economic Journal 70* (1960), 197–256.

Prest, A. R., and R. Turvey, "Cost-Benefit Analysis: A Survey," *Economic Journal 75* (1965), 683–735.

INDEX

A

B

G

H

I